God's Heart As It Relates To Depravity

Written by Bob Warren

Much thanks to the following saints who devoted countless
hours to the production of this work:

Trey Alley
Brent Armstrong
Dan Carter
Myra Cleaver
Jhonda Johnston
Rick Underhill

ISBN: 978-1-62727-040-3

All Scripture, unless otherwise noted, is from the New American Standard
Bible.

Table of Contents

CHAPTER ONE

INTRODUCTION

Why This Book

A PROPER VIEW OF GOD'S HEART should be the intent of every Biblical study. Moreover, how we define key terms addressed in God's Word influences how we perceive Him and represent him to others. God wrote His letter to man to reveal Who He is. Hence, every word, of every phrase, of every verse, of His infallible letter must be viewed in the context of the whole. Taking Scripture out of context results in not only a tarnished view of the Scriptures, but a flawed view of God Himself.

Every word, of every phrase, of every verse, of His infallible letter must be viewed in the context of the whole.

Depravity, election, atonement, grace, perseverance, and faith are the subjects of much "talk" these days. Consequently, the perceptions and definitions of these subjects vary significantly. In fact, hearing familiar "terminology" does not always indicate that we are on the same theological page as the person with whom we are speaking. Every word uttered by a man is influenced by what he believes in *"his heart"* (Matthew 12:34; Luke 6:45). One can't assume to be in harmony with what is heard or read until knowing the context of the words spoken or written. For instance, never assume that someone's definition of depravity agrees with your own.

These inconsistencies, and an abundance of others, necessitated this study. Many people conclude that parallel vocabulary yields identical thinking, identical theology, and an identical perception of God. This series exposes the danger that lurks behind this erroneous conclusion. Subjects addressed in our previous two *God's Heart* publications, *God's Heart as it Relates to Foreknowledge-Predestination,* and *God's Heart as it Relates to Sovereignty-Free Will,* will be of great value as we tackle the topics covered in *God's Heart as it Relates to Depravity.*

Do you enjoy thinking? Are you interested in knowing why you believe what you believe? Does it make any difference, whatsoever, if your view of God is correct; can it be somewhat distorted and not affect you in any way? Does a study of "doctrine" (the truth taught in the Scriptures) interest you? If you answered "No" to any of the previous four questions, I have three more questions. Through what means are you finding rest for your soul? Is fellowshipping in "unity" with other believers (at the expense of truth) more appealing than having God's Word instruct you in the way of Scriptural unity? Have you realized that meaningful relationships stand on the core truths of God's Word rather than on common interests or common causes? The depth of meaningful fellowship (with God and man) is directly proportional to the measure of truth that has permeated one's heart.

The Scriptures teach that fellowship, true *koinonia*, flourishes where truth abounds. In Philemon 6 Paul wrote:

> *and I pray that the fellowship of your faith may become effective through the knowledge of every good thing which is in you for Christ's sake.* (Philemon 6)

Paul realized that a proper understanding *"of every good thing"* which Christ has given the New Testament believer is the foundation of all Scriptural fellowship. Why? Misinterpreting what Christ accomplished through His death, burial, resurrection, and ascension leads to a faulty view of His heart and generates a lack of desire to know Him intimately, which, in turn, prevents us from knowing ourselves—since He, our Creator, knows us best. If we fail to know ourselves, we cannot utilize what God has fashioned us into through our new birth in Christ. Without this knowledge, we will likely fall prey to the lie that what we do is who we are.

Believing that what we do is who we are automatically places us on a performance-based acceptance with God—resulting in our also judging others by their performance. This situation becomes extremely problematic, because measuring others by such an impossible standard (we all falter at times) creates a rigid environment where friendships last only as long as behavior meets the demands of perfection. Unconditional love vanishes, leaving superficial relationships that cannot withstand adversity—a sad, lifeless, and powerless condition indeed.

Yes, a proper view of God, gleaned from the Scriptures, must be the foundation if deep, meaningful relationships are to prevail. Without it, we jump from one "friendship" to another, never finding the intimacy made possible only through Jesus. For this reason, a host of marriages end in what is commonly labeled "irreconcilable differences"—none of the "differences" being the root cause of the dissension. Therefore, until we can identify (and address) the root cause of the tensions within our human relationships, we will seldom experience Scriptural *koinonia*. Only a proper understanding of God's heart allows us to recognize that the "issue" is very seldom the "issue," and that God is up to something special in all "issues" of life. This understanding is true wisdom, which is attained only through trusting God, no matter what!

When fellowship is emphasized at the expense of doctrine, true *koinonia* excuses itself. However, doctrine illumined by God's Spirit allows us to know Who God is, the cornerstone of all meaningful relationships. Then, and only then, will the world know that we are Christ's disciples:

> *I in them, and Thou in Me, that they may be perfected in unity, that the world may know that Thou didst send Me, and didst love them, even as Thou didst love Me.* (John 17:23)

> *"By this all men will know that you are My disciples, if you have love for one another."* (John 13:35)

We can expect this study, because it is inundated with doctrine, to enhance not only our fellowship with God (due to an enriched understanding of His heart), but also our fellowship with others. I trust that you will be blessed and encouraged by its content!

Note: Words are sometimes underlined for emphasis, and statements enclosed in brackets for clarity.

CHAPTER TWO

THE ORIGIN OF THE DEBATE BETWEEN ARMINIANISM AND CALVINISM

WHEN DETERMINING WHAT TO BELIEVE regarding depravity, election, predestination, atonement, sovereignty, free will, and related topics, many people perceive Arminianism and Calvinism (although miles apart doctrinally) to be the only systems of thought that address these highly debated theological matters. I disagree. In fact, Bible scholars (along with people in general) have viewed these subjects from a variety of perspectives for centuries. We will begin our journey by examining the debate between Arminianism and Calvinism (why, as well as how, the five points of Arminianism and Calvinism were generated) and branch out from there.

*M**any people believe as they do solely because someone told them it was proper.*

Many Arminians and Calvinists believe as they do solely because someone told them it was "proper." However, the Scriptures alone must be the final say when addressing issues as critical as these.

We must understand, to some degree at least, the origin and persistence of the differences that separate Arminians and Calvinists if we are to speak intelligently with the followers of either camp. How their differences were birthed, and what has followed, is so captivating that volumes could be written without exhausting the subject. Therefore, I have exercised excessive restraint while writing this portion of the study. Nevertheless, what follows should equip you to dig deeply into the matter, the remainder of your days.

John Calvin was born in 1509 and died in 1564. Jacobus (James) Arminius was born in 1560 and died in 1609. Calvin is the man behind Calvinism and author of *Institutes of the Christian Religion*, a literary work that explains his views regarding depravity, election, predestination, salvation, grace, atonement, faith, and an assortment of other subjects. Arminius was a Calvinist in his earlier years; in fact, he studied at Calvin's seminary in Geneva, Switzerland under Calvin's disciple, Beza. After struggling with the extreme views of Calvinism, he concluded that, in some respects, Calvinism was unbiblical. As a result, he opposed Calvinism vigorously until his death in 1609. After his death, his ministers met in Gould, Holland, in 1610, to draw up a *Remonstrance* (protest) against Calvinism. The *Remonstrance,* which came to be known as the five points of Arminianism, consisted of only five short paragraphs. They are cited below:

1. God elects on the basis of His "eternal, unchangeable purpose" only "those who, through the grace of the Holy Ghost, shall believe on this His Son Jesus." He also wills "to leave the incorrigible and unbelieving in sin and under wrath."

2. Christ "died for all men and for every man, so that he has obtained for them all...redemption and forgiveness of sins; yet that no one actually enjoys this forgiveness of sins except the believer..."

3. "That man has not saving grace of himself, nor of the energy of his free will...can of and by himself neither think, will, nor do any thing that is truly good (such as saving faith eminently is); but that it is needful that he be born again of God in Christ...."

4. "That this grace of God is the beginning, continuance, and accomplishment of all good, even to this extent, that the regenerate man himself, without prevenient or assisting, awakening, following, and co-operative grace, can neither think, will, nor do good...." It adds, "But as respects the mode of the operation of this grace, it is not irresistible...."

5. "That those who are incorporated into Christ by a true faith...have thereby full power to...win the victory...but whether they are capable...of becoming devoid of grace, that must be more particularly determined out of the Holy Scriptures, before we ourselves can teach it with the full persuasion of our minds."

The Calvinists responded a few months later with a *Counter-Remonstrance*. Vance, *Other Side*, pages 151-152, summarize the Calvinists' *Counter-Remonstrance*:

1. Because the whole race has fallen in Adam and become corrupt and powerless to believe, God draws out of condemnation those whom he has chosen unto salvation, passing by the others.

2. The children of believers, as long as they do not manifest the contrary, are to be reckoned among God's elect.

3. God has decreed to bestow faith and perseverance and thus save those whom he has chosen to salvation.

4. God delivered up his Son Jesus Christ to die on the cross to save only the elect.

5. The Holy Spirit, externally through the preaching of the Gospel, works a special grace internally in the hearts of the elect, giving them power to believe.

6. Those whom God has decreed to save are supported and preserved by the Holy Spirit so that they cannot finally lose their true faith.

7. True believers do not carelessly pursue the lusts of the flesh, but work out their own salvation in the fear of the Lord.

The Arminian response to the Calvinists' *Counter-Remonstrance* was a lengthy document (*The Opinion of the Remonstrants*) which explained in greater depth their view of the Scriptures—plus their objections to Calvinism. Although this document was not in total harmony with James Arminius' theology, it was perceived as containing five points. On November 13, 1618, the Calvinists met at the Synod of Dort and drew up five answers (responses), or Canons, which are viewed today as the *Five Points of Calvinism*. Later, in 1643, a group of "divines" (many of whom were Calvinists) met in England and formulated *The Westminster Confession of Faith*, which some theologians have labeled as "the most systematically complete statement of Calvinism ever devised" (a quote addressed in *Other Side*, page 159, Vance). An understanding of the intriguing history surrounding these events can be gleaned from the civil and religious environment of that day, and greatly enhances one's perception of this critical season of church history. A variety of reliable resources that supply additional input are available in book form, on the Internet, and a host of other venues.

The Five Points of Calvinism: TULIP

Having previously listed the five points of Arminianism, a need exists to list *The Five Points of Calvinism*—often referred to by the acronym, *TULIP* (Total Depravity; Unconditional Election; Limited Atonement; Irresistible Grace; Perseverance of the Saints). (The TULIP was covered in more depth in *God's Heart as it Relates to Foreknowledge-Predestination*, so a review of that material might be helpful.) While proceeding, we will explore the ever-present tension between Arminianism and all forms of Calvinism. We will also discuss why the extreme and hyper-Calvinists (Reformed theologians) embrace all five points of the TULIP while the moderate Calvinists embrace (to some degree at least) only four, totally rejecting the "L" (Limited Atonement). Thus, the moderate Calvinists normally define the "T," "U," "I," and "P" differently than do the extreme and hyper-Calvinists.

The following excerpt from Dave Hunt's work, *What Love Is This?*, pages 108-109, defines the basic tenants of extreme and hyper-Calvinism (Reformed Theology):

> Some readers may have never heard of TULIP. Others, though knowing that it has something to do with Calvinism, find it difficult to remember what each letter stands for. Here, in brief, is a summary of common explanations. In each case, in order to avoid the charge that they are not properly stated, they are presented in the words of the major Calvinistic creeds or confessions:
>
>> "T" stands for Total Depravity: that man, because he is spiritually dead to God "in trespasses and in sins" (Ephesians 2:1; Colossians 2:13), is incapable of responding to the gospel, though able to make other moral choices.
>>
>> The Westminster Confession of Faith declares, "Our first parents...became dead in sin, and wholly defiled in all the faculties and parts of soul and body...wholly inclined to all evil.... Man, by his fall into a state of sin, hath wholly lost all ability of will to any spiritual good accompanying salvation...being altogether averse from that good, and dead

in sin, is not able by his own strength, to convert himself, or to prepare himself thereunto."

"U" stands for Unconditional Election: that God decides on no basis whatsoever but by the mystery of His will to save some, called the elect, and to allow all others to go to hell, even though He *could* save *all* mankind if He so desired.

The Canons of Dort declare, "That some receive the gift of faith from God, and others do not receive it proceeds from God's eternal decree...[by] which decree, he graciously softens the hearts of the elect, however obstinate, and inclines them to believe, while he leaves the non-elect in his just judgment to their own wickedness and obduracy."

"L" stands for Limited Atonement: that the elect are the only ones for whom Christ died in payment of the penalty for their sins, and that His death is efficacious for no others, nor was intended to be.

Dort declares: "For this was the sovereign counsel, and most gracious will and purpose of God the Father, that...the most precious death of his Son should extend to all the elect...all those, and those only, who were from eternity chosen to salvation...he purchased by his death."

"I" stands for Irresistible Grace: that God is able to cause whomever He will to respond to the gospel; that without this enabling, no one could do so; and that He only provides this Irresistible Grace to the elect and damns the rest.

The Westminster Confession states: "All those whom God hath predestinated unto life, and those only, he is pleased, in his appointed and accepted time, effectually to call, by his Word and Spirit, out of that state of sin and death...effectually drawing them to Jesus Christ; yet so, as they come most freely, being made willing by his grace."

"P" stands for Perseverance of the Saints: that God will not allow any of the elect to fail to persevere in living a life consistent with the salvation that He has sovereignly given them.

The Westminster Confession states: "They, whom God hath accepted in his Beloved, effectually called, and sanctified by His Spirit, can neither totally nor finally fall

> away from the state of grace, but shall certainly persevere
> therein to the end, and be eternally saved. This
> perseverance of the saints depends not upon their own free
> will, but upon the immutability of the decree of election.[1]

As this study unfolds, we will examine additional remarks from a variety of Calvinists pertaining to this subject matter. We will observe that their comments echo Hunt's preceding quotes from Dort and The Westminster Confession, confirming that Hunt was fair in his presentation of these remarks, though in disagreement with them.

I am not a follower of Arminianism. Nor do I adhere to any form of Calvinism, be it moderate, extreme, or hyper (extreme and hyper-Calvinism being Reformed Theology). Interestingly, the extreme and hyper-Calvinists normally classify as Arminian (or Pelagian—a term we will define shortly) anyone who views the depraved (those living in a spiritually unregenerated state) as free to choose Christ. Norm Geisler, a moderate Calvinist, believes that man can choose to accept Christ while depraved. Consequently, some Reformed theologians label him Arminian. No wonder the great Spurgeon (a Calvinist) was accused by many Calvinists of being Arminian as a result of his sermon, *"Compel them to come in."* Dave Hunt in *What Love Is This?,* pages 154-155, writes:

> ...Calvinists eagerly cite Spurgeon for support, and there is no
> doubt that Spurgeon often declared himself to be a Calvinist.
> Yet he frequently made statements that contradicted Calvinism.
> The following is from a British scholar who thoroughly knew
> Spurgeon's writings and sermons:
>
>> Charles Haddon Spurgeon always claimed to be a
>> Calvinist.... His mind was soaked in the writings of the
>> Puritan divines; but his intense zeal for the conversion of
>> souls led him to step outside the bounds of the creed he
>> had inherited. His sermon on "Compel them to come in" was
>> criticized as Arminian and unsound. To his critics he replied:
>> "My Master set His seal on that message. I never preached
>> a sermon by which so many souls were won to God.... If it be
>> thought an evil thing to bid the sinner lay hold of eternal life,
>> I will yet be more evil in this respect and herein imitate my
>> Lord and His apostles."
>>   More than once Spurgeon prayed, "Lord, hasten to bring
>> in all Thine elect, and then elect some more." He seems to
>> have used that phrase often in conversation, and on his lips
>> it was no mere badinage. With its definite rejection of a

> limited atonement, it would have horrified John Calvin.... The truth seems to be that the old Calvinistic phrases were often on Spurgeon's lips but the genuine Calvinistic meaning had gone out of them.
>
> J. C. Carlile admits that "illogical as it may seem, Spurgeon's Calvinism was of such a character that while he proclaimed the majesty of God *he did not hesitate to ascribe freedom of will to man and to insist that any man might find in Jesus Christ deliverance from the power of sin* (emphasis added)."[2]

Spurgeon struggled with what to believe regarding the free will of man. At times he seemed to adhere to free will, as was addressed above, while at other times reject it, as in his sermon titled, "The Holy Spirit in the Covenant," preached in 1856.

> What a vain pretense it is to profess to honor God by a doctrine that makes salvation depend on the will of man!...Beloved, do not any of you swerve from the free grace of God, for the babblings about man's free agency are neither more nor less than lies, right contrary to the truth of Christ, and the teachings of the Spirit.
>
> How certain, then, is the salvation of every elect soul! It does not depend on the will of man; he is "made willing" in the day of God's power. He shall be called at the set time, and his heart shall be effectually changed, that he may become a trophy of the Redeemer's power. That he was unwilling before, is no hindrance; for God giveth him the will, so that he is then of a willing mind. Thus, every heir of heaven must be saved, because the Spirit is put within him, and thereby his disposition and affections are molded according to the will of God.[3]

In the following quote from, "God's will and man's will," (No. 442; Newington, Metropolitan Tabernacle; a sermon delivered Sunday morning, March 30, 1862), Spurgeon describes certain types of Calvinists. In so doing, he contradicts his strong stand against the free will of man previously addressed (this quote can also be found in Dave Hunt's *What Love Is This?*, page 158):

> "a class of strong-minded hard-headed men who magnified sovereignty at the expense of [human] responsibility"[4]

Such inconsistencies resulted from Spurgeon's submission to the irregularities within Calvinism. This same problem arises with everyone who fails to allow the full counsel of God's Word to govern all areas of thought. Thus, we will permit all of the Scriptures (rather than a select few—interpreted out of context) to have their way as we proceed.

Now that we have a "general" idea of how depravity is perceived by Arminianism and Calvinism, we will study the term in more depth, addressing the seven most prevalent views (Pelagianism, Semi-Pelagianism, Arminianism, Moderate Calvinism, Extreme Calvinism, Hyper-Calvinism, and what I call "The Scriptural View"). What follows should be enormously intriguing, especially due to the controversy surrounding "depravity" since the days of Augustine.

CHAPTER THREE

SEVEN VIEWS OF DEPRAVITY: TO WHAT DEGREE IS MAN DEPRAVED?

Pelagianism and Depravity

PELAGIANISM GAINED ITS VIEW OF DEPRAVITY from Pelagius (354-420 AD), who believed that mankind is born with the innocence Adam possessed prior to his (Adam's) falling into sin. Followers of this system perceive all persons as created moral and in God's image since (according to their view) man did not sin *"in"* Adam, thus inheriting his fallen nature. This fact explains why Pelagianism perceives Adam as serving only as a bad example for mankind. This system does, however, hold to the view that man is capable of sinning *"like"* Adam. They consider themselves free to obey or disobey, viewing their choices as determining their destiny—and that those who choose Christ do so without the aid of the Holy Spirit. They also perceive physical death as resulting from man's sin, not Adam's. This view is in the minority today and can be easily refuted by verses such as Romans 5:12-21 and Ephesians 2:1-3. Dave Hunt, in *What Love Is This?,* page 36, confirms my previous comments.

> Born in Britain near the end of the fourth century, Pelagius rose to prominence after the fall of Rome in August 410 forced him to flee to North Africa. There he came into open conflict with Augustine for his views that there had been sinless beings before Christ and that it was possible through human effort, aided by grace, for anyone to live above sin. He claimed that Adam was mortal when created and that his sin did not bring death upon mankind but affected only himself. Consequently,

> infants are born in the same state Adam was in before he
> sinned. Moreover, good works were essential to salvation,
> especially for the rich to give their goods to the poor to help
> effect the moral transformation of society, which he believed
> possible. He considered "forgive us our sins" to be a prayer
> involving false humility and unsuitable for Christians, inasmuch
> as sin is not a necessity but man's own fault.[5]

Pelagius' and Augustine's views of depravity could not have been more
polarized. After all, Augustine (in his latter years) viewed man as incapable of
choosing Christ in his depraved (spiritually unregenerated) state. Augustine's latter
writings greatly influenced Calvin's view of depravity, which will become evident
as we proceed. Note: Augustine, in the early years of his ministry, believed that
man is free to choose Christ while depraved. The circumstances that led to his
change of heart (doctrine) are worth researching when time permits. Augustine's
situation serves as a warning to all persons who desire to remain true to God's
Word when facing the pressures of a popular yet heretical viewpoint.

Semi-Pelagianism and Depravity

Dave Hunt, in *What Love Is This?,* page 36, writes:

> Semi-Pelagianism was developed a few years later [a few
> years after the birth of Pelagianism] by a French monk, John
> Cassianus, who modified Pelagianism by denying its extreme
> views on human merit and accepting the necessity of the power
> of the Holy Spirit but retaining the belief that man can do good,
> that he can resist God's grace, that he must cooperate in
> election, does have the will to choose between good and evil,
> and can lose his salvation. Those who reject Calvinism are often
> accused of promoting semi-Pelagianism, which is a broad label
> and often not true.[6]

Semi-Pelagianism, like Pelagianism, views man as capable of choosing Christ.

Arminianism and Depravity

Jerry Walls and Joseph Dongell, followers of Arminianism, write about depravity
in, *Why I am Not a Calvinist*, page 11:

> ...The Arminian and Wesleyan answer is that the death of
> Christ provided grace for all persons and that, as a result of his
> atonement, God extends sufficient grace to all persons through
> the Holy Spirit to counteract the influence of sin and to enable a
> positive response to God (Jn 15:26-27; 16:7-11). The initiative
> here is entirely God's; the sinner's part is only to respond in
> faith and grateful obedience (Lk 15; Rom 5:6-8; Eph 2:4-5; Phil
> 2:12-13). However, it is possible for sinners to resist God's
> initiative and to persist in sin and rebellion. In other words,
> God's grace enables and encourages a positive and saving
> response from everyone, but it does not determine a saving
> response for anyone (Acts 7:51).... [7]

Apparently, Walls and Dongell agree that man possesses the freedom, assisted by God's grace, to choose Christ in his depraved state.

Norm Geisler, a moderate Calvinist, writes regarding Arminianism in *Systematic Theology, Volume 3, Sin/Salvation*, pages 143-144:

> This view [Arminianism] gets its name from Jacob (James)
> Arminius (1560-1609), a Reformed theologian from Holland,
> although "Arminianism" also bears resemblance to a view called
> semi-Pelagianism. However, the popular version of what we
> know *today* as "Arminianism" springs from John Wesley (1703-
> 1791) and is more properly called "Wesleyanism."
>
> Since subviews in the overall Arminian camp differ
> significantly, it is difficult to point to a single person who held to
> all the elements listed here. Even so, a general Arminian view
> of depravity, in contrast to Pelagianism, maintains that all
> people are born depraved and *cannot* on their own power obey
> God. Each human was either potentially or seminally in Adam
> when he chose evil, and, hence, he or she is born with a corrupt
> nature, under the stigma of Adam's sin.
>
> Arminianism (Wesleyanism) believes that all human beings
> are born with both the bent toward sin and the unavoidability of
> physical death; and should they not repent of their sins, they will
> die eternally. The image of God in humans is so effaced that
> they need His grace to overcome it and to move in His direction,
> as He alone can save them. In contrast to the insistence of
> extreme Calvinism, however, God's grace does not work
> *irresistibly* on all (or on the elect only). Rather, God's grace
> works *sufficiently* on all, awaiting their free cooperation before it
> becomes savingly...effective.[8]

The following description of Arminianism is taken from the website the-highway.com:

> Although human nature was seriously affected by the fall, man has not been left in a state of total spiritual helplessness. God graciously enables every sinner to repent and believe, but He does not interfere with man's freedom. Each sinner possesses a free will, and his eternal destiny depends on how he uses it. Man's freedom consists of his ability to choose good over evil in spiritual matters; his will is not enslaved to his sinful nature. The sinner has the power to either cooperate with God's Spirit and be regenerated or resist God's grace and perish. The lost sinner needs the Spirit's assistance, but he does not have to be regenerated by the Spirit before he can believe, for faith is man's act and precedes the new birth. Faith is the sinner's gift to God; it is man's contribution to salvation. [9]

Arminianism adheres to the mindset that unregenerate man (assisted by God's grace while in his depravity) can choose to accept Christ—confirming that "believe" in the following quote from James Arminius means to choose to believe while depraved:

> "God decreed to save and damn certain particular persons. This decree has its foundation in the foreknowledge of God, by which he knew from all eternity those individuals who would, through his...grace, believe, and, through his subsequent grace would persevere" (*The Works of James Arminius*, Vol. 1, My own Sentiments on Predestination)[10]

Moderate Calvinism and Depravity

Norm Geisler, a moderate Calvinist, discusses depravity in his work, *Systematic Theology, Volume 3, Sin/Salvation*, page 144:

> Unlike Arminianism, moderate Calvinism holds that we inherit a judicial guilt from Adam's sin and that we are legally (and/or naturally) connected to him. As a result of Adam's choice for evil, all human beings, apart from salvation, suffer spiritual death and will undergo both physical and eternal death. Further, God's grace is not merely *sufficient* for all; it is *efficient*

> for the elect. In order for God's grace to be effective, there must
> be cooperation by the recipient on whom God has moved.
>   In common with strong Calvinism [Extreme and Hyper
> Calvinism], moderate Calvinism maintains that all human
> beings sinned in Adam, either legally or naturally, and that we
> all inherit a sinful nature—Adam's guilt is imputed to all his
> posterity. This guilt can only be overcome by God's saving
> grace, which, according to moderate Calvinism, is irresistible
> only on the *willing*.[11]

The moderate Calvinists view all of mankind as having sinned in Adam, and as a result, possessing a sin nature at conception (and, therefore, at birth). They also view man as capable of choosing Christ in this depraved state, but not without the assistance of God's grace. In other words, they generally believe that man's depravity disallows him from *initiating* any move toward God on his own—but that man, through God's drawing, can exercise his free will (while depraved) and repent and believe.

Extreme Calvinism and Depravity

The extreme and hyper-Calvinists, like the moderate Calvinists, perceive man as inheriting a sin nature from Adam. They differ from the moderates by assuming that God must spiritually regenerate the depraved, and follow by granting the spiritually regenerated repentance and faith, before they can choose to repent, believe, and be saved. Thus, their view of depravity is that the spiritually unregenerated (depraved) lack the ability to choose Christ. John Piper (a Reformed theologian), in his DVD series, *TULIP*, Disk 2, Title 1, Chapters 1-3, states:

> We don't seek Him [God], we don't delight in Him, we don't
> pursue Him, apart from His enabling grace because of how
> depraved we are. ...there is a kind of bondage of the human
> heart to sin that makes it unable to choose good, and it's a real
> unable....We have to agree with the Biblical assumption—I am so
> sinful I cannot see or savor Jesus Christ as my supreme value
> and I am guilty for my failure to see Him and savor Him...[12]

Wikipedia's definition of the Reformed view of total depravity is in agreement:

> Because of the fall, man is unable of himself to savingly believe
> the gospel. The sinner is dead, blind, and deaf to the things of
> God; his heart is deceitful and desperately corrupt. His will is not

free, it is in bondage to his evil nature, therefore, he will not - indeed he cannot - choose good over evil in the spiritual realm.[13]

Dr. Arnold Fruchtenbaum, a moderate Calvinist, states the following regarding extreme and hyper-Calvinism in his CD series, *God's Will, Man's Will*:

Total Depravity [within extreme and hyper-Calvinism] means total inability...man cannot do anything toward his salvation, not even believe. That's why the strict [extreme] and the hyper-Calvinist both teach that regeneration precedes faith, and that man must become spiritually alive before he can believe.... For example, one of the Calvinists says, "Faith is not the cause of the new birth, but the consequence of it." In other words, you first are born again, then you believe. That's how they teach it. That's because of their extreme view of what total depravity means.... Another writer says this, and I quote, "We have nothing to do with our spiritual birth. It occurs with or without our consent being asked." So it doesn't matter whether you want to be saved or not. You are forced to be saved.... If any person believes, it is because God has quickened him, and if any person fails to believe, it is because God has withheld that grace. Only the soul, dead in sin, when it is first transferred to spiritual life—then it exercises faith and repentance. And that's why the strict [extreme] Calvinists and the hyper-Calvinists do not stress believing all that much, because until God zaps you, you can't believe. But with that view, mind you, you are already saved before you believe, so why even bother telling people to believe....[14]

Edwin H. Palmer (a Reformed theologian), in *The Five Points of Calvinism*, page 16, writes:

...all minds are blind, unless they are regenerated....
Not only is the non-Christian unable to do anything that is truly good, not only is he unable to understand the good, but, worse still, he is not even able to desire the good....[15]

Extreme Calvinism's view of depravity (and hyper-Calvinism's view as well—which is discussed next) requires that God spiritually regenerate the depraved (and follow by giving them the gifts of repentance and faith) before they can choose to repent, believe, and be saved. But isn't this order a reversal of what is taught in

God's Word? Don't the Scriptures teach that repentance and faith precede spiritual regeneration? We will soon consider Acts 16:31, Romans 4:3, 5, 9, 5:1, 10:9-10 (along with an abundance of additional passages), all of which teach that repentance and faith must <u>precede</u> spiritual regeneration (Scriptural salvation). We will also include the extreme and hyper-Calvinists' interpretation of these passages, that is, the passages they are willing to address.

Hyper-Calvinism and Depravity

Even with the many conflicting ideas that permeate Calvinism, one can safely say that hyper-Calvinism views the depravity of man in basically the same manner as extreme Calvinism. Thus, the previous input regarding extreme Calvinism's view of depravity is applicable.

The following quote from the moderate Calvinist, Dr. Norm Geisler's *Systematic Theology, Volume 3, Sin/Salvation*, page 147, is interesting food for thought:

> Ironically, if one takes total depravity too far, he destroys a person's ability to be depraved. For if *total depravity* means "one's ability to know and choose good over evil is destroyed," then the person whose knowledge and volition have been eliminated is no longer able to sin, because then he would have had no access to the good (only evil would have been available to him). There *are* creatures without these abilities, but they are subhuman animals and plants that cannot sin. What has no moral capacity and ability has no moral responsibility.[16]

The Scriptural View of Depravity

God's Word does not teach that total depravity means "total inability." Yes, all of mankind is born with a sin nature due to their genes having been in Adam's gene pool when Adam sinned (Romans 5:12-21; Ephesians 2:1-2; etc.). However, with the assistance of God's grace, man can choose to accept Christ, even in a depraved state. We will confirm this truth, not through the use of logic or tradition, but through the Scriptures alone. Keep in mind that our goal is to know God's heart, and in the process, protect His impeccable name and reputation.

Because free will ties in nicely with depravity, we will attend to many passages that, due to time restraints, were bypassed in our previous study of *God's Heart as it Relates to Sovereignty-Free Will*. These verses will be beneficial as we pursue God's perspective of this critical doctrinal matter. We will begin by allowing Scripture (rather than logic) to properly define "death."

CHAPTER FOUR

THE SCRIPTURAL MEANING OF "DEATH"

A HEALTHY VIEW OF DEPRAVITY is not possible without understanding the Scriptural meaning of the term *"death" (or "dead")*. *"Death"* is basically used in four ways in God's Word: (1) Physical death (2) Spiritual death (3) *"The second death"* (4) The *"death"* (eradication, annihilation, or extinction) of the Adamic nature in a New Testament believer.

1. <u>*Physical death*</u> occurs when the soul and spirit separate from the body. Lazarus and the rich man in Luke 16:19-31 are examples of this type of death. Lazarus' soul and spirit, as well as the rich man's soul and spirit, continued in conscious existence after body function had ceased—Lazarus departing to *"Abraham's bosom"* (where the righteous deceased dwelt prior to the cross) and the rich man departing to *"Hades"* (hell in this case).

2. *Spiritual death* is spiritual <u>separation</u> from God, God being *"spirit"* (John 4:24). Man is born in this condition, as illustrated by Paul in Ephesians 2:1:

    And you were <u>dead</u> in your trespasses and sins (Ephesians 2:1)

    An abundance of additional verses confirm this same truth, several of which will be addressed later in the study.

3. *"<u>The second death</u>"* is mentioned in Revelation 21:8:

"But for the cowardly and unbelieving and abominable and murderers and immoral persons and sorcerers and idolaters and all liars, their part will be in the lake that burns with fire and brimstone, which is the second death." (Revelation 21:8)

This passage points to that day when the lost are cast into *"the lake that burns with fire and brimstone,"* an event described in the Scriptures as *"the second death."* Obviously, a *"second death"* requires that a death precede it. The "first" death results from Adam's descendants being born spiritually *"dead"* (Ephesians 2:1). Therefore, the lost who refuse to accept the gift of life offered by Christ (John 5:40; 10:10) are cast into hell, an environment void of the presence of God—total separation from God the Father, Son, and Spirit.

The *"second death"* (Revelation 21:8), obviously, is different from the *"first."* It occurs in conjunction with the *"great white throne"* judgment of Revelation 20:11-15, a judgment that transpires after Christ's Second Coming. At the completion of this judgment, the lost are separated from God for all eternity. This sequence proves that the term *"death"* (or *"dead"*) in Scripture can point to separation rather than extinction, especially since the lost will exist as conscious beings while suffering eternally in the lake of fire.

4. *The death (eradication, annihilation, or extinction) of the Adamic nature in a New Testament believer* (Romans 6:6; 7:4). This "death" transpires when the depraved exercise personal repentance and faith and are crucified *"in Christ"* (1Corinthians 12:13; 2Corinthians 5:17; Galatians 2:20). The *Romans 1-8* course distributed by this ministry explores this subject in much detail.

Conclusion

Spiritual death (resulting from Adam's sin—Romans 5:12-19) does not make the depraved spiritual corpses, totally unable to respond to God's grace. Spiritual death is separation, which can be rectified if the depraved will but choose Christ—God drawing and convicting all mankind (John 6:44; 12:32; 16:8) due to His desiring that none perish (1Timothy 2:4; 2Peter 3:9). Once a depraved individual chooses to repent and believe, he is placed into Christ through the power of the Holy Spirit (1Corinthians 12:13), *"crucified"* with Christ (Galatians 2:20; Romans 6:6; 7:4), *"buried"* with Christ (Colossians 2:12), and made *"new"* (2Corinthians 5:17). The fact that the depraved can exercise personal repentance and faith (prior to spiritual regeneration) is confirmed throughout the remainder of this study.

Now that we have presented the four basic views of *"death"* addressed in the Scriptures, let's return to the subject of depravity (spiritual death) by revisiting Paul's words of Ephesians 2:1:

> *And you were <u>dead</u> in your trespasses and sins* (Ephesians 2:1)

Without doubt, man is born spiritually dead, totally separated from God. Is Paul communicating that the unregenerate (depraved) are totally incapable of responding to God? In other words, does the spiritual deadness associated with total depravity point to a "total inability" to repent and believe? What follows answers these questions.

CHAPTER FIVE

TOTAL DEPRAVITY INCOMPATIBLE WITH "TOTAL INABILITY"

God makes even the Heathen Aware of the Truth

Romans 1:18-32

These verses describe the progression of sin in man when man chooses to exchange God's truth for a lie. In fact, Romans 1:8-32 portrays the lifestyle of the heathen—those who, through their own choosing, reject the truth that God so graciously supplies.

> *For the wrath of God is revealed from heaven against all*
> *ungodliness and unrighteousness of men, who suppress the truth in*
> *unrighteousness,* (Romans 1:18)

The spiritually depraved can *"suppress the truth,"* proving that they are conscious (aware) of the truth. You can't *"suppress"* what has not been made accessible.

> *because that which is known about God is evident within them; for*
> *God made it evident to them.* (Romans 1:19)

Here, God makes what can be *"known"* about Himself *"evident"* to not just the elect, but to all mankind.

> *For since the creation of the world His invisible attributes, His*
> *eternal power and divine nature, have been clearly seen, being*
> *understood through what has been made, so that they are without*
> *excuse.* (Romans 1:20)

Creation reveals God's *"attributes," "power,"* and *"divine nature."* Thus, no man can accuse God of withholding from mankind the certainty of His existence—not even the unrepentant heathen.

> *For even though they knew God, they did not honor Him as God,*
> *or give thanks; but they became futile in their speculations, and*
> *their foolish heart was darkened.* (Romans 1:21)

Paul teaches that all persons (all of the depraved) know about God—know of His existence and characteristics regarding His Person. The depraved who choose to dishonor Him, however, find their hearts progressively *"darkened."* The fact that the choice to dishonor God results in an intensified darkening of the heart proves that man is not at his worst at the point of physical birth, much less a spiritual corpse (the depraved are spiritual corpses according to Reformed Theology). His heart can (in the midst of his depravity) become increasingly darkened through intensified rebellion. A spiritual corpse experiencing an exacerbated state of darkness proves that he previously possessed a measure of light—negating the spiritual corpse theory altogether. Also, would God have stretched out His hands (offered salvation) to lost Jews who never believed (referenced in Romans 10:21) should the depraved be incapable of exercising personal repentance and faith? Such an arrangement would make Him anything but the all-wise Sovereign the Scriptures declare Him to be.

> *Professing to be wise, they became fools,* (Romans 1:22)

Persons who prefer *"to be wise"* in their own eyes become fools due to their own choices.

> *and exchanged the glory of the incorruptible God for an image in*
> *the form of corruptible man and of birds and four-footed animals*
> *and crawling creatures.* (Romans 1:23)

Once the depraved reject God's truth, they worship what has been created. In making that choice, they exchange *"the glory of...God"* (Who He is in His essence) for what will perish.

*Therefore God gave them over in the lusts of their hearts to
impurity, that their bodies might be dishonored among them.*
(Romans 1:24)

As a result of the depraved rejecting His truth, "*God*" gives "*them over*" to "*impurity.*" Note that He gives "*them over*" <u>after</u> they chose to disobey.

*For they exchanged the truth of God for a lie, and worshiped and
served the creature rather than the Creator, who is blessed forever.
Amen.* (Romans 1:25)

The depraved (as they progress in sin) are given "*over...to impurity*" (Romans 1:24) for one reason only—they exchange "*the truth of God for a lie,*" which results in their worshipping "*the creature rather than the Creator*" (Romans 1:25). To exchange "*the truth,*" they must have access to the truth. You can't exchange something for an alternative if you don't first possess what you are exchanging. All along, God loves the sinner but hates his sin.

*For this reason God gave them over to degrading passions; for
their women exchanged the natural function for that which is
unnatural,* (Romans 1:26)

After the depraved reject the truth, God gives "*them over to degrading passions*"—which are defined in the following verse.

*and in the same way also the men abandoned the natural function
of the woman and burned in their desire toward one another, men
with men committing indecent acts and receiving in their own
persons the due penalty of their error.* (Romans 1:27)

The "*degrading passions*" of verse 26 are passions that cause women to desire improper (and "*unnatural*") physical relationships with women (v.26) and men to desire improper (unnatural and "*indecent*") physical relationships with men (v.27)—homosexual and lesbian relationships in other words. Again, God loves the sinner but hates his sin.

*And even as they did not like to retain God in their knowledge, God
gave them over to a reprobate mind, to do those things which are
not convenient;* (Romans 1:28 KJV)

The depraved possess a *"knowledge"* of God, although they many times despise retaining it. Therefore, their rejection of the truth causes their minds to become *"reprobate."*

> *being filled with all unrighteousness, wickedness, greed, evil; full*
> *of envy, murder, strife, deceit, malice; they are gossips, slanderers,*
> *haters of God, insolent, arrogant, boastful, inventors of evil,*
> *disobedient to parents, without understanding, untrustworthy,*
> *unloving, unmerciful;* (Romans 1:29-31)

The fruit of rebellion, an appalling state indeed, is described in verses 29-31!

> *and, although they know the ordinance of God, that those who*
> *practice such things are worthy of death, they not only do the*
> *same, but also give hearty approval to those who practice them.*
> (Romans 1:32)

The *"depraved"* (verse 28 NASB) *"know the ordinance of God"* (verse 32) prior to their extreme rebelliousness. Thus, a huge difference exists between knowing God's truth and yearning to apply it. Once the depraved repent and believe, however, they are made new—resulting in a passionate desire to know and exercise God's absolutes to the greatest degree possible.

Romans 1:18-32 validates (beyond doubt) that man, even in his depraved state, has a conscience awareness of God's existence—proving that man's depravity does not make him totally unaware of spiritual matters, and thus, a spiritual corpse. No wonder the Psalmist penned:

> *The heavens are telling of the glory of God; and their expanse is*
> *declaring the work of His hands. Day to day pours forth speech,*
> *and night to night reveals knowledge. There is no speech, nor are*
> *there words; their voice is not heard.* (Psalm 19:1-3)

Conclusion

Depravity does not mean that unregenerate man is "incapable" of knowing about God and His truth. Neither does depravity validate the idea that unregenerate man possesses an "inability" to exercise personal repentance and faith—as verified by the remainder of this study.

The Law Convicts the Depraved of their Depravity

Galatians 3:24

> *Therefore the Law has become our tutor to lead us to Christ, that*
> *we may be justified by faith.* (Galatians 3:24)

Our gleanings from Romans 1:18-32 tie in perfectly with Galatians 3:24. The Law, given to Moses in the Old Testament, serves a very special purpose. Paul describes it as a *"tutor,"* for through the Law man can recognize his need for a Savior. However, if totally depraved means "total inability," what need would there be for the Law? If man, in his lost state, cannot recognize sin and exercise personal repentance and faith, why would God give a Law, whose purpose it is to convict the depraved of their lostness?

Paul, in (1Timothy 1:8-10), confirms that the Law is for the ungodly—not the righteous:

> *But we know that the Law is good, if one uses it lawfully, realizing*
> *the fact that law is not made for a righteous man, but for those who*
> *are lawless and rebellious, for the ungodly and sinners, for the*
> *unholy and profane, for those who kill their fathers or mothers, for*
> *murderers and immoral men and homosexuals and kidnappers and*
> *liars and perjurers, and whatever else is contrary to sound*
> *teaching,* (1Timothy 1:8-10)

These verses prove, beyond doubt, that the Law was given to convict the hearts of the ungodly (depraved) only. Paul confirms this same truth in Romans 3:19:

> *Now we know that whatever the Law says, it speaks to those who*
> *are under the Law, that every mouth may be closed, and all the*
> *world may become accountable to God;* (Romans 3:19)

The Law speaks to one class of individuals: *"to those who are under the Law."* Once again we observe that the Law convicts the depraved of their sin so they might recognize their need for a Savior. Paul adds to the argument in Romans 6:14 where he states that the New Testament believer is *"not under law, but under grace"*:

> *For sin shall not be master over you, for you are not under law, but*
> *under grace.* (Romans 6:14)

This verse reinforces the fact that only the ungodly (the depraved) are under the Law. Paul also states (in Romans 7:4-6) that believers died to the Law through the body of Christ, freeing them to *"serve in the newness of the Spirit and not in the oldness of the letter"*:

> *Therefore, my brethren, you also were made to die to the Law*
> *through the body of Christ, that you might be joined to another, to*
> *Him who was raised from the dead, that we might bear fruit for*
> *God. For while we were in the flesh, the sinful passions, which*
> *were aroused by the Law, were at work in the members of our body*
> *to bear fruit for death. But now we have been released from the*
> *Law, having died to that by which we were bound, so that we serve*
> *in newness of the Spirit and not in oldness of the letter.* (Romans
> 7:4-6)

Unquestionably, the Law serves to convict the ungodly only. It was given, in other words, to lead the ungodly (the depraved) to Christ (Galatians 3:24). Thus, the depraved are capable of having the Law convict them of their ungodliness so they might repent and believe—disproving that total depravity means "total inability."

To perceive the depraved as spiritual corpses is in violation of the full counsel of God's Word. Again we observe the consistency of the Scriptures regardless of the subject under examination.

God's Spirit Convicts the World of Sin, Righteousness, and Judgment

John 16:8

> *"And He, when He comes, will convict the world concerning sin,*
> *and righteousness, and judgment;* (John 16:8)

Jesus taught that the Holy Spirit would *"convict the world"* (*kosmos*—the entire inhabited earth) of *"sin."* Should depravity indicate that man (while depraved) is incapable of responding to God, would God not be unwise if, through the power of the Holy Spirit, He convicted individuals who are unable to respond? Even John MacArthur (a Reformed theologian) states that John 16:8 points to a:

‖ ...conviction of the need for a Savior[17]

Titus 2:11-12 also agrees:

36

> *For the grace of God has appeared, bringing salvation to all men,*
> *instructing us to deny ungodliness and worldly desires and to live*
> *sensibly, righteously and godly in the present age,* (Titus 2:11-12)

If depravity makes man a spiritually lifeless corpse (according to the Reformed view of depravity), why would Paul record such statements? Note: Some Calvinists view the *"all men"* in verse 11 as the "elect" of Calvinism in an attempt to hold to their view of total depravity (and other aspects of the TULIP). This conclusion is contextually impossible. Titus 2:11-12 is also misused by the Universalists in an attempt to prove that all mankind will be saved. When taken through the full counsel of the Scriptures, however, proper context indicates that God offers *"salvation to all men,"* many of whom reject it to their own demise. 2Thessalonians 1:6-10 refutes the error that all mankind will be saved:

> *For after all it is only just for God to repay with affliction those*
> *who afflict you, and to give relief to you who are afflicted and to us*
> *as well when the Lord Jesus shall be revealed from heaven with*
> *His mighty angels in flaming fire, dealing out retribution to those*
> *who do not know God and to those who do not obey the gospel of*
> *our Lord Jesus. And these will pay the penalty of eternal*
> *destruction, away from the presence of the Lord and from the glory*
> *of His power, when He comes to be glorified in His saints on that*
> *day, and to be marveled at among all who have believed — for our*
> *testimony to you was believed.* (2Thessalonians 1:6-10)

A wealth of additional passages could be cited, but we must continue with our present topic of interest by considering Stephen's words of Acts 7:51:

> *"You men who are stiff-necked and uncircumcised in heart and*
> *ears are always resisting the Holy Spirit; you are doing just as*
> *your fathers did.* (Acts 7:51)

Observe that Stephen's accusers resisted the Holy Spirit and its work of conviction. Therefore, their *"resisting"* proves that the Holy Spirit convicts the depraved. It also proves (coupled with what we will study shortly) that Stephen's accusers' choice, not God's choice, determined where they would spend eternity. Again, if God is all knowing (omniscient), sovereign, and wise, He would be totally unwise (foolish—relinquishing His sovereignty) should He convict a person of sin whom He knew could not possibly believe? Thus, depravity and "total inability" are anything but synonymous. Isn't the full counsel of God's Word amazing!

CHAPTER SIX

MORE VERSES THAT RELATE TO DEPRAVITY

2Corinthians 4:3-4 and Depravity

And even if our gospel is veiled, it is veiled to those who are perishing, in whose case the god of this world has blinded the minds of the unbelieving, that they might not see the light of the gospel of the glory of Christ, who is the image of God. (2 Corinthians 4:3-4)

No need would exist for Satan to blind the minds of the depraved should they be incapable of comprehending truth. This fact is even more convincing proof that the depraved <u>can</u> recognize their need for a Savior and repent and believe.

Mark 16:15 and Depravity

... *"Go into all the world and preach the gospel to all creation.* (Mark 16:15)

Why would Jesus desire that *"all the world"* hear the gospel if *"all"* people are not given opportunity to believe the gospel while depraved?

John 7:37 and Depravity

"If any man is thirsty, let him come to Me and drink. (John 7:37)

To possess a thirst for the Lord, one must desire to know the Lord. Because thirst precedes drinking, a person can thirst for God (in his/her depraved state) before he/she drinks of His Spirit—that is, experiences spiritual regeneration—salvation.

Revelation 22:17 and Depravity

And the Spirit and the bride say, "Come." And let the one who hears say, "Come." And let the one who is thirsty come; let the one who wishes take the water of life without cost. (Revelation 22:17)

Again, we see that a thirst for the things of God must precede the partaking of *"the water of life"* (spiritual regeneration—salvation). Thus, the depraved can recognize their need for a Savior and choose to repent and believe. Also note that the act of partaking of *"the water of life"* is without cost. Hence, to accept the free gift of salvation through faith (while depraved) is not a work (read Romans 3:27-28 and 4:4-5 for verification). This topic is addressed on several occasions in the remainder of the study.

Acts 16:31 and Depravity

And they said, "Believe in the Lord Jesus, and you shall be saved,... (Acts 16:31)

Faith (believing) precedes salvation, confirming that the lost (depraved) can choose to accept Christ before they are spiritually regenerated ("saved"). Note that spiritual regeneration and salvation are one and the same.

We will study additional verses relating to depravity momentarily, but a short detour is required to cover an amazing truth. Can man respond contrary to his strongest inclination? If so, Total Depravity, the "T" of the TULIP (as defined by extreme and hyper-Calvinism), cannot stand. In fact, none of the five points of Calvinism can stand. The four letters (ULIP), which follow the T, are wholly dependent on the T pointing to total "inability."

As to whether man can or cannot respond contrary to his strongest inclination is one of the cornerstones of theological deliberation. In fact, one should start here when considering how man's depravity affects his ability to repent and believe. This topic was covered previously in *God Heart as it Relates to Sovereignty-Free Will* (pages 14-18), but a review is necessary at this time. Additional input is included as well, so enjoy yourself!

The Hill

CHAPTER SEVEN

CAN MAN RESPOND CONTRARY TO HIS STRONGEST INCLINATION?

Romans 7:1-25

Or do you not know, brethren (for I am speaking to those who know the law), that the law has jurisdiction over a person as long as he lives? For the married woman is bound by law to her husband while he is living; but if her husband dies, she is released from the law concerning the husband. So then if, while her husband is living, she is joined to another man, she shall be called an adulteress; but if her husband dies, she is free from the law, so that she is not an adulteress, though she is joined to another man. Therefore, my brethren, you also were made to die to the Law through the body of Christ, that you might be joined to another, to Him who was raised from the dead, that we might bear fruit for God. For while we were in the flesh, the sinful passions, which were aroused by the Law, were at work in the members of our body to bear fruit for death. But now we have been released from the Law, having died to that by which we were bound, so that we serve in newness of the Spirit and not in oldness of the letter. What shall we say then? Is the Law sin? May it never be! On the contrary, I would not have come to know sin except through the Law; for I would not have known about coveting if the Law had not said, "YOU SHALL NOT COVET." But sin, taking opportunity through the commandment, produced in me coveting of every kind; for apart from the Law sin is dead. And I was once alive apart from the Law; but when the commandment came, sin became alive, and I died; and this commandment, which was to result in life, proved to result in death for me; for sin, taking opportunity through the commandment, deceived me, and through it killed me. So then, the Law is holy, and the commandment is holy and righteous and good. Therefore did that which is good become a cause of death for me? May it never be! Rather it was sin, in order that it might be shown to be sin by effecting my death through that which is good, that through the commandment sin might become utterly sinful. For we know that the Law is spiritual; but I am of flesh, sold into bondage to sin. For that which I am doing, I do not understand; for I am not practicing what I would like to do, but I am doing the very thing I hate. But if I do the very thing I do not wish to do, I agree with the Law, confessing that it is good. So now, no longer am I the one doing it, but sin which indwells me. For I know that nothing good dwells in me, that is, in my flesh; for the wishing is present in me, but the doing of the good is not. For the good that I wish, I do not do; but I practice the very evil that I do not wish. But if I am doing the very thing I do not wish, I am no longer the one doing it, but sin which dwells in me. I find then the principle that evil is present in me, the one who wishes to do good. For I joyfully concur with the law of God in the inner man, but I see a different law in the members of my body, waging war against the law of my mind, and making me a prisoner of the law of sin which is in my members. Wretched man that I am! Who will set me free from the body of this death? Thanks be to God through Jesus Christ our Lord! So then, on the one hand I myself with my mind am serving the law of God, but on the other, with my flesh the law of sin. (Romans 7:1-25)

To properly interpret Romans 7:1-25, the following backdrop is absolutely essential.

The genes of all mankind were in Adam when he sinned (Romans 5:17-18). As a result, man is born with a sinful nature, the same nature that Adam possessed after he sinned—a nature that is dead to (separated from) God (Ephesians 2:3, 5). (Scripture refers to this nature in different ways—Adamic nature, sinful nature, old self, old man, or dead spirit—all being synonymous.) To have introduced me properly during the twenty-seven-year span that I was without Christ, you would have needed to say, "This is Bob Warren, the sinful nature," or "This is Bob Warren, the Adamic nature," etc. In fact, before I became a believer I woke up enjoying sin and went to bed enjoying sin. I was on the throne of my life like you were on the throne of yours when you were without Christ. We were good sinners weren't we, even though we could conceal our sin from others at times? Consequently, our absolute "strongest inclination" was to wallow in sin.

When a person makes a choice to receive Christ (John 1:12; Acts 16:31; Acts 26:18; Romans 10:9-10; etc.), God kills (eradicates) that person (Romans 6:6; 7:4; etc.). As a result, the individual who loved to sin no longer exists (Galatians 2:20). This transformation means that God, after killing (eradicating) the person who originally lived in my body (the sinful nature, or old self, etc.), created a totally new person to live inside my same body (2Corinthians 5:17). The person who inhabited it originally was Bob Warren, the old man (old self, sinful nature, etc.). The person inhabiting it now is Bob Warren, the new man (new self).

Do you see what the Scriptures are communicating? If you are a believer, the person you used to be is gone, never to be dealt with again. That person was crucified with Christ on His cross in 30 AD (Romans 6:6; 7:4; Galatians 2:20). How could this change occur? Once you repented and believed (while depraved),

The new Testament believer is crucified with Christ.

God took who you were (the sinful nature; old man; old self; etc.), placed that nature into Christ through the avenue of the Holy Spirit (1Corinthians 12:13), "*crucified*" that nature (Romans 6:6; 7:4; Galatians 2:20), "*buried*" that nature (Romans 6:4; Colossians 2:12), and made you into a "*new*" creation (2Corinthians 5:17). You were then the new man, or the new self—both synonymous.

Having received Christ's kind of life (Colossians 3:4) at the point of salvation/justification, this new man (new creation) is an eternal being, with no beginning and no end. If the new creation (the New Testament believer) has no beginning and no end, he/she was in Christ when Christ was crucified, buried, and raised. For this reason Paul could say, "*I have been crucified with Christ*" (Galatians 2:20), for the old man was placed in Christ and eradicated. Paul could also teach that the New Testament believer has been "*buried*" (Romans 6:4; Colossians 2:12) and "*raised*" with Christ (Ephesians 2:6; Colossians 2:12). (Diagram 8 in the Reference Section displays this truth graphically.)

With the above in mind, we can conclude that in your unredeemed state, you were (fill in your name), _____ the sinful nature (sometimes called the old man, old self, Adamic nature, or dead spirit—all synonymous). Today you are (fill in your name) _____, the new man (sometimes called the new self, or new creation—all synonymous). God did more than just wound who you were. He eradicated who you were as an unbeliever. How could He possibly allow the old man (sinful nature) to live inside your body alongside the new man? If both the old man and the new man were to cohabit your body, you would be part evil and part good, making you nothing more than a lowly sinner saved by grace.

The Scriptures teach that you became anything but a saved, lowly sinner when you accepted Christ. In fact, you were made into a righteous (2Corinthians 5:21), holy (Ephesians 1:4), perfect (Hebrews 10:14), complete (Colossians 2:10), forgiven (Ephesians 4:32; Colossians 2:13; 1John 2:12), glorified (Romans 8:30), justified (Romans 5:1), never to be condemned (Romans 8:1) saint (1Corinthians 1:2) who sometimes sins. The most natural thing you do, therefore, is walk in righteousness—proving that the most unnatural thing you do is walk in sin. Yes, you disobey at times, but disobedience is unnatural and very troubling to your soul.

If the old man (sinful nature) were alive in you, though wounded, living alongside the holy, blameless, and glorified new man (as some have taught and continue to teach), to desire to sin would remain somewhat natural. However, with the old man eradicated, your "strongest inclination" is to walk as righteously as possible. To state it differently, your "strongest inclination," the moment you accepted Christ, was (and continues to be) to abandon sin.

All New Testament believers are ushered into the presence of God the moment their earthly bodies cease operating (2Corinthians 5:8). Consequently, when my body dies, I (my soul and spirit—the real me) will be taken into heaven. The same applies to you if you are a believer. Once in heaven, we will walk in sinless perfection for the first time in our existence (1John 3:2), never once disobeying the Master, because we will no longer dwell in an unredeemed body (1Corinthians 15:50-55), a body which houses Satan's agent, the power of sin (Romans 7:23)—the means through which Satan tempts the New Testament believer during his/her stay on earth. We can conclude, therefore, that the only reason we sin is due to the power of sin's presence in our unredeemed bodies (Romans 7:23), a power which regularly tempts us to sin. When we sin, we hate our sin, because our strongest inclination is to avoid sin.

Because our souls and spirits were perfected (made holy, righteous, and complete) the moment we accepted Christ, the holiness, righteousness, and completeness of our souls and spirits will not be enhanced when we are taken to

Believer, your strongest inclination is to abandon sin.

heaven. Our behavior becomes increasingly holy as we mature in the faith while on earth (and will be made completely holy once we are in heaven), but our souls and spirits (who we really are) were made holy and blameless (never to be improved upon) at the point of new birth/spiritual regeneration/salvation/justification. (All of this wonderful news is addressed to a much greater degree in our *Romans 1-8* course.)

Conclusion

The moment I accepted Christ, my "strongest inclination" was to walk in holiness. In fact, my "strongest inclination" remains the same today. I never want to sin again, but at times I find myself sinning due to believing the enemy's lie. When I sin, however, I hate my sin because my "strongest inclination" is to not sin. How do I know that not sinning is my "strongest inclination?" Let my heart stop beating and I will never sin again. In heaven, the new man (Bob Warren) will cease being tempted and will respond according to his "strongest inclination" one hundred percent of the time. Consequently, my "strongest inclination," from the moment I became a child of God, has been to avoid sin. Not sinning was Paul's desire as well, but the Scriptures confirm that he, the great apostle, disobeyed at times:

> *For that which I am doing, I do not understand; for I am not practicing what I would like to do, but I am doing the very thing I hate.* (Romans 7:15)

He also said:

> *...for the wishing is present in me, but the doing of the good is not.* (Romans 7:18)

He followed by saying:

> *For the good that I wish, I do not do; but I practice the very evil that I do not wish.* (Romans 7:19)

As a believer, Paul's "strongest inclination" was to walk in unwavering obedience. These verses verify, however, that in certain situations he made choices contrary to his "strongest inclination." Consequently, Jonathan Edwards' assumption (that man is incapable of responding contrary to his strongest inclination—a teaching accepted by followers of Reformed Theology) is in error. We will discuss Edwards' theology in more depth shortly.

In an attempt to circumvent the idea that Paul is speaking about acting against his strongest inclination in Romans 7, some theologians (including some Calvinists) teach that almost all of Romans 7 addresses Paul's experience prior to becoming a believer. Verses such as Romans 7:24 are cited:

> *Wretched man that I am! Who will set me free from the body of this death?* (Romans 7:24)

This reasoning is incorrect, for the word *"wretched"* in this case actually means "distressed" or "miserable." Thus, Paul is not saying that he is a wretched person in the sense of being spiritually separated from God (lost). He is basically communicating that, as a believer, he is "distressed" over the battle that rages in his mind as a result of the power of sin working through the avenue of his body *("the body of this death")*. The great news is that he, as a believer, finds victory through the life of Jesus within (Romans 7:25) strictly because he has discovered that the lies that penetrate his mind have not been generated by him but by the power of sin (living in his body) <u>pretending to be the sinful nature.</u> Yes, Satan longs to have us incorrectly conclude that the sin nature is still alive. Yet, Romans 7:1-4 teaches that we would live in a state of spiritual adultery should the sinful nature remain in us, living alongside the new man.

The idea that man is incapable of responding contrary to his "strongest inclination" is wrong; for Paul, describing his battle with the power of sin subsequent to salvation (Romans 7), discredits such thinking. Therefore, the depraved can make a choice to accept Christ <u>before</u> being spiritually regenerated. Why else would Paul teach that, *"the Law has become our tutor to lead us to Christ"* (Galatians 3:24), and John write, *"And He (the Spirit), when He comes, will convict the world concerning sin, and righteousness, and judgment"* (John 16:8)? What purpose would the Law serve, along with the conviction of the Spirit, should the depraved be spiritual corpses, totally incapable of responding to God's truth?

This rock-solid truth refutes R.C. Sproul Jr.'s line of thinking as he addresses Jonathan Edward's thoughts regarding man's "strongest inclination" in *Almighty Over All*, pages 46-47:

> ...Edwards wrote that all men everywhere always act according to their strongest inclination at a given time....
>
> Stop to consider whether there was ever a time when you acted against your strongest inclination....
>
> ...Edwards was right; we always choose according to our strongest inclination given our choices.[18]

We have just proven such statements to be in error.

John Piper, in his DVD series *TULIP*, Disk 2, Title 6, Chapters 4-5, associates Edwards' view of "strongest inclination" with total depravity:

> "Total Depravity" means so depraved that you can't do what you have to do. You can't. In that sense it is total. It's not like there's ninety nine percent bondage to sin and a one percent window, that if you are smart enough, or spiritual enough, or fortunate enough, you can produce what's required of you. There's no one percent. It is one hundred percent dead in

> trespasses and sins, and we are unable. Now that is what
> creates huge theological discussions about whether or not a
> person who is described that way can be held accountable for
> his behavior....Jonathan Edwards' book, *The Freedom of the
> Will,* may be the most important book outside of the Bible
> written on the problem of the human will in relation to the
> sovereignty of God in salvation. So, if you are really intent on
> grappling at the most rigorous level with these things, that's
> where you have to go. Any other book, even Luther's, *Bondage
> of the Will,* which is right up there in the top three, won't take
> you where this book takes you in terms of remarkably hard
> thinking about the issue of the will....He [Edwards] describes an
> important distinction in understanding what we mean by saying
> that irresistible grace and total depravity are based on the
> biblical conviction that people are in themselves unable to
> believe on Christ and yet are morally accountable for doing so.
> So there's the mystery, there's the paradox, there's the
> tension....What does "unable" mean in that sentence, and
> Edwards is the one who has labored hardest, I think, to explain
> this?.... moral inability consists in the opposition or lack of
> *inclination* [emphasis added]. Now, just in simple laymen's
> terms: You can love evil so much you can't do good. And that's
> the kind of "can't" that total depravity is referring to....[19]

Sproul and Piper must agree with Edwards' view of "strongest inclination" if their view of depravity is to stand. After all, if man should be capable of choosing Christ in his depraved state (with the assistance of God's grace, of course), extreme and hyper-Calvinism would become extinct because God would <u>not</u> be required to spiritually regenerate the elect and give them repentance and faith before they could repent and believe—a scenario that would destroy, not just one point of the TULIP, but the other four points as well. Neither would moderate Calvinism stand; for although it rejects much of what the extreme and hyper-Calvinists believe regarding Total Depravity, it relies heavily on Unconditional Election, the "U" of the TULIP.

Clearly, the Scriptures teach that man (in his depravity) possesses a free will that allows him to choose Christ <u>before</u> being spiritually regenerated. In other words, repentance and faith precede spiritual regeneration—never spiritual regeneration followed by repentance and faith. This fact confirms that total depravity cannot mean total "inability," as the extreme and hyper-Calvinists (Reformed theologians) advocate. It also proves Jonathan Edwards' logic incorrect, for Romans 7 (along with an abundance of additional passages) validates that man most definitely <u>can</u> respond contrary to his "strongest inclination." (For more input regarding Reformed Theology, refer to Diagrams 10 and 11 in the Reference Section.)

Do you see the need to dig deeply when addressing such key doctrinal issues? I am excited about what we will discover as this study unfolds.

C H A P T E R   E I G H T

MORE VERSES THAT RELATE TO DEPRAVITY

REFORMED THEOLOGIANS FOLLOW Jonathan Edwards' lead by viewing the depraved as incapable of responding contrary to their strongest inclination. They view man's depravity to be so severe that God must: (1) Spiritually regenerate the depraved and cause them to be born again—at which time they receive the *"hidden wisdom"* of 1Corinthians 2:7 (2) Grant them repentance and faith once they are spiritually regenerated (3) Save them after they repent and believe. This arrangement, however, advocates that the elect are born again <u>before</u> they exercise repentance and faith and are saved. Does this mindset line up with the full counsel of God's Word?

We will begin answering this question by asking some questions. If man, in his depravity, is incapable of making even the slightest move toward God (as extreme and hyper-Calvinists suppose), why would so many verses address Paul's attempts to persuade the depraved, many of whom refused to believe (read Acts 28:17-29 for instance)? If the depraved must be spiritually regenerated (born again) and granted the *"hidden wisdom"* of 1Corinthians 2:7 (along with repentance and faith) before they can repent, choose Christ, and be saved (the Reformed view), what need would there have been for Paul to persuade anyone to believe. To state it differently, why would those whom God has granted Reformed Theology's *"hidden wisdom"* through spiritual regeneration need to be persuaded? Would God's *"hidden wisdom"* in itself not be sufficient to convince them? Therefore, the fact that Paul reasoned with (and attempted to persuade) the depraved totally refutes Reformed Theology's system of beliefs. As was verified in *God's Heart as it Relates to Foreknowledge-Predestination*, the *"hidden wisdom"* of 1Corinthians 2:7 is granted to the New Testament believer who chooses to go on to spiritual maturity. Never is it given to: (1) The believer who remains immature nor (2) The spiritually regenerated of Reformed Theology prior to salvation. The following passages relate to this subject matter—with words underlined for emphasis:

Acts 9:22

But Saul kept increasing in strength and confounding the Jews who lived at Damascus by <u>proving</u> that this Jesus is the Christ. (Acts 9:22)

Acts 17:17

So he was <u>reasoning</u> in the synagogue with the Jews and the God-fearing Gentiles, and in the market place every day with those who happened to be present. (Acts 17:17)

Acts 18:4

And he was <u>reasoning</u> in the synagogue every Sabbath and trying to persuade Jews and Greeks. (Acts 18:4)

Acts 26:28

And Agrippa replied to Paul, "In a short time you will <u>persuade</u> me to become a Christian." (Acts 26:28)

Acts 28:23

And when they had set a day for him, they came to him at his lodging in large numbers; and he was explaining to them by solemnly testifying about the kingdom of God, and trying to <u>persuade</u> them concerning Jesus, from both the Law of Moses and from the Prophets, from morning until evening. (Acts 28:23)

1Corinthians 9:22-23

To the weak I became weak, that I might win the weak; I have become all things to all men, that I may by all means save some. (1Corinthians 9:22-23)

2Corinthians 5:11-12

> *Therefore knowing the fear of the Lord, we <u>persuade</u> men, but we*
> *are made manifest to God; and I hope that we are made manifest*
> *also in your consciences.* (2Corinthians 5:11-12)

Paul viewed the gospel as a means through which the Holy Spirit revealed God's *"righteousness"* to the lost (depraved—read Romans 1:16-17)—who had the capacity to repent and believe while depraved. Why else would he have preached so passionately and fervently to so many people, many of whom did not believe? His words to the church at Thessalonica describe how the gospel brought conviction upon those who had listened to his words, many of whom had first heard of Christ through his preaching:

1Thessalonians 1:5

> *for our gospel did not come to you in word only, but also in power*
> *and in the Holy Spirit and with full <u>conviction</u>;* (1Thessalonians
> 1:5)

1Thessalonians 1:9

> *For they themselves report about us what kind of a reception we*
> *had with you, and how <u>you turned to God</u> from idols to serve a*
> *living and true God,* (1Thessalonians 1:9)

These believers *"turned to God."* The verse says nothing about God spiritually regenerating them (and giving them the *"hidden wisdom"* of 1Corinthians 2:7 along with repentance and faith—the Reformed view) before they could repent, believe, and be saved. They turned while living in their depraved state.

John MacArthur, in Appendix 1 of *The Love of God*, records excerpts from a sermon delivered by Thomas Chalmers (a Calvinist). Chalmers was not only a pastor, but also a professor of theology at the University of Edinburgh in the early 1800's. Observe how much life Chalmers grants to the corpse of Calvinism's total depravity (without realizing it) as he speaks to individuals in need of salvation. Keep in mind that extreme and hyper Calvinists adhere to the idea that the depraved are incapable of making even the slightest move toward Christ.

> And if you have not yet begun to place this confidence in the
> assurances of the gospel, lay hold of them now. They are
> addressed to you. "The Spirit and the bride say, Come. And let

him that heareth say, Come. And let him that is athirst come. And *whosoever will*, let him take of the water of life freely" (Rev. 22:17, emphasis added). It is not a vague generality of which I am speaking. You are invited to take up with Christ, and trust in Him for yourself. God Himself urges you to repent and live (Ezek. 18:31).

I am well aware that unless the Spirit reveal to you, all I have said about Him will fall fruitless upon your ears, and your hearts will remain as cold and as heavy and as alienated as ever. Faith is His gift, and it is not of ourselves. But the minister is at his post when he puts the truth before you; and you are at your posts when you hearken diligently, and have a prayerful spirit of dependence on the Giver of all wisdom, that He will bless the Word spoken, and make it reach your souls in the form of a salutary and convicting application.

And it is indeed incredible—it is more than incredible—that we should entertain any thought that our Father who is in heaven is less than benevolent. With all the ways He sets Himself forth to us, isn't it disgraceful that we do not have more confidence in His goodness and His willingness to save? How can we account for the barrier of unbelief that stands so obstinately firm in spite of His every remonstrance? Why does the hardness continue? Not the hardness of God toward us, for He has said everything to woo us to put our trust in Him, but our hardness toward God. In the face of His kind and compassionate entreaties, how can we persist in being cold and distant and afraid of Him?

I know not, my brethren, in how far I may have succeeded, as an humble and unworthy instrument, in drawing aside the veil which darkens the face of Him who sits on the throne. But oh, how imposing is the attitude, and how altogether affecting is the argument with which He comes forward to us in the text we are considering!...[20]

As was stated earlier, Reformed Theology (extreme and hyper-Calvinism) teaches that man is incapable of making even the slightest move toward God in the midst of his depravity. Yet, Chalmers encourages the lost to "lay hold of" [the gospel]—to "...hearken diligently, and have a prayerful spirit of dependence on the Giver of all wisdom, that He will bless the Word spoken..." How could the depraved, according to the Reformed view of depravity, "have a prayerful spirit of dependence on the Giver of all wisdom" if they are void of all forms of spiritual awareness? Chalmers later states, "...isn't it disgraceful that we do not have more confidence in His goodness and His willingness to save?" Why should anything but unbelief be expected from those who, according to the total depravity of extreme and hyper-Calvinism, are incapable of responding to the truth prior to spiritual regeneration? Chalmers follows by saying, "How can we account for the barrier of unbelief that stands so obstinately firm in spite of His every remonstrance?" How can he make such statements without realizing that he has contradicted everything that the Reformed view of total depravity espouses? "Total Depravity," as defined by Reformed Theology, won't allow the depraved to respond in even the slightest manner to the truth. If Chalmers' listeners could have overcome the "barrier of unbelief" that stood "so obstinately firm in spite of His (God's) remonstrance," their positive response would have destroyed the entire TULIP. Yet, he follows by saying, "Why does the hardness continue?... for He has said everything to woo us to put our trust in Him....In the face of His kind and compassionate entreaties, how can we persist in being cold and distant and afraid of Him?" How can Chalmers make such statements and remain true to his Calvinistic beliefs? Chalmers then follows with a most alarming statement. He says, "I know not, my brethren, in how far I may have succeeded, as an humble and unworthy instrument, in drawing aside the veil which darkens the face of Him who sits on the throne." Surely he didn't perceive himself as capable of removing the veil from the eyes of the unbelieving. The removal of the veil is God's doing alone, accomplished subsequent to the depraved recognizing their depravity and turning to the Lord:

> *but whenever a man turns to the Lord, the veil is taken away.*
> (2Corinthians 3:16)

2Corinthians 3:16 does not say that God must first spiritually regenerate man before the veil can be removed. It does say, however, that *"man turns to the Lord,"* then *"the veil is taken away"*—discrediting Reformed Theology altogether!

Chalmers is a prime example of how the contradictions within Reformed Theology (extreme and hyper-Calvinism) weave their way into the message of its advocates. John Piper, another Reformed Theologian, contradicts himself in his DVD series *TULIP*, Disk 1, Title 6, Chapter 1:

> ...You didn't understand how depraved you were before you got
> saved. You had a little inkling, a little inkling that you were a sinner
> and needed a Savior ...[21]

The Reformed position views the lost as so spiritually dead that they could never, under any circumstance, recognize (to any degree whatsoever) their need for a Savior. According to this view, the depraved are nothing more than corpses with no spiritual awareness whatsoever. Yet, Piper gives them a small amount of life. So which is it? Can, or cannot, the depraved realize that they are depraved? Piper, evidently, believes both are true. Adam realized his nakedness immediately after his sin—<u>after</u> becoming depraved (Genesis 3:7).   Thus, the inconsistencies generated by Calvinistic reasoning continue. These inconsistencies bleed over into other areas of their theology pertaining to the salvation of man.

The Hill

CHAPTER NINE

WHAT DOES IT MEAN TO BE BORN AGAIN?

THE WORDS *"BORN AGAIN"* are used in John 3:3 and 3:7, verses which are part of Jesus' dialog with Nicodemus, a Jewish teacher and member of the Sanhedrin. Our commentary, *The Gospels from a Jewish Perspective*, addresses these verses in much greater depth.

John 3:3-6

> *Jesus answered and said to him, "Truly, truly, I say to you, unless one is born again, he cannot see the kingdom of God." 4 Nicodemus said to Him, "How can a man be born when he is old? He cannot enter a second time into his mother's womb and be born, can he?" 5 Jesus answered, "Truly, truly, I say to you, unless one is born of water and the Spirit, he cannot enter into the kingdom of God. 6 That which is born of the flesh is flesh, and that which is born of the Spirit is spirit.* (John 3:3-6)

Jesus confirms that through being *"born again"* (saved) man is allowed to *"see the kingdom of God"* (v.3), meaning that the small amount of understanding possessed by the depraved is greatly enlarged through salvation. Jesus is <u>not</u> teaching that man must be born again and granted the *"hidden wisdom"* of 1Corinthians 2:7 (along with repentance and faith) before he can see the kingdom of God, exercise repentance and faith, and be saved (the Reformed position). A proper view of *"born again"* is necessary if Jesus' words to Nicodemus are to be "rightly divided."

57

Interestingly, the Reformed view perceives *"born again"* as playing the following role in one's salvation:

1. Man is so depraved that God must cause him to be *"born again"* void of a choice on man's part.

2. In conjunction with God causing man to be *"born again,"* He gives man the *"hidden wisdom"* of 1Corinthians 2:7.

3. This *"hidden wisdom"* allows man to *"see the kingdom of God"* (John 3:3).

4. Along with the hidden wisdom, God gives man the gifts of repentance and faith.

5. God's gifts of repentance and faith suddenly become the possession of the individual receiving them.

6. Repentance and faith are exercised and God's salvation is bestowed.

Is this a proper view of *"born again"*? Must man be born again before he can be saved? In other words, does a difference exist between being *"born again"* and receiving salvation? Some would answer "No!" Others would answer in the affirmative. What causes this difference of opinion? The source of the debate stems from whether man in his depravity can or cannot choose to accept the salvation made available through Christ. Reformed theologians believe it to be impossible while the non-Reformed view "normally" considers it to be one-hundred percent Scriptural. Let's consider for a moment how the Reformed view has impacted its followers' perception of 1John 5:1.

> *Whoever believes that Jesus is the Christ is born of God; and*
> *whoever loves the Father loves the child born of Him.* (1John 5:1)

Because *"believes"* is in the present tense (continuous action) and *"is born"* is in the perfect tense (past action with ongoing results), many Reformed theologians use this verse in an attempt to prove that spiritual regeneration (being born again) must precede repentance, faith, and salvation. As a result, John Piper states in his DVD series, *TULIP*, Disk 1, Title 6, Chapter 4:

> The new birth enables us to receive Christ....Whoever believes
> that Jesus is the Christ is born of God. Whoever believes,
> literally, perfect tense, has been born of God. I think that's

> crystal clear, that the reason you believe is because you have
> been born again. Not the other way around.[22]

This argument is easily defused by understanding that 1John 5:1 is teaching that all believers (all whose lives are characterized by believing—present tense action, ongoing action since they are already believers) have been born of God (saved/justified) at a specific time in the past (perfect tense action, never to be repeated). Thus, the fact that believers continue to believe confirms that they were born again (saved/justified) at an earlier date.

John 1:12, 5:40, 3:15-18, 20:31, Acts 16:31, Romans 3:22, 3:26, 4:3, 4:5, 5:1, and 10:9-10, unmistakably teach that faith (believing in Christ in our depraved state) precedes spiritual regeneration (being born again—salvation/justification). 1John 5:1 does not validate the Reformed view: That "the elect" are born again before they exercise repentance and faith and are saved. Note what Norm Geisler, a moderate Calvinist, states in his work titled *Systematic Theology, Volume 3, Sin/Salvation*, pages 484-485. Keep in mind that moderate Calvinists, who believe that man <u>can</u> choose Christ in his depraved state, are in disagreement with Reformed Theology (extreme and hyper-Calvinism) over this issue:

> First of all, this text [1John 5:1] says nothing about how one
> becomes born of God. It is simply noting that all who confess
> Jesus as the Messiah have been converted; that is, born of God.
>   Second, John makes it clear elsewhere that one has to
> believe in order to be born of God. He told Nicodemus that one
> had to "believe" (John 3:15-18) in order to be "born again"
> (vv.3, 5, 7). Indeed, the very theme of his gospel declared that
> faith was prior to salvation. He wrote: "But these are written
> that you may believe that Jesus is the Christ, the Son of God,
> and *that by believing* you may have life in his name" (20:31; cf.
> 5:24).
>
> In every New Testament instance, faith is prior to salvation.
> Faith is the means, and salvation is the end. Nowhere does
> God's Word teach that we must be saved in order to believe; by
> contrast, everywhere it affirms that we must believe in order to
> be saved. Extreme Calvinism has the soteriological cart before
> the horse.[23]

This quote explains the disparity that exists between moderate Calvinism and Reformed Theology (extreme and hyper-Calvinism). Yet <u>all</u> the moderate, extreme, and hyper-Calvinists believe that God chose/elected the elect to salvation in eternity past. My question remains: What difference would it make should the elect of moderate Calvinism be capable of choosing Christ in their depravity if only the elect of moderate Calvinism are capable of choosing to believe? That isn't free will. In fact, such a mindset totally negates moderate Calvinism's "free will."

Geisler's interpretation of 1John 5:1 is correct in the sense that it allows those who believe in the present tense (those who are already saved) to have been born again (saved/justified) at a particular point in the past (when they exercised repentance and faith while depraved). He is right in that nowhere does this passage require a person to be born again <u>before</u> he/she can make a choice to repent, believe, and be saved. Therefore, Piper's argument is <u>not</u> "crystal clear" as he supposes.

Jesus taught that until man *"is born again, he cannot see the kingdom of God"* (John 3:3). To be *"born again"* is, as has been established, synonymous with salvation/justification. In other words, if you are born again, you are saved—a truth that will be validated to a greater degree shortly. Verse 3 does not require man to be *"born again"* <u>before</u> he can see the kingdom, repent, believe, and be saved (the Reformed view). It states that man must be *"born again"* (saved) <u>before</u> he can *"see the kingdom."* The Scriptures teach that the depraved must exercise repentance and faith (based on the limited revelation available to them) <u>before</u> they can be *"born again"* (saved) and *"see the kingdom:"*

> *"While you have the light, believe in the light, in order that you may become sons of light."* (John 12:36)

> *And they said, "Believe in the Lord Jesus, and you shall be saved, you and your household."* (Acts 16:31)

God's Word says nothing about individuals being required to see the kingdom <u>before</u> they repent, believe, and receive salvation (the Reformed view). God's letter to man clearly states that seeing the kingdom comes once one is spiritually regenerated (born again/saved/justified). However, R.C. Sproul, in *Chosen by God*, page 72, states that man must be *"born again"* and capable of seeing the kingdom prior to choosing Christ as Savior and experiencing salvation:

> ...The Reformed view of predestination teaches that before a person can choose Christ his heart must be changed. He must be born again.... How can a man choose a kingdom he cannot see? How can a man enter the kingdom without being first reborn?[24]

Sproul's view stems from Jonathan Edwards' idea that man always responds according to his "strongest inclination" (an idea refuted earlier in our study). On page 72 of *Chosen by God* Sproul writes:

> Non-Reformed views have people responding to Christ who are not reborn.... If a person who is still in the flesh, who is not yet reborn by the power of the Holy Spirit, can incline or dispose himself of Christ, what good is rebirth? This is the fatal flaw of non-Reformed views. They fail to take seriously man's moral inability, the moral impotency of the flesh....
>
> A cardinal point of Reformed theology is the maxim: "Regeneration precedes faith."[25]

Sproul believes that man must be spiritually regenerated (born again) and granted repentance and faith (by God) before he can repent, believe, and be saved. Yet, this contradicts the Reformed view of "strongest inclination."

Remember, the Reformed view perceives man as incapable of responding contrary to his strongest inclination—contrary to his nature. However, if Reformed Theology's "*born again*" is what brings about a new inclination, then the elect of Reformed Theology receive a new inclination (and, therefore, a new nature) before they are saved. Yet, 2Corinthians 5:17 teaches that receiving a new nature (a new inclination) is synonymous with salvation—a salvation received in conjunction with being placed in Christ subsequent to repenting and believing while depraved. Paul consistently teaches that once the depraved repent and exercise faith, God saves them by making them new "*in Christ.*" Thus, Paul totally invalidates the Reformed view which depicts the elect as receiving a new inclination (new nature) prior to salvation.

John 3:3 states that one must be *"born again"* (saved) to *"see the kingdom of God."* The Reformed and non-Reformed schools of thought are polarized regarding this verse's interpretation. For clarification, the two views are presented in a simplified form:

Reformed—The elect are first "born again" (spiritually regenerated) by God (God's choice of the elect, not the elect's choice of God, brings this about) and given the hidden wisdom of 1Corinthians 2:7. This new birth releases the elect from their depravity and frees them to see the kingdom, after which they repent, exercise faith, and are saved—repentance and faith being God's gift to the elect according to this view.

Non-Reformed (in general, not all)—Man understands that he is a sinner in the midst of his depravity, repents, believes, and is "born again" (saved). The fruit of the new birth is an ability to see the kingdom. The depraved are capable of repenting and believing due to the limited (but sufficient) truth made available to all mankind.

61

Titus 3:5 adds intriguing insight to this highly debated theological matter:

> *He saved us, not on the basis of deeds which we have done in righteousness, but according to His mercy, by the washing of regeneration and renewing by the Holy Spirit,* (Titus 3:5)

The term *"regeneration"* (Titus 3:5) points to new birth (salvation/justification). Note what *Barnes' Commentary* records regarding the subject:

> It means, properly, a new birth, reproduction, or renewal. It would properly be applied to one who should be begotten again in this sense, that a new life was commenced in him in some way corresponding to his being made to live at first. To the proper idea of the word, it is essential that there should be connected the notion of the commencement of life in the man, so that he may be said to live anew; and as religion is in the Scriptures represented as life, it is properly applied to the beginning of that kind of life by which man may be said to live anew.[26]

This commentary agrees with what we have concluded—that the New Testament believer receives "new life" at the point of spiritual regeneration. This "new life" is equivalent to being *"born again"* (John 3:3). Therefore, to be *"born again"* means to be spiritually regenerated, to experience new birth. This new birth for the New Testament believer is salvation/justification, which results from being placed *"in Christ"* (2Corinthians 5:17) through the avenue of the Holy Spirit (1Corinthians 12:13) <u>after</u> repenting and believing while depraved.

Charles Spurgeon (a Reformed theologian) agreed, confirmed by his sermon, *The Warrant of Faith.*

> If I am to preach faith in Christ to a man who is regenerated, then the man, being regenerated, is saved already, and it is an unnecessary and ridiculous thing for me to preach Christ to him, and bid him to believe in order to be saved when he is saved already, being regenerate. Am I only to preach faith to those who have it? Absurd, indeed! Is not this waiting till the man is cured and then bringing him the medicine? This is preaching Christ to the righteous and not to sinners.[27]

Spurgeon's comments were extremely non-Reformed in nature.

All of the above makes Paul's words of 2Corinthians 5:17 enormously significant:

> *Therefore if any man is in Christ, he is a new creature; the old*
> *things passed away; behold, new things have come.* (2Corinthians
> 5:17)

Paul states that each believer at Corinth became "*a new creature*" (creation) in association with being placed "*in Christ.*" Thus, being "*in Christ*" is what allows a New Testament believer to become a new creation (experience salvation/justification), or as John 3:3 describes it, to be "*born again.*"

Being placed "*in Christ*" (into Christ's body) occurs through the avenue of the Holy Spirit:

> *For by one Spirit we were all baptized into one body, whether Jews*
> *or Greeks, whether slaves or free, and we were all made to drink of*
> *one Spirit* (1Corinthians 12:13).

We can conclude, therefore, that when a New Testament believer is "*born again*" (John 3:3), he/she is made a "*new*" creation through being placed "*in Christ*" (2Corinthians 5:17) through the avenue of the "*Spirit*" (1Corinthians 12:13) the moment he/she repents and believes while depraved. This truth lines up perfectly with Jesus' words to Nicodemus in John 3:5-6:

> *Jesus answered, "Truly, truly, I say to you, unless one is born of*
> *water and the Spirit, he cannot enter into the kingdom of God. 6*
> *That which is born of the flesh is flesh, and that which is born of*
> *the Spirit is spirit.* (John 3:5-6)

Jesus spoke of being "*born of water and the Spirit*" (v.5). To be "*born of water*" (v.5) means to be "*born of the flesh*" (v.6), pointing to physical birth. To be "*born of...the Spirit*" (v.5) means just what it says, to be "*born of the Spirit*" (v.6)—to be "*born again*" (v.3). Combining 2Corinthians 5:17, 1Corinthians 12:13, and John 3:5-6, we can conclude that to be "*born again*" (John 3:3) means to become a new creation in Christ, a spiritually regenerated (saved/justified) member of God's Family. This truth confirms that man is not "*born again*" (John 3:3) prior to being saved (as extreme and hyper-Calvinism suppose). To be "*born again*" points to salvation—to becoming a new creation as a result of: (1) Realizing our depravity (2) Repenting and exercising faith while depraved (3)

*M**an is not "born again" prior to being saved, as extreme and hyper-Calvinism suppose.*

Being placed *"in Christ"* through the avenue of the Holy Spirit and receiving new life (a new nature).

The words *"in Christ"* are used in Romans 3:24; 6:11, 23, 8:1, 2, 39; 12:5; 1Corinthians 1:2, 4, 30 (this verse will be studied later in its context and is very encouraging); 2Corinthians 5:17; Ephesians 1:3; 2:6, 13; and 2Timothy 1:1; 2:10 to confirm that those who are *"born again"* are not only saved, but saints of God and much, much more. Yes, to be *"born again"* (John 3:3) means to become a son of God and member of the kingdom.

As was addressed earlier, these wonderful truths are problematic for Reformed Theologians due to their improper view of "regeneration." Note again R.C. Sproul's words from *Chosen by God*, page 72:

> A cardinal point of Reformed theology is the maxim:
> "Regeneration precedes faith."[28]

Extreme and hyper-Calvinism's idea that man must be spiritually regenerated (and given the *"hidden wisdom"* of 1Corinthians 2:7, along with God's gifts of repentance and faith) before he can repent, believe, and be saved has been proven invalid. Why would a spiritually regenerated ("born again") individual, who has been placed "in Christ," need to be saved a second time after repenting and believing? Yet Edwin Palmer, in *The Five Points of Calvinism*, page 19, writes:

> ...the unsaved, the unregenerate, is spiritually dead (Eph. 2). He is unable to ask for help unless God changes his heart of stone into a heart of flesh, and makes him alive spiritually (Eph. 2:5). Then, once he is born again, he can for the first time turn to Jesus, expressing sorrow for his sins and asking Jesus to save him.[29]

What causes Palmer to draw such unscriptural conclusions regarding depravity? The answer is simple. His misunderstanding results from the error of elevating God's sovereignty above all His other glorious attributes, even His love (a subject addressed in much depth in our previous study titled *God's Heart as it Relates to Sovereignty-Free Will*.) Palmer's God must be the cause of all things, including who will or will not believe. This incorrect assumption is the core source of Palmer's error and all who follow the Reformed view of God's dealings with man.

Let's take what we have gleaned from John 3:3-6 and tie it in to the following verses:

John 3:7-15

> *Do not marvel that I said to you, 'You must be born again.' 8 The*
> *wind blows where it wishes and you hear the sound of it, but do not*
> *know where it comes from and where it is going; so is everyone*
> *who is born of the Spirit." 9 Nicodemus answered and said to*
> *Him, "How can these things be?" 10 Jesus answered and said to*
> *him, "Are you the teacher of Israel, and do not understand these*
> *things? 11 Truly, truly, I say to you, we speak that which we know,*
> *and bear witness of that which we have seen; and you do not*
> *receive our witness. 12 If I told you earthly things and you do not*
> *believe, how shall you believe if I tell you heavenly things? 13 And*
> *no one has ascended into heaven, but He who descended from*
> *heaven, even the Son of Man. 14 And as Moses lifted up the serpent*
> *in the wilderness, even so must the Son of Man be lifted up; 15 that*
> *whoever believes may in Him have eternal life.* (John 3:7-15)

While speaking to Nicodemus in John 3:7-15, Jesus equated salvation with being *"born of the Spirit."* Yet, Jesus taught Nicodemus that he could *"be born again"* (*"born of the Spirit"*) through one avenue only—through receiving (believing) His words. Consequently, believing precedes spiritual regeneration (the new birth)—the impartation of *"eternal life"* (John 3:15) to the one who chooses while depraved to exercise personal repentance and faith. This *"eternal life"* is found *"in Him"* (in Christ), of course (v.15). Once again we see that the depraved can repent and believe.

The new birth is also addressed in:

1Peter 1:3

> *Blessed be the God and Father of our Lord Jesus Christ, who*
> *according to His great mercy has caused us to be born again to a*
> *living hope through the resurrection of Jesus Christ from the dead,*
> (1Peter 1:3 NASB)

1Peter 1:3

> *Blessed be the God and Father of our Lord Jesus Christ, which*
> *according to his abundant mercy hath begotten us again unto a*
> *lively hope by the resurrection of Jesus Christ from the dead,*
> (1Peter 1:3 KJV)

The NASB uses *"born again"* while the KJV uses *"begotten,"* both pointing to the fact that the Father is the Author of the eternal life given to those who choose (in their depravity) to repent and believe. Thus, He *"caused us to be born again"* (1Peter 1:3 NASB) in that He saved us once we repented and believed while depraved.

1Peter 1:23

> *for you have been born again not of seed which is perishable but*
> *imperishable, that is, through the living and abiding word of God.*
> (1Peter 1:23 NASB)

Peter confirms that God's *"word"* (Scripture) is used to convict the souls of the depraved, encouraging them to exercise personal repentance and faith in Christ. Once repentance and faith are exercised, God bestows new birth/salvation.

CHAPTER TEN

CAN THE DEPRAVED CHOOSE CHRIST?

John 1:11-13—Receiving Christ

He came to His own, and those who were His own did not receive Him. 12 But as many as received Him, to them He gave the right to become children of God, even to those who believe in His name, 13 who were born not of blood, nor of the will of the flesh, nor of the will of man, but of God. (John 1:11-13)

The words, *"receive Him,"* in verse 11 as well as the terms, *"received Him,"* in verse 12, will be addressed first because the word *"receive"* (v.11) is responsible for much of the disparity that exists between Reformed theology (extreme and hyper-Calvinism) and a variety of other views. The quotes included in this section from James White, John Calvin, Martin Luther, Norm Geisler, and Dave Hunt, expose the gap that exists between Reformed Theology and the other systems of thought.

Verse 11, *"He came to His own, and those who were His own did not receive Him."* describes how the Jews generally responded to Jesus, for eleven of the original twelve apostles, along with other Jews, did *"receive"* Him as Savior. John 1:12 also confirms that some of the individuals exposed to Jesus' ministry *"received Him."* Therefore, verse 11 is not stating that all Jews rejected Him. What, then, does it mean to *"receive"* Christ?

Many Calvinists (especially extreme and hyper) disagree that the words, *"received Him"* (verse 12), point to the depraved choosing to accept Christ through exercising personal repentance and faith. After all, if *"received"* (John 1:12) should point to man choosing to believe while in his depraved state, Reformed

67

Theology's definition of total depravity could not stand (Reformed Theology being extreme and hyper-Calvinism).

Dave Hunt (a non-Calvinist), in *What Love Is This?* (pages 445-446), addresses this issue through bringing John 3:3-6 into the discussion. Hunt's quote adds additional insight to what we gleaned from John 3:3-15:

> John 1:11-13 simply states that flesh and blood have no relationship to the new birth, which is spiritual and completely unrelated to physical birth. Treating the two as analogous was the very mistake Nicodemus made: "How can a man be born when he is old? Can he enter the second time into his mother's womb, and be born" (John 3:4)? Christ makes a clear distinction: "That which is born of the flesh is flesh; and that which is born of the Spirit is spirit" (John 3:6). These are two different births, and any seeming similarities are only superficial and cannot become the basis of sound conclusions.
>
> John also explains that the new birth—which Christ tells Nicodemus is essential for entering the kingdom of God (John 3:3,5)—does not come by man's will but by the will of God. Man did not conceive of the new birth nor can he effect it by his efforts. Nor does the non-Calvinist believe that he can. Yet we are accused of that....[30]

Hunt is correct. The Scriptures clearly teach that once man chooses to repent and believe (in his depraved state), God unleashes the salvation He has made available through Christ. At the same time, John 1:13 establishes that man cannot save himself, for "*Salvation is from the Lord*" (Jonah 2:9). Thus, man asks—then God saves. Through an exercise of the will, man (in his depravity) repents and believes, but the salvation that results is from God alone. Therefore, John 1:13 is not teaching that unregenerate man lacks free will (that he is incapable of choosing Christ while depraved), but rather that the willing are saved through God alone.

Yet, James White (a Reformed theologian), regarding the passage states:

> Nothing is said in the text that the new birth is "received" by an "act of free will." In fact, *the exact opposite is stated clearly,* "the ones born *not* of the will of man...." It is an amazing example of how preconceived notions can be read into a text that CBF [Geisler's *Chosen But Free*] can say the text makes the new birth dependent upon an act of the "free will" when the text says the opposite.
>
> [Furthermore], if a person can have saving faith without the new birth, then *what does the new birth accomplish?* Evidently

> one does not need the new birth to obey God's commands or
> have saving faith. (Taken from Dave Hunt's *What Love Is This?*,
> page 451, where he quotes from James White's, *The Potter's
> Freedom*)[31]

The Scriptures clearly teach that man (in his depravity) is free to accept (through the exercise of his will) the gift of salvation. Man does the repenting and believing; God does the regenerating—in that order and exactly the reverse of White's order (read John 5:40, Acts 16:31, Romans 3:22, 4:5, and 5:1.). White's problem is that he confuses what God does (regenerate) with what man is required to do prior to regeneration (repent and believe). Dave Hunt in *What Love Is This?*, page 451, states:

> ...That the new birth is "not of the will of man, but of God" does
> not deny that man must believe for God to effect this work in
> him. Man's faith in Christ no more causes the new birth than
> faith causes forgiveness of sins and reconciliation to God.
> Forgiveness of sins, the new birth into God's family, and the
> many other blessings we have in Christ are all the work of God—
> but they are only bestowed on those who believe. Believing did
> not *create* these blessings; it merely fulfilled God's condition for
> receiving them. Yes, regeneration is not by man's fleshly will but
> is all of God; however, God regenerates only those who have
> received and believed on Christ, as the passage clearly states.[32]

Hunt's quote confirms that the Scriptural view of free will does not make man the source of his salvation. The Scriptures teach that God is always the source of salvation—never man. On this one point the Calvinists and non-Calvinists can agree.

As was stated previously, White's problem is that he confuses what God does (regenerate) with what man is required to do prior to regeneration (exercise personal repentance and faith)—faith never being a work (Romans 3:27-28; 4:4-5; 9:32). In fact, White's dilemma is the dilemma that Reformed Theology faces in general.

White's ideology would be true if faith brought about regeneration (new birth/salvation); but the Scriptures clearly teach that grace, not faith, ushers in new life. Therefore, man's choice to believe through faith is merely the *means* through which the new birth is <u>received</u>, God being the Source through which the new birth is <u>imparted</u>. Salvation is "*<u>by</u> grace...<u>through</u> faith*" (Ephesians 2:8a). Hence, God is the source of salvation, not man in his willingness to believe. By perceiving the non-Reformed view of faith (believing) as the source of regeneration, White totally misses the truth that man can possess faith (and believe) prior to spiritual regeneration and God remain the cause of man's new birth (regeneration/salvation).

White, by using logic (instead of Biblical truth), reveals the problem that has plagued Calvinism for centuries: They have the proverbial cart before the proverbial horse. One's perception of Who God is and how He deals with mankind must never be based on logic, but on the Scriptures alone. As a result of considering the depraved as incapable of believing, Reformed Theology must perceive God as: (1) Spiritually regenerating the depraved (2) Giving the spiritually regenerated repentance and faith—along with the "*hidden wisdom*" of 1Corinthians 2:7 (3) Saving those whom He has already spiritually regenerated once they choose to repent and believe. White, in hopes of validating his thinking, quotes John Calvin on page 183 of *The Potter's Freedom*:

> ..."Hence it follows, first, that faith does not proceed from ourselves, but is the fruit of spiritual regeneration; for the Evangelist affirms that no man can believe, unless he be begotten of God; and therefore faith is a heavenly gift."...[33]

No amount of support, even from Calvin himself, can make John 1:12-13 teach that depravity deprives man of his ability to make a willing choice, through repentance and faith, to accept Christ. Nor can the tradition of Jonathan Edwards, a man who has greatly impacted Reformed Theology (extreme and hyper-Calvinism), make John 1:12-13 teach such a view. Romans 7, as was verified earlier, refutes Edwards' idea that man only responds according to his "strongest inclination." Without Edwards' flawed theory of "strongest inclination" to support their thinking, extreme and hyper-Calvinism's "Total Depravity" cannot stand.

White, along with other Reformed theologians, fails to make a distinction between man's responsibility (to repent and believe) and God's responsibility (to save). Again, man's choice to repent and believe (while depraved) is merely the *means* through which the new birth is <u>received</u>, God being the Source through which it is <u>bestowed</u>. Salvation is <u>by</u> grace, <u>through</u> faith (Ephesians 2:8). Consequently, God is the source of salvation, not man in his willingness to repent and believe.

Most extreme and hyper-Calvinists avoid John 1:12. Dave Hunt comments on page 450 of *What Love Is This?*:

> It is no coincidence that most Calvinists avoid John 1:12. No reference is made to it in the 600 pages of the *Selected Writings of John Knox,* and Pink avoids it in *The Sovereignty of God.* Piper makes two oblique references to it in *The Justification of God,* but without substantive comment. Not one of the thirteen authors in *Still Sovereign: Contemporary*

> *Perspectives on Election, Foreknowledge and Grace* confronts
> it. To his credit, White gives it four and one-half pages because
> Norm Geisler mentions it in his book, *Chosen But Free* (Bethany
> House, 1999), and White's book was written specifically as a
> rebuttal to Geisler.[34]

We have already addressed how White differs with Geisler's view of regeneration, so no need exists for further comment.

Intriguingly, the word *"born"* (John 1:13) is in the aorist *passive* form, meaning that the subject is being acted upon by an outside source. The subject is those who *"received Him,"* the *"children of God...who believe in His name"* (v.12). The source (Source) is God. These verses confirm, beyond doubt, that God does the saving—not the will of man. Thus, man is free to choose Christ in the midst of his depravity, receive salvation, and enjoy the eternal benefits of God's saving grace. This truth is communicated by John in John 1:12-13.

In the following quotes from Martin Luther, a man whose name will forever be tied to The Great Reformation, note the degree to which he contradicts the Scriptures. I am thankful for how the Lord used him to help partially reshape Christianity, but much of his theology is inaccurate.

The following is taken from Norm Geisler's, *Systematic Theology, Volume 3, Sin/Salvation*, pages 133-134.

> The main point of the Reformation was, at its heart, that "the
> just shall live *by faith*—and faith alone." Therefore, the exercise
> of faith is the one condition (action) necessary for a person to
> receive justification before God. Nevertheless, both ironically
> and contradictory, Martin Luther (1483-1546) insisted, against
> the mainstream of fifteen hundred years of church teaching and
> history, that a free act of belief is *not* a condition for receiving
> salvation at all. Rather, he argued that "this is plainly to ascribe
> *divinity* to 'free will,' for to will to embrace the Law and the
> Gospel...belongs to the power of God alone."...
>
> Addressing John's statement that a man must "receive"
> Christ (John 1:12), Luther contended,
>
> > This man is merely passive (as the term is used), nor
> > does he do anything, but is wholly mad; and John is
> > speaking of being made; he saith we are made the
> > sons of God by a power given unto us from above, not
> > by the power of "free will" inherent in ourselves....

He added,

> How could reason then think that faith in Jesus as
> the Son of God and man was necessary, when even at
> this day it could neither receive nor believe it?...so far
> is it from possibility that it should either will it, or
> believe it....

Luther was not timid in carrying his view to its logical
conclusion, namely, that *even evil men are caused to act by
God*:

> He [God] uses evil instruments, which cannot
> escape the sway and motion of [His] omnipotence....
> Hence it is, that the wicked man cannot but always err
> and sin; because, being carried along by the motion of
> the Divine Omnipotence, he is not permitted to remain
> motionless, but must will, desire, and act according to
> his nature. All this is fixed certainly, if we believe that
> God is Omnipotent![35]

Luther believed that man is incapable of responding against (contrary to) his
"strongest inclination," an idea that we proved invalid earlier.

We will now address additional verses that teach the necessity of personal
repentance and faith preceding spiritual regeneration, verses that confirm, beyond
doubt, that man in his depravity can repent and believe.

John 3:14-15—Moses Lifting Up The Serpent In The Wilderness

With John 3:1-15 fresh on our minds, we need to address verses 14-15 in more
depth:

> *And as Moses lifted up the serpent in the wilderness, even so must
> the Son of Man be lifted up; 15 that whoever believes may in Him
> have eternal life.* (John 3:14-15)

Because the context of Jesus' words to Nicodemus is crucial, let's look at
Numbers 21:4-9:

> *Then they set out from Mount Hor by the way of the Red Sea, to go
> around the land of Edom; and the people became impatient*

because of the journey. 5 And the people spoke against God and
Moses, "Why have you brought us up out of Egypt to die in the
wilderness? For there is no food and no water, and we loathe this
miserable food." 6 And the LORD sent fiery serpents among the
people and they bit the people, so that many people of Israel died.
7 So the people came to Moses and said, "We have sinned, because
we have spoken against the LORD and you; intercede with the
LORD, that He may remove the serpents from us." And Moses
interceded for the people. 8 Then the LORD said to Moses, "Make
a fiery serpent, and set it on a standard; and it shall come about,
that everyone who is bitten, when he looks at it, he shall live." 9
And Moses made a bronze serpent and set it on the standard; and it
came about, that if a serpent bit any man, when he looked to the
bronze serpent, he lived. (Numbers 21:4-9)

Israel rebelled by speaking *"against God and Moses"* (vv.4-5). As a result, *"the Lord sent fiery serpents among the people,"* they were bitten, and *"many people of Israel died"* (v.6). Once the people repented, *"Moses interceded"* (v.7), and God presented the remedy. Moses was to *"Make a fiery serpent, and set it on a standard"* (v.8) so those *"bitten"* could *"live"* (v.8) through one means only—through looking at the *"serpent"* (v.8). So *"Moses made a bronze serpent and set it on the standard; and it came about, that if a serpent bit any man, when he looked to the bronze serpent, he lived"* (v.9).

Now that we comprehend the context, we will address Jesus' words to Nicodemus in John 3:14-15. Follow closely.

When Israel sinned in Numbers 21, anyone *"bitten"* could be healed through looking at the *"fiery serpent."* The choice was left, not to God, but to those who had been *"bitten."* The correlation is simple. All mankind has been *"bitten"* by sin, being Adam's descendants. The *"bronze serpent,"* (Numbers 21:9; John 3:14) points to Jesus, Who was *"lifted up"* (John 3:14) on a cross so that *"whoever believes may in Him have eternal life"* (John 3:15). Just as a *"bronze serpent"* was raised by Moses as the remedy to the poison injected by the *"serpents,"* Jesus became *"sin"* (2Corinthians 5:21) while on the cross, taking on the misdeeds of all mankind. As a result, the poison of sin is eradicated in all who choose (while depraved) to repent and believe. The Jews in Numbers 21, through choosing to gaze upon God's provision, made the choice to obey. The fact that the choice was made <u>before</u> they were healed illustrates that the depraved can choose Christ <u>before</u> being born again (saved). After all, not all who made that choice were believers in Jehovah when the rebellion of Numbers 21:4-5 broke out. These verses again refute Jonathan Edwards' teaching regarding "strongest inclination" (addressed earlier when we studied Romans 7:1-25). They also explain why most Reformed theologians fail to address them. Dave Hunt comments on pages 338 of *What Love Is This?*:

> ...Like most other apologists for Calvinism, White [James White, a Reformed theologian] avoids John 3:14-15...[36]

On pages 451-452 of that same work, Hunt writes:

> In response to Nicodemus's question about how a man can be born again into God's kingdom, Christ explains that He is going to be "lifted up" for sin upon the cross like the brazen serpent in the wilderness, "that whosoever believeth in him should not perish, but have everlasting life" (John 3:15–16). Salvation is not of works, but by faith: "But to him that worketh not, but believeth on him that justifieth the ungodly, his faith is counted for righteousness" (Romans 4:5). As Paul repeatedly says, the sinner is "justified by faith" (Romans 5:1).
>
> The sinner must hear and believe the gospel *before* regeneration, not after it. That is why we must preach the gospel and seek, like Paul, to persuade men. Calvin reversed the biblical order, as do his followers today, declaring that no one can believe the gospel until he has first been regenerated. As Spurgeon said, however, one who has been regenerated has no need of the gospel, being saved already.[37]

John 11:43-44—The Resurrection of Lazarus

> *And when He had said these things, He cried out with a loud voice, "Lazarus, come forth." 44 He who had died came forth, bound hand and foot with wrappings; and his face was wrapped around with a cloth. Jesus said to them, "Unbind him, and let him go."* (John 11:43-44)

The extreme and hyper-Calvinists use John 11:1-44 in an attempt to strengthen their view of total depravity. They perceive the raising of Lazarus as an illustration of God's regenerating power upon the totally depraved so they might repent and believe. The problem with such thinking is that Lazarus was raised back to natural life, not to spiritual life, which negates their argument altogether. Nevertheless, John Piper (a Reformed theologian), in his DVD series *TULIP*, Disk 1, Title 6, Chapter 4, uses the account of Lazarus in an attempt to prove that the depraved must be spiritually regenerated <u>before</u> they can believe. He uses C.S. Lewis' conversion as an example:

> If you are called, you live. The calling here is the calling of Lazarus out of the tomb, "Lazarus come forth.".…Well what happened to him [Lewis] is that God called him.…God said, somewhere along that road, He said, "Lazarus, live, Lewis, see." And,…the eyes of his heart embraced the truth.[38]

Piper's argument is invalid, for Lazarus was a true physical corpse before being raised back to natural life in John 11:1-44. Just how much of a corpse he was is explained by the following quote from my commentary on the four Gospels titled, *The Gospels from a Jewish Perspective*, page 69:

> Jesus was deeply moved with anger when He arrived at the tomb, for He was angry at death (v.38), the last hurdle that must be abolished before Jesus presents the kingdom to the Father (1Corinthians 15:26-28). Jesus then asked that the stone which sealed the tomb be taken away, prompting Martha to point out that her brother had been dead for "four days" (v.39). "Four days" is significant in that, "It was a common Jewish idea that corruption commenced on the fourth day, that the drip of gall, which had fallen from the sword of the Angel and caused death, was then working its effect, and that, as the face changed, the soul took its final leave from the resting-place of the body" (*The Life and Times of Jesus the Messiah*—Book IV, pp.324-325). According to the Jewish mindset of Jesus' day, the spirit hovered over the body of the deceased individual for three days only, after which it departed to Hades or Sheol. As far as most Jews were concerned, the miracle of resurrection back to natural life was only possible for three days after death. Lazarus had died four days earlier, adding much gravity to Martha's words of verse 39, proving she thought it impossible for her brother to be raised. The belief that a body could only be raised back to life within three days also explains why Jesus waited an additional two days in Perea (v.6) before departing for Bethany. The raising of Lazarus was to be an extraordinary event in the ministry of Jesus, so He ensured that all conditions were met for it to fulfill its ultimate purpose.

A corpse cannot respond to any type of stimuli (including sin), for the being that once inhabited the body no longer dwells there. After four days, even Lazarus's body was perceived by the Jews as a body void of the spirit.

We discovered earlier that the Scriptures view spiritual "death" as separation, never extinction—meaning that the depraved are not corpses without a spiritual consciousness. The depraved have the Law (Galatians 3:24) and the Spirit (John 16:8) to reveal not only their sin, but also their need for a Savior. Hence, equating Lazarus, a true physical corpse while in the tomb, with a person living in a state of spiritual depravity is erroneous. We have already noted that Romans 1:18-32 grants the depraved opportunity to know truth.

Reformed Theology's view of John 11:1-44 breaks down for several reasons. Lazarus was raised to physical life, not to spiritual life—and spiritual regeneration so greatly supersedes restoration to natural life that the two cannot be compared. Also, a corpse can't respond to anything, even sin—and the spiritually depraved are superb sinners. Consequently, the resurrection of Lazarus back to natural life in no way supports Reformed Theology's total depravity.

2Corinthians 3:16—The Depraved Can Turn

> *but whenever a man turns to the Lord, the veil is taken away.*
> (2Corinthians 3:16)

This verse was addressed, in passing, earlier in our discussion of John 3, but a need exists to examine it more thoroughly. First, note what it communicates: "*but whenever a man turns to the Lord, the veil is taken away.*" A choice is required on behalf of those who come to Christ (in this particular case, the Jews), and the choice results in the veil being "*taken away.*" This fact confirms that man can choose Christ in his depraved state, resulting in God revealing Himself more vividly (through His truth, activated by the Holy Spirit) once the choice is made. Interestingly, John Piper, in *The Justification of God* and *The Pleasures of God*, mentions 2Corinthians 3:14-15 and 2Corinthians 3:18, but bypasses 2Corinthians 3:16 (according to the Scripture indices in those works). John MacArthur also avoids 2Corinthians 3:16 in his *MacArthur Study Bible* commentary, yet comments on 2Corinthians 3:14-15 and 2Corinthians 3:17-18. James White, in *The Potter's Freedom*, fails to mention 2Corinthians 3:16 as well. Extreme and hyper-Calvinism's definition of total depravity cannot withstand the truth of 2Corinthians 3:16 due to their belief that God must spiritually regenerate the depraved and grant them repentance and faith before they can choose to repent, believe, and be saved. Unquestionably, Paul taught that man's choice to repent and believe occurs <u>before</u> God removes "*the veil.*" He did not imply, by any stretch of the imagination, that God removes the veil (through Reformed Theology's spiritual regeneration) and man follows by choosing to repent and believe. Note how 2Corinthians 3:16 applies to Romans 9:16, the next verse that directly affects our perception of depravity.

Romans 9:16—Man's Will and God's Mercy

> *So then it does not depend on the man who wills or the man who runs, but on God who has mercy.* (Romans 9:16)

God's Heart as it Relates to Sovereignty-Free Will, the second (previous) book of this four part *God's Heart* series, presents a more detailed explanation of this passage.

After Israel sinned with the golden calf in Exodus 32, Moses willed that God's presence dwell among the nation (Exodus 33:15-16)—an unwise choice indeed. Had God done so, the nation would have been consumed (Exodus 33:3). God's mercy (on Moses and Israel) prevailed in that His presence (glory) entered the camp on Moses' face rather than dwelling amid all the people (read 2Corinthians 3:1-18). Thus, what resulted was not dependent upon what man (Moses in this instance) willed, *"but on God who has mercy."* This verse does not teach that man is incapable of choosing (willing) to follow Christ in his depraved state.

CHAPTER ELEVEN

DEPRAVITY AND THE NEW COVENANT

Ezekiel 11:19-20

> *And I shall give them one heart, and shall put a new spirit within them. And I shall take the heart of stone out of their flesh and give them a heart of flesh, 20 that they may walk in My statutes and keep My ordinances, and do them. Then they will be My people, and I shall be their God.* (Ezekiel 11:19-20)

Jeremiah 32:40

> *And I will make an everlasting covenant with them that I will not turn away from them, to do them good; and I will put the fear of Me in their hearts so that they will not turn away from Me.* (Jeremiah 32:40)

John Piper uses Ezekiel 11:19-20 and Jeremiah 32:40 in an attempt to solidify his view of the "T" of the TULIP, Total Depravity—that man in his depraved state <u>cannot</u> choose Christ. In his DVD series *TULIP*, Disk 1, Title 6, Chapter 5, Piper states:

> So there is coming a New Covenant day, Ezekiel and Jeremiah say, in which God will act decisively so that we stop rebelling against Him.[39]

Piper, due to incorrectly viewing the church as fulfilling the unconditional covenants God enacted with physical Israel, takes passages that relate to the nation of Israel (the physical Jews) and applies them to the church by interpreting these unconditional covenants allegorically rather than literally. (Our study, *Jacob I Loved—A Study of Romans 9*, addresses these unconditional covenants from a literal standpoint.) One of these unconditional covenants is the New Covenant of Jeremiah 31:31-34:

> *"Behold, days are coming," declares the LORD, "when I will make a new covenant with the house of Israel and with the house of Judah, 32 not like the covenant which I made with their fathers in the day I took them by the hand to bring them out of the land of Egypt, My covenant which they broke, although I was a husband to them," declares the LORD. 33 "But this is the covenant which I will make with the house of Israel after those days," declares the LORD, "I will put My law within them, and on their heart I will write it; and I will be their God, and they shall be My people. 34 And they shall not teach again, each man his neighbor and each man his brother, saying, 'Know the LORD,' for they shall all know Me, from the least of them to the greatest of them," declares the LORD, "for I will forgive their iniquity, and their sin I will remember no more."* (Jeremiah 31:31-34)

Although this covenant is being fulfilled in the general sense during the church age (this present age), it will not be fulfilled in its ultimate sense until the Jews living on the earth at the end of the Tribulation repent of their sins and accept Christ as Savior. This magnificent occasion will occur when the Jewish survivors of the Tribulation recognize their need for a Savior and call Christ back. Their prayer of repentance is recorded in Isaiah 53:1-9:

> *Who has believed our message? And to whom has the arm of the LORD been revealed? 2 For He grew up before Him like a tender shoot, And like a root out of parched ground; He has no stately form or majesty That we should look upon Him, Nor appearance that we should be attracted to Him. 3 He was despised and forsaken of men, A man of sorrows, and acquainted with grief; And like one from whom men hide their face, He was despised, and we did not esteem Him.*
>
> *4 Surely our griefs He Himself bore, And our sorrows He carried; Yet we ourselves esteemed Him stricken, Smitten of God, and afflicted. 5 But He was pierced through for our transgressions, He was crushed for our iniquities; The chastening for our well-being fell upon Him, And by His scourging we are healed. 6 All of us like*

sheep have gone astray, Each of us has turned to his own way; But the LORD has caused the iniquity of us all To fall on Him. 7 He was oppressed and He was afflicted, Yet He did not open His mouth; Like a lamb that is led to slaughter, And like a sheep that is silent before its shearers, So He did not open His mouth. 8 By oppression and judgment He was taken away; And as for His generation, who considered That He was cut off out of the land of the living, For the transgression of my people to whom the stroke was due? 9 His grave was assigned with wicked men, Yet He was with a rich man in His death, Because He had done no violence, Nor was there any deceit in His mouth. (Isaiah 53:1-9)

Hosea 5:15 states that the Jews (physical Israel) must recognize their sin, believe, and call Christ back before He can return:

I will go away and return to My place until they acknowledge their guilt and seek My face; in their affliction they will earnestly seek Me. (Hosea 5:15)

Hosea 6:1-3 communicates that Christ will grant these Jews spiritual life as a result of their repentance and faith:

"Come, let us return to the LORD. For He has torn us, but He will heal us; He has wounded us, but He will bandage us. 2 He will revive us after two days; He will raise us up on the third day that we may live before Him. 3 So let us know, let us press on to know the LORD. His going forth is as certain as the dawn; and He will come to us like the rain, like the spring rain watering the earth." (Hosea 6:1-3)

The Jews who survive the Tribulation will be capable of repenting of their sin in their depravity (v.1) *before* receiving spiritual rebirth—note the phrase in verse 2, *"That we may live before Him."* This new life will be dispensed *after* they repent and believe, totally negating Piper's idea that God must spiritually regenerate the depraved before they can turn to Christ. Interestingly, even if this context applied to the church alone (which it does not), repentance and faith would still precede new life—the new birth addressed in John 3:1-15.

Piper also uses the following verses in an attempt to prove that God must give man a new heart before he can repent, believe, and be saved. As you read them, note how easily they are interpreted, without contradiction, by considering that man can exercise repentance and faith while depraved prior to God's gift of spiritual regeneration (salvation).

> *Oh that they had such a heart in them, that they would fear Me,*
> *and keep all My commandments always, that it may be well with*
> *them and with their sons forever!;* (Deuteronomy 5:29)

> *And Moses summoned all Israel and said to them, "You have seen*
> *all that the LORD did before your eyes in the land of Egypt to*
> *Pharaoh and all his servants and all his land; 3 the great trials*
> *which your eyes have seen, those great signs and wonders. 4 Yet to*
> *this day the LORD has not given you a heart to know, nor eyes to*
> *see, nor ears to hear.* (Deuteronomy 29:2-4)

> *Moreover the LORD your God will circumcise your heart and the*
> *heart of your descendants, to love the LORD your God with all*
> *your heart and with all your soul, in order that you may live.*
> (Deuteronomy 30:6)

The full counsel of God's Word teaches that Jehovah will grant these Jews a new *"heart"* only after they repent (in their depraved state) and believe—as evidenced by the verses addressed thus far, as well as a wealth of additional passages. They most definitely will not be given a new heart prior to their repenting and believing. The Jewish remnant's prayer at the end of the Tribulation, recorded in Isaiah 64:1-12, confirms that man must repent and believe before receiving a new heart through spiritual rebirth:

> *Oh, that Thou wouldst rend the heavens and come down, That the*
> *mountains might quake at Thy presence— 2 As fire kindles the*
> *brushwood, as fire causes water to boil—To make Thy name known*
> *to Thine adversaries, That the nations may tremble at Thy*
> *presence! 3 When Thou didst awesome things which we did not*
> *expect, Thou didst come down, the mountains quaked at Thy*
> *presence. 4 For from of old they have not heard nor perceived by*
> *ear, neither has the eye seen a God besides Thee, Who acts in*
> *behalf of the one who waits for Him. 5 Thou dost meet him who*
> *rejoices in doing righteousness, Who remembers Thee in Thy ways.*
> *Behold, Thou wast angry, for we sinned, we continued in them a*
> *long time; and shall we be saved? 6 For all of us have become like*
> *one who is unclean, and all our righteous deeds are like a filthy*
> *garment; and all of us wither like a leaf, and our iniquities, like the*
> *wind, take us away. 7 And there is no one who calls on Thy name,*
> *who arouses himself to take hold of Thee; for Thou hast hidden Thy*
> *face from us, and hast delivered us into the power of our iniquities.*

8 But now, O LORD, Thou art our Father, we are the clay, and Thou our potter; and all of us are the work of Thy hand. 9 Do not be angry beyond measure, O LORD, Neither remember iniquity forever; behold, look now, all of us are Thy people. 10 Thy holy cities have become a wilderness, Zion has become a wilderness, Jerusalem a desolation. 11 Our holy and beautiful house, where our fathers praised Thee, has been burned by fire; and all our precious things have become a ruin. 12 Wilt Thou restrain Thyself at these things, O LORD? Wilt Thou keep silent and afflict us beyond measure? (Isaiah 64:1-12)

Psalm 79:1-13 also verifies that man must repent and believe <u>before</u> being saved, <u>before</u> receiving a new heart. After all, these passages describe the repentance and faith of the believing remnant of Jews at the end of the Tribulation <u>before</u> they are spiritually regenerated:

O God, the nations have invaded Your inheritance; they have defiled Your holy temple; they have laid Jerusalem in ruins. 2 They have given the dead bodies of Your servants for food to the birds of the heavens, the flesh of Your godly ones to the beasts of the earth. 3 They have poured out their blood like water round about Jerusalem; and there was no one to bury them. 4 We have become a reproach to our neighbors, a scoffing and derision to those around us. 5 How long, O LORD? Will You be angry forever? Will Your jealousy burn like fire? 6 Pour out Your wrath upon the nations which do not know You, and upon the kingdoms which do not call upon Your name. 7 For they have devoured Jacob and laid waste his habitation.

8 Do not remember the iniquities of our forefathers against us; let Your compassion come quickly to meet us, for we are brought very low. 9 Help us, O God of our salvation, for the glory of Your name; and deliver us and forgive our sins for Your name's sake. 10 Why should the nations say, "Where is their God?" Let there be known among the nations in our sight, vengeance for the blood of Your servants which has been shed. 11 Let the groaning of the prisoner come before You; according to the greatness of Your power preserve those who are doomed to die. 12 And return to our neighbors sevenfold into their bosom the reproach with which they have reproached You, O Lord. 13 So we Your people and the sheep of Your pasture will give thanks to You forever; to all generations we will tell of Your praise. (Psalm 79:1-13)

83

Psalm 80:1-19 also describes the repentance of the believing remnant of Jews at the end of the Tribulation <u>before</u> they are spiritually regenerated:

> *...Oh, give ear, Shepherd of Israel, Thou who dost lead Joseph like a flock; Thou who art enthroned above the cherubim, shine forth! 2 Before Ephraim and Benjamin and Manasseh, stir up Thy power, and come to save us! 3 O God, restore us, and cause Thy face to shine upon us, and we will be saved.*
>
> *4 O LORD God of hosts, How long wilt Thou be angry with the prayer of Thy people? 5 Thou hast fed them with the bread of tears, and Thou hast made them to drink tears in large measure. 6 Thou dost make us an object of contention to our neighbors; and our enemies laugh among themselves. 7 O God of hosts, restore us, and cause Thy face to shine upon us, and we will be saved.*
>
> *8 Thou didst remove a vine from Egypt; Thou didst drive out the nations, and didst plant it. 9 Thou didst clear the ground before it, and it took deep root and filled the land. 10 The mountains were covered with its shadow; and the cedars of God with its boughs. 11 It was sending out its branches to the sea, and its shoots to the River. 12 Why hast Thou broken down its hedges, so that all who pass that way pick its fruit? 13 A boar from the forest eats it away, and whatever moves in the field feeds on it.*
>
> *14 O God of hosts, turn again now, we beseech Thee; look down from heaven and see, and take care of this vine, 15 even the shoot which Thy right hand has planted, and on the son whom Thou hast strengthened for Thyself. 16 It is burned with fire, it is cut down; they perish at the rebuke of Thy countenance. 17 Let Thy hand be upon the man of Thy right hand, upon the son of man whom Thou didst make strong for Thyself. 18 Then we shall not turn back from Thee; revive us, and we will call upon Thy name. 19 O LORD God of hosts, restore us; Cause Thy face to shine upon us, and we will be saved.* (Psalm 80:1-19)

The nation calls on God to "*revive*" them in the midst of their depravity (v.18)— prior to spiritual regeneration (salvation).

Deuteronomy 30:1-10 addresses the restoration of the Jews to their land <u>after</u> they repent and return to Jehovah for salvation. They will receive a new heart (circumcised heart) <u>after</u> turning to the Lord—not beforehand. This circumcised heart will result in a sustained obedience:

"So it shall be when all of these things have come upon you, the blessing and the curse which I have set before you, and you call them to mind in all nations where the LORD your God has banished you, 2 and you return to the LORD your God and obey Him with all your heart and soul according to all that I command you today, you and your sons, 3 then the LORD your God will restore you from captivity, and have compassion on you, and will gather you again from all the peoples where the LORD your God has scattered you. 4 If your outcasts are at the ends of the earth, from there the LORD your God will gather you, and from there He will bring you back. 5 The LORD your God will bring you into the land which your fathers possessed, and you shall possess it; and He will prosper you and multiply you more than your fathers. 6 Moreover the LORD your God will circumcise your heart and the heart of your descendants, to love the LORD your God with all your heart and with all your soul, so that you may live. 7 The LORD your God will inflict all these curses on your enemies and on those who hate you, who persecuted you. 8 And you shall again obey the LORD, and observe all His commandments which I command you today. 9 Then the LORD your God will prosper you abundantly in all the work of your hand, in the offspring of your body and in the offspring of your cattle and in the produce of your ground, for the LORD will again rejoice over you for good, just as He rejoiced over your fathers; 10 if you obey the LORD your God to keep His commandments and His statutes which are written in this book of the law, if you turn to the LORD your God with all your heart and soul. (Deuteronomy 30:1-10)

We could cite numerous verses, but for the sake of space and time we will move on. Reformed theologians, disregarding the full counsel of God's Word, blind themselves to the Scriptural view of the depravity of man. Their mishandling of John 6:44 and John 12:32 exposes the depth of their faulty theology.

Do John 6:44 and John 12:32 Teach the "T" (Total Depravity) of the TULIP?

John 6:44

No one can come to Me, unless the Father who sent Me draws him; and I will raise him up on the last day. (John 6:44)

Scripture plainly teaches that no man can be saved unless he is drawn by the Father (John 6:44).

John 12:32

> *And I, if I be lifted up from the earth, will draw all men to Myself."*
> (John 12:32)

John 12:32 and John 6:44 are easily harmonized by realizing that all people are drawn by God (John 12:32), but only the drawn who choose to repent and believe while depraved *"can come"* to Christ (John 6:44). Man does the repenting and believing, but God does the drawing and saving, which allows us to "draw" the following conclusions.

God requires the depraved to exercise personal repentance and faith before He will make them part of His family—before He will make them new through spiritual regeneration (salvation). In other words, man's choice to repent and believe does not mean that man is capable of saving himself through repentance and faith, but rather that man's repentance and faith result in God's bestowal of salvation. This foundational truth allows Mark 10:52 to be interpreted in proper context:

> *And Jesus said to him, "Go your way; your faith has made you*
> *well." And immediately he regained his sight and began following*
> *Him on the road.* (Mark 10:52)

Jesus was <u>not</u> saying to this blind man that his faith, in itself, had made him well. Jesus was communicating that the God in Whom he believed had made him well. This truth is vital, so it will be covered in much depth when "faith" is examined as an independent subject in chapter fourteen.

Extreme and hyper-Calvinism must view the words *"all men"* (John 12:32) as the "elect only"—that is, if their definition of total depravity is to stand. Such a rendering, however, violates the heart and soul of the text, leaving it at the mercy of a contradictory system that must consistently yield to "mystery."

CHAPTER TWELVE

CAN DEPRAVITY AND GOD'S CONDITIONAL STATEMENTS BE RECONCILED?

ARE THE REPENTANCE AND FAITH exercised prior to salvation God's gifts, or do they originate with man? This question will be exciting to answer in subsequent chapters. But for now, the question is: Can depravity and God's conditional statements be reconciled void of contradiction? John Piper, in his DVD series, *TULIP*, makes assertions regarding this subject that will be examined for reliability. Piper addresses Irresistible Grace, the "I" of the TULIP—an idea that is entirely dependent on the "T" of the TULIP, Total Depravity. The "I," in fact, stems from the notion that man is so totally depraved that God must bring him to Himself through irresistible grace, spiritually regenerate him, and grant him repentance and faith, <u>before</u> he can repent, believe, and be saved. Therefore, Reformed Theology's irresistible grace is entirely dependent on its view of total depravity. Thus, disprove Reformed Theology's total depravity and you do away with the "I" of Calvinism's TULIP, "Irresistible Grace." In fact, you would abolish the entire TULIP. Charles Spurgeon's words, from his sermon titled, *Exposition of the Doctrines of Grace*, agree with my conclusion:

> "You cannot vanquish a Calvinist. You may think you can, but you cannot. The stones of the great doctrines so fit into each other, that the more pressure there is applied to remove them the more strenuously do they adhere together. And you may see, that you cannot receive one of these doctrines without believing all of them. Hold for instance that man is utterly

87

> depraved, and you draw the inference then that certainly if God
> has such a creature to deal with salvation must come from God
> alone, and if from him, the offended one, to an offending
> creature, then he [God] has a right to give or withhold his mercy
> as he wishes; you are thus forced upon election, and when you
> have received that you have all: the others must follow. Some by
> putting the strain upon their judgments may manage to hold two
> or three points and not the rest, but sound logic I take it
> requires a man to hold the whole system or reject it entirely;"[40]

Are you seeing why we are examining total depravity in such depth? Refute Calvinism's "T" of the TULIP, "Total Depravity," and you demolish their entire system of thought.

Piper's comments from his DVD series *TULIP*, Disk 1, Title 7, Chapters 2-4, are recorded next. What he states violates the full counsel of God's Word as much as anything I have researched regarding the Reformed position. As we address Piper's view of God's "conditional language" in the Scriptures, note the degree to which Reformed Theology has influenced his thinking. I need to warn you. Reading this section once may not suffice. It will probably take multiple readings to understand what Piper is attempting to communicate. If the information becomes overwhelming, just transition into **Depravity and God's Conditional Statements in Deuteronomy 28** (which follows this section), and press on. I do suggest, however, that you at least skim over what is included here:

> ...Faith is a gift, or repentance is a gift. So, we don't get nudged
> merely as in the Arminian understanding that grace brings us to
> a point and then leaves us to provide the decisive impulse to
> finish it. We are brought to the place where grace gives us faith,
> gives us repentance. Now, one of the obstacles to believing
> that is that...all over the Bible you run into God speaking to
> humans in conditional language—if you do this, I will do this; if
> you do this, I will do this...which, on the face of it, inclines us to
> think, "Well God is telling us what we have to do and then
> waiting to see if we will do it, to which He then, if we do it, will
> respond with the appropriate thing." And when we see that,
> we're inclined to think, "Well..., it doesn't seem to work then to
> say that God is irresistibly bringing us to where we need to be
> because He's telling us if we will go to a certain place then He
> will bring us to where we need to be...." I was reading this
> passage [2Chronicles 30:12], and it hit me. Now this is by way
> of illustration extremely helpful for seeing how conditional talk
> from God to us should not be taken to mean He is depending on

us to meet the condition, or that we should consider ourselves as self-reliant in meeting the condition that He just laid out. But that, in fact, it may be that when God says if you do this I will do this, He intends to enable us to do that so that He can do this. And once you see that in several places then you are relieved of the burden to take all those conditional places that you read about in the Bible and say, "Oh, we are being left to ourselves there to meet the condition, so there really is no such thing as irresistible grace." You don't have to make that conclusion once you see a few texts like this, so let's look at this one. It's 2Chronicles 30:6-12, and I'm going to read the whole thing to point out the conditionality language that God is using through Hezekiah's call. Hezekiah is calling for repentance. He's going to send messengers throughout the land with a summons for repentance. So here we read in verse 6:

Oh sons of Israel, return to the Lord God of Abraham, Isaac, and Israel, that He may return to those of you who escaped and are left from the hand of the kings of Assyria.[41]

Piper continues by saying:

So now notice. That's what God intends or wants to do. And it looks like He's saying, "You return so that I may return, you return so that God may return to you." That's conditional....My, you find that a dozen times in the Bible,..."you come to me and I'll come to you. Draw near to God and He'll draw near to you." Things like that.[42]

Piper then reads 2Chronicles 30:8:

Now do not stiffen your neck like your fathers, but yield to the Lord and enter his sanctuary which He has consecrated forever, and serve the Lord your God, that His burning anger may turn away from you.[43]

Piper then states:

So don't stiffen your neck, don't be resistant. He's telling them to stop being resistant....He's telling them to yield; it's what you've got to do. Do this, don't stiffen, yield, enter His

> sanctuary, and the result will be so that His burning anger may
> turn away from you....So, just think how an Arminian would use
> this against a Calvinist. Right off the bat they would say, "See,
> you have to do this and then His anger will turn away. So clearly
> His anger doesn't turn away first, help you, and then you
> respond. It's you respond and then He turns His anger away."
> You find this all over the Bible, talk like this.[44]

Piper then reads 2Chronicles 30:9-12:

> *9 For if you return to the LORD, your brothers and your sons will
> find compassion before those who led them captive, and will
> return to this land. For the LORD your God is gracious and
> compassionate, and will not turn His face away from you if you
> return to Him." 10 So the couriers passed from city to city
> through the country of Ephraim and Manasseh, and as far as
> Zebulun, but they laughed them to scorn, and mocked them. 11
> Nevertheless some men of Asher, Manasseh and Zebulun
> humbled themselves and came to Jerusalem. 12 The hand of
> God was also on Judah to give them one heart to do what the
> king and the princes commanded by the word of the LORD.*[45]

Piper's following comments are self-revealing, governed totally by the Reformed
view of Total Depravity:

> And when I got to verse 12...I'm reading along; I'm circling all
> the "if's" and "so that's," showing the structure of the
> conditionality of the language God is using toward me—I must
> do this and then He'll do this. And when I get to verse 12, I say,
> "Aw, look at that. Changes everything! It just changes
> everything." *"The hand of God was on Judah to give them one
> heart."* So the people here, they laughed them to scorn;
> nevertheless men from Asher and Manasseh and Zebulon, they
> didn't laugh them to scorn; they humbled themselves; they
> responded appropriately. And they came to Jerusalem and they
> did what they were told to do. He doesn't say why; it just says
> they did it. So if you stopped right there, you'd say, "Well see,
> they've got sovereign, decisive, ultimate, self-determining free
> will; and they did what they were told to do. Now God will
> respond and do what He promised to do. But then verse 12
> says, *"The hand of God was also"*; and I checked this out in the
> Hebrew..."*also on Judah.*" So not only Asher, Manasseh,

Zebulun, but also Judah; and it's the word *"also"* that clues me in to what's going to be said about why the Judah folks responded the way they did is also true of why Manasseh, Zebulun, and Asher responded the way they did. *"The hand of God was also on Judah to give them one heart to do what the king and the princes commanded by the word of the Lord."*

So Judah responded positively for the call to repentance because God gave them a heart to do it. And all the other responses of Manasseh, Zebulun, and Asher were also owing to that same cause. So, here's the conclusion. The condition stands! You don't go back and read and say, "Oh, there were no conditions." The conditions are real. "Return to the Lord God of Abraham, that He may return to you." "Don't stiffen your neck; yield to the Lord that His burning anger may turn away." But now we know from verse 12 you must not infer from that conditionality that God is folding His arms, standing back, and waiting for us unaided to fulfill the condition. That's not what's going on in this text. Not in any text I would argue. I mean, what if this text had stopped right there at verse 11 and I didn't get any help at all in seeing this. That's the case in many texts. Many texts do not provide verse 12. They just say, "Do this, and God will do this." So I am saying that the structure of thinking in the Bible is such that you should never infer from the Bible that when a condition is given to man that he do a thing, in order for God to do another thing, you jump to the conclusion that He leaves us to ourselves in fulfilling the condition that He just gave us. Because this text says He doesn't leave us to ourselves. He did the work in Judah that needed to be done in order for him to respond....[46]

We will discover shortly that Piper's words (thus far) don't fully reveal what he believes regarding total depravity. He says, "...you should never infer from the Bible that when a condition is given to man that he do a thing, in order for God to do another thing, you jump to the conclusion that He leaves us to ourselves in fulfilling the condition that He just gave us." I (Bob Warren) agree that God doesn't leave man to himself in his depravity; John 6:44 states:

> *No one can come to Me, unless the Father who sent Me draws him;...* (John 6:44)

All men are drawn by the Lord, for He desires that none perish:

And I, if I be lifted up from the earth, will draw all men to Myself."
(John 12:32)

*The Lord is not slow about His promise, as some count slowness,
but is patient toward you, not wishing for any to perish but for all
to come to repentance.* (2Peter 3:9)

John 12:32 and 2Peter 3:9 confirm that the Lord desires all people to be saved—although many choose to disregard His offer and remain lost. Thus, these passages do <u>not</u> teach Universalism—that all men will be saved. Neither does John 6:44 communicate that God must (through irresistible grace) draw the elect (alone) to Himself, spiritually regenerate the elect, grant them repentance and faith, <u>before</u> they can repent, believe, and be saved. Nor does God leave man to himself to fulfill the calling on his life once he believes. Nehemiah said:

"...But now, O God, strengthen my hands." (Nehemiah 6:9)

Even Paul stated:

*"But by the grace of God I am what I am, and His grace toward
me did not prove vain; but I labored even more than all of them,
yet not I, but the grace of God with me."* (1Corinthians 15:10)

Both Nehemiah and Paul knew that God sustained them (worked through them) as they chose to walk in His will for their lives.

Considering the subject matter addressed thus far, we realize: All men are drawn by the Lord (John 12:32). No man can come to Christ without the Father's drawing (John 6:44), but the Father's drawing does not result in God imparting salvation unless the drawn one chooses to repent and believe while depraved. Nor is one, who after being drawn, makes the choice to repent and believe, required to fulfill God's calling on his/her life without God's energizing. This fact, however, is unrelated to my source of concern. My concern is who Piper views as responsible for making the <u>decisive</u> choice (providing the "decisive impulse," to use Piper's words) regarding man's departure from depravity. After all, Piper seems to view the parties of 2Chronicles 30:11-12 as in need of salvation, especially considering his upcoming quote. Can man in his depravity repent and choose Christ, or must God make the choice for him? Does not 2Chronicles 30:11 state, *"Nevertheless, some men of Asher, Manasseh, and Zebulun humbled themselves* [repented] *and came to Jerusalem"*? Undoubtedly, these men humbled themselves, that is, repented (yielded to the Lord) as a result of their own decision to do so. However, note Piper's view of these events as he applies them to Revelation 3:20:

> ...Probably the most common example you think of is, "Behold I stand at the door and knock, whoever will open the door I will come in to him, sup with him, and he with Me" (Revelation 3:20). The issue here is not whether that's being addressed to Christians or non-Christians. It's really being addressed to Christians, but the point is the principle of: If God says that to an unbeliever, "Behold I stand at the door and knock, if you will open your heart I will come in." That's a conditional statement just like this: "If you return to Him, He will come to you." Should you conclude from that, that Christ should be only pictured as outside the door knocking? That's all: You don't have any other picture in your mind beside that; and I would say on the basis of dozens and dozens of other texts, "No, we shouldn't." And there are different ways you can think about it. One is the Holy Spirit simply enters by the chimney, or window, or just osmosis through the wall; and He...just pulls the latch from the inside, or you could say: "He inclines your heart to pull the latch from the inside, and Jesus walks in, and He is actually responding to your choice." But there has been another factor brought into the situation that inclines you to open the door from the inside. The way we are saved involves language that is conditional and prevenient or preemptive. "If you come to me I will save you." "Believe on the Lord Jesus Christ and you will be saved." The Bible is replete with summons for us to make choices in response to God. But I'm pointing out here: Don't ever infer from those summons to make choices, to which God will then respond, don't ever infer from those that God leaves you to yourself with no <u>decisive</u> help in providing the response that He requires you to give. [emphasis associated with "<u>decisive</u>" added][47]

The key statement in Piper's quote is, "But I'm pointing out here, don't ever infer from those summons to make choices, to which God will then respond, don't ever infer from those that God leaves you to yourself with no <u>decisive</u> help in providing the response that He requires you to give."

Piper perceives the depraved as void of the ability to provide the "<u>decisive</u> impulse" (choice) that leads to God bestowing salvation, for he views God's "<u>decisive</u> help" as necessary if anyone is to exit his/her depravity. "<u>Decisive</u>" is the key word that reveals Piper's commitment to the Reformed view of total depravity—a view that depicts the depraved as incapable of providing the "<u>decisive</u> impulse" (choice) required to come to Christ. He supposes that the <u>decisive</u> impulse is God's prerogative, never man's, especially when salvation is involved.

This mindset is easily disproved by the wealth of verses that require man to choose Christ in his depravity <u>before</u> being saved (read John 1:12, Acts 16:31, Romans 4:5, Romans 10:9-10 for starters).   Reformed Theology, therefore, reverses the Scriptural order of events regarding the salvation of man.

As we have addressed on numerous occasions (please be patient with the required redundancy), Reformed Theology views God as bringing man out of his depravity by spiritual regeneration, which causes him (man) to be born again. God is then free to grant him repentance and faith, after which he (man) can choose to repent, believe, and be saved.   But, as was verified earlier, this scenario would mean that man is saved twice—first, when he is born again and, second, when he chooses to repent and believe after having received God's gifts of repentance and faith—that is, if the proper definition is assigned to "born again," meaning "salvation." Because Reformed Theology perceives man as spiritually regenerated before he repents and believes, a reversal of the Scriptural order, Piper must reverse the meaning of God's conditional statements included in His Word. If you are confused at this point, you will likely not be when the study is completed. This subject matter is not only fascinating to work through, but exceedingly important for the health of our souls.

Now back to 2Chronicles 30:11-12.

> *Nevertheless some men of Asher, Manasseh, and Zebulun <u>humbled</u>*
> *<u>themselves</u> and came to Jerusalem. 12 The hand of God was <u>also</u>*
> *on Judah to give them <u>one heart</u> to do what the king and the*
> *princes commanded by the word of the LORD.* (2Chronicles
> 30:11-12 —emphasis added)

Piper uses these verses in an attempt to validate his definition of total depravity, for he seems to assume that the people mentioned in verses 11-12 were in need of salvation when the couriers of verses 6 and 10 invited them to the Passover. He, therefore, takes the word *"also"* in verse 12 and attempts to prove two presuppositions: (1) That God's *"hand"* provided the <u>decisive</u> impulse for Judah *"to do what the king and the princes commanded by the word of the LORD"* (v.12); (2) That it was *"also"* His *"hand"* (v.12) that provided the <u>decisive</u> impulse for Asher, Manasseh, and Zebulun to humble themselves, come to Jerusalem (v.11), and *"do what the king and the princes commanded by the word of the LORD"* (v.12). Is this feasible? Does the fact that verse 12 mentions God's *"hand"* as being upon these individuals mean that they were incapable of providing the <u>decisive</u> impulse to respond in this manner? Did God make the decision for them? If you took Piper's assumptions through all the Scriptures, would his thinking be deemed accurate?

We will begin by examining Ezra 8:22, a verse that uses parallel terminology:

> *"...The hand of our God is favorably disposed to [upon] all those who seek Him, but His power and His anger are against all those who forsake Him."* (Ezra 8:22 NASB)

> *The hand of our God is upon all them that seek him, for good; but his power and his wrath is against all them that forsake him.* (Ezra 8:22 ASV)

> *The hand of our God is upon all them for good that seek him; but his power and his wrath is against all them that forsake him.* (Ezra 8:22 KJV)

This verse does <u>not</u> state that God's *"hand"* caused these individuals to *"seek Him."* The verse also contains the phrase, *"The hand of our God,"* and mentions that His *"hand"* is *"upon all them that seek him"* (ASV). We can conclude, therefore, that God's *"hand"* is upon <u>all</u> individuals who choose to obey, whether they are desiring salvation or yielding to the Lord subsequent to salvation. The order of events shows that Ezra 8:22 clearly teaches that man first seeks God—after which God's *"hand"* is *"upon"* him. Yet, Piper supposes that God's *"hand"* is *"upon"* man (to provide the <u>decisive</u> impulse regarding salvation and obedience) <u>before</u> man is capable of seeking the Lord. This sequence is exactly backwards. Verses such as Ezra 8:22 grant a person the freedom to provide not only the <u>decisive</u> impulse to believe unto salvation but also the <u>decisive</u> impulse to yield to God once he/she is saved.

That God *"draws"* the depraved (John 6:44; 12:32) is undeniable, *"not wishing for any to perish but for all to come to repentance"* (2Peter 3:9) and *"be saved"* (1Timothy 2:4). As has been verified, God draws all of mankind (John 12:32); but only those who choose to repent and believe (yield to Him while depraved) can come to Christ and receive God's salvation (John 6:44; John 1:12; Acts 16:31; Romans 10:9-10; etc.). Once man provides the <u>decisive</u> impulse to yield to the Lord, not only does God's *"hand"* bring him to salvation, but once saved, His *"hand"* rests upon him as he pursues a life of obedience and faithfulness (as was Ezra's case in Ezra 8:22). This truth is vividly displayed in Romans 6:6, 6:11, and 6:13, verses that describe the victorious life made available to the New Testament believer.

> *knowing this, that our old self was crucified with Him, that our body of sin might be done away with, that we should no longer be slaves to sin; 7 for he who has died is freed from sin.* (Romans 6:6)

To experience victory, the New Testament believer must first know that *the "old self"* (sinful nature, Adamic nature, old man, dead spirit—all synonymous terms) has been *"crucified"*—in other words, know that it no longer exists. Only through *"knowing"* that we are dead to temptation can we realize the unnaturalness of yielding to temptation. After *"knowing"* the truth regarding the eradication of the *"old self"* (Romans 6:6), we must, according to Romans 6:11, follow by believing the truth that we possess regarding the eradication of the *"old self"*:

> *Even so consider yourselves to be dead to sin, but alive to God in*
> *Christ Jesus.* (Romans 6:11)

Paul is saying in verse 11 that it takes more than just *"knowing"* that the "*old self*" has been eradicated (Romans 6:6) if we are to see sin's power defeated in our lives. It takes considering (believing) ourselves *"to be dead to sin, but alive to God in Christ Jesus"* (Romans 6:11), that is, considering as true what we know from verse 6. A vast difference exists between knowing the truth and believing the truth. Once we come to believe what we already know concerning the eradication of the *"old self,"* the next step, addressed by Romans 6:13 is the most critical:

> *and do not go on presenting the members of your body to sin as*
> *instruments of unrighteousness; but present yourselves to God as*
> *those alive from the dead, and your members as instruments of*
> *righteousness to God.* (Romans 6:13)

If victorious living is to be experienced by New Testament believers, more than *"knowing"* that the eradication of the *"old self"* has freed us from slavery to the power of sin (Romans 6:6) is necessary. Also, more than believing that the eradication of the *"old self"* has freed us from slavery to the power of *"sin"* (Romans 6:11) is required. We are to *"present"* ourselves *"to God as those alive from the dead"* (Romans 6:13). Wow! What an amazing thought! Thus, victory is realized by the New Testament believer only through yielding to Christ's life within (Galatians 2:20)—Christ being *"God"* (Hebrews 1:8). Observe how Romans 6:13 is rendered in the KJV:

> *Neither yield ye your members as instruments of unrighteousness*
> *unto sin: but yield yourselves unto God, as those that are alive*
> *from the dead, and your members as instruments of righteousness*
> *unto God.* (Romans 6:13 KJV)

Don't overlook the word *"yield."* The New Testament believer must *"yield"* to Christ to live abundantly, for Paul understood that no amount of self-discipline could produce victorious living (Colossians 2:20-23). Paul possessed a thorough understanding of Ezra's words in Ezra 8:22:

> *The hand of our God is upon all them for good that seek him; but his power and his wrath is against all them that forsake him.* (Ezra 8:22 KJV)

Paul stated in Romans 5:10:

> *For if while we were enemies, we were reconciled to God through the death of His Son, much more, having been reconciled, we shall be saved by His life.* (Romans 5:10 NASB)

Paul viewed himself (as a believer) as being saved daily from sin's power by Christ's very *"life."* We can conclude, therefore, that we were saved from the penalty of our sin (once and for all) through Christ's death (when we chose, while depraved, to repent and believe), and are now being *"saved"* from the power of sin (on an ongoing basis) through yielding to *"His life."* This truth lines up perfectly with Ezra's words, for God's *"hand"* is truly *"upon all"* who *"seek him"* (Ezra 8:22). Thus, His power is also upon all New Testament saints who *"yield"* (Romans 6:13) to Christ in their pursuit of God's best for their lives. No wonder Paul viewed the ministry to which he was called as being fulfilled through *"the grace of God"* as he chose to obey:

> *But by the grace of God I am what I am, and His grace toward me did not prove vain; but I labored even more than all of them, yet not I, but the grace of God with me.* (1Corinthians 15:10)

Peter says:

> *Humble yourselves, therefore, under the mighty hand of God, that He may exalt you at the proper time,* (1Peter 5:6)

Ezra 7:6 and 10 apply here as well:

> *This Ezra went up from Babylon, and he was a scribe skilled in the law of Moses, which the LORD God of Israel had given; and the king granted him all he requested because the hand of the LORD his God was upon him.* (Ezra 7:6)

> *For Ezra had set his heart to study the law of the LORD, and to*
> *practice it, and to teach His statutes and ordinances in Israel.*
> (Ezra 7:10)

God exalts those who make the choice to humble themselves before Him. In other words, God's hand is always on those who possess a yielded heart, whether they are yielding for salvation or yielding for strength to live abundantly as a believer.

The word *"yield"* in 2Chronicles 30:8 ties in extremely well with our discussion:

> *Now do not stiffen your neck like your fathers, but yield to the*
> *LORD and enter His sanctuary which He has consecrated forever,*
> *and serve the LORD your God, that His burning anger may turn*
> *away from you.* (2Chronicles 30:8 — emphasis added)

In some editions of the *New American Standard Bible*, the word *"yield"* in 2Chronicles 30:8 has a number beside it, serving as a reminder to reference the margin. The margin then verifies that *"yield"* can also be rendered, *"give a hand."* Note what *Keil & Delitzsch Commentary on the Old Testament* says regarding *"yield"* in 2Chronicles 30:8:

> ...it denotes the giving of the hand as a pledge of fidelity, as in 2
> Kings 10:15; Ezra 10:19; Ezek 17:18.[48]

Interesting! This meaning is clearly seen in 2Kings 10:15:

> *Now when he had departed from there, he met Jehonadab the son*
> *of Rechab coming to meet him; and he greeted him and said to*
> *him, "Is your heart right, as my heart is with your heart?" And*
> *Jehonadab answered, "It is." Jehu said, "If it is, give me your*
> *hand." And he gave him his hand, and he took him up to him into*
> *the chariot.* (2Kings 10:15 —emphasis added)

First, Jehonadab made the choice to come to Jehu. Jehu then asked Jehonadab, *"Is your heart right, as my heart is with your heart?"* Stated differently, Jehu asked Jehonadab if his heart was committed to him. When Jehonadab answered, *"It is,"* Jehu said, *"If it is, give me your hand,"* in other words, *"If it is, yield."* Then Jehonadab gave Jehu his yielded *hand, and he* [Jehu] *took him up to him into the chariot.* Thus, the relationship established between the two men was greatly enhanced by Jehonadab's desire (and choice) to associate with Jehu. Once Jehu saw Jehonadab's commitment, he grasped Jehonadab's yielded *hand* and *took him up* into the chariot.

I realize that most illustrations break down at some point. However, the exchange between Jehonadab and Jehu illustrates, to some degree at least, how God deals with man. Man must first choose (and desire) to meet Him with a yielded heart (while depraved), the type of heart that God requires. God responds by asking him to extend his hand, a yielded hand that has been influenced by the man's yielded heart. God then grasps his yielded hand and brings him into the kingdom. What do we take away from this illustration? We can learn from this illustration that both the heart of the seeker and the heart of God must desire that the relationship begin. Because God longs for a relationship with all mankind, He continually desires that none perish (1Timothy 2:4; 2Peter 3:9). For this relationship to occur, however, man in his depraved state must yield his heart to God through repentance and faith. God does all the rest, including grasping his yielded hand and taking him up into the "chariot" (the kingdom). The personal faith exercised by the depraved is not a work on man's part (Romans 3:27-28; 4:4-5; 9:32). Once man is saved, God continues to place His hand on the yielded servant by performing the work of the ministry through him (as previously confirmed by Romans 6:6, 11, and 13, along with Romans 5:10 and 1Corinthians 15:10). By trusting God's indwelling presence to perform the impossible (rather than working "for" God to the point of exhaustion), the New Testament believer enters *"Sabbath rest"* (Hebrews 4:9-10)—a truth dealt with in much detail in the *Hebrews* course distributed by this ministry.

We have proven that God draws the depraved to Himself in the midst of their depravity (John 6:44; 12:32) without providing the "decisive impulse" as to whether they will or will not repent and believe. Thus, if they choose to repent and believe, the decisive impulse (choice) is left to the one desiring salvation (Acts 16:31 and John 1:12), not to God. So how does this truth apply to 2Chronicles 30:11-12?

> *Nevertheless some men of Asher, Manasseh, and Zebulun humbled themselves and came to Jerusalem. 12 The hand of God was also on Judah to give them one heart to do what the king and the princes commanded by the word of the LORD.* (2Chronicles 30:11-12)

Let's allow the Scriptures to speak for themselves. First, *"some men"* from Asher, Manasseh, and Zebulun *"humbled themselves,"* in other words, yielded themselves to the Lord (verse 11). However, *"also,"* in verse 12, points to the fact that *"The hand of God"* was not only *"on Judah,"* but also on the men from Asher, Manasseh, and Zebulun. What must be answered is: (1) Was God's *"hand"* on the men from Asher, Manasseh, and Zebulun for the purpose of providing the decisive impulse (choice) that caused them to humble themselves, come *"to Jerusalem,"* and *"do what the king and the princes commanded by the word of the Lord,"* or (2)

Did these men first choose to humble themselves and come to Jerusalem *"to do what the king and the princes commanded by the word of the Lord,"* after which God's *"hand"* strengthened them for the task? Ezra 8:22 reveals the answer:

> ... *"The hand of our God is favorably disposed to all those who seek Him, but His power and His anger are against all those who forsake Him."* (Ezra 8:22)

Man first seeks the Lord, after which God's *"hand"* is *"favorably disposed"* to him. Hence, all the individuals addressed in 2Chronicles 30:11-12 were strengthened by God after they chose to obey, whether for salvation or for service. Stated differently, God's hand supplied the power to do what they had already chosen to do. Paul was in agreement with this view of the Scriptures. Read Acts 16:31, Romans 4:5, 5:1, and 10:9-10 for verses addressing man's freedom to choose Christ (in his depraved state), after which God saves the ones who have chosen to repent and believe. Read Ephesians 3:16, Colossians 1:11, 1Timothy 1:12, and 2Timothy 4:17 for verses pertaining to God's strengthening of believers for service. Oh, the value of the full counsel of God's Word!

Conclusion

God's Word contains a wealth of conditional statements. However, God does not have to provide the decisive impulse (choice) before man can obey. Man can choose, for himself, whether he will or will not yield to what God prescribes. Therefore, the man who yields (while depraved) will find God's hand ready to save and usher him into the kingdom. Once in the kingdom, he will be granted the power to live abundantly (as he yields to God) the remainder of his days.

Scripture confirms as well that God draws *"all men"* to Himself (John 12:32), in fact, no man *"can come"* to Christ unless *"the Father...draws him"* (John 6:44). However, drawing men is totally different from making decisions for the men being drawn. Thus, God drew us without providing the decisive impulse for us to repent and believe, for we provided the decisive impulse while depraved.

Depravity and God's Conditional Statements in Deuteronomy 28

Let's suppose for a moment that Piper is correct in assuming that God must provide the decisive impulse before one can respond appropriately to His conditional statements, especially those statements pertaining to salvation. We will take this hypothesis through Deuteronomy 28 to see how God's reputation would be affected should Piper be correct.

Before attending to any of the verses found in Deuteronomy 28, we must realize that many of the Jews who heard these words died without having believed, reaping the full consequence of their unbelief. If God must provide the decisive impulse for the "elect" to come to faith, as Piper supposes, then God communicated these conditional statements to many people from whom He withheld the freedom to believe. In this case, why would He state them in the first place? Why prescribe conditional proclamations to individuals who can't obey? How could a just God punish anyone, yes, anyone, for failing to do the impossible? Surely God isn't in heaven playing games with men's souls, is He?

John Piper attempts to circumvent this issue in *TULIP*, Disk 2, Title 6, Chapters 4 and 5, where he begins by quoting Jonathan Edwards' work, *The Freedom of the Will*:

> "God's moral government over mankind, his treating them as moral agents, making them the objects of His commands, counsels, calls, warnings, expostulations, promises, threatenings, rewards, punishments, is not inconsistent with a determining disposal of all events [total control of everything], of every kind, throughout the universe, in his providence; either by positive efficiency, or permission." (Conclusion, p. 258 in Bobb-Merrill, 1969 edition)

> So there's the thesis....That's the goal, that's my belief, assumption. And ultimately it's an assumption I cannot probably philosophically demonstrate to your satisfaction. I simply embrace it because it is assumed everywhere in the Bible, that God both has a determining disposal of all events, that's one thing that's all over the Bible, and that we are dealt with as morally accountable creatures in making commands to us and threatening punishments to us and offering rewards to us if we will think and feel and do certain things. He [Edwards] describes an important distinction in understanding what we mean by saying that irresistible grace and total depravity are based on the biblical conviction that people are in themselves "unable" to believe on Christ and yet are morally accountable for doing so. So there's the mystery; there's the paradox; there's the tension.[49]

Piper realizes his "assumption" cannot be "philosophically" demonstrated (explained) to our "satisfaction"; yet he states, without reservation, that his "assumption" is "all over the Bible." —His assumption is that "people are in themselves unable to believe on Christ and yet are morally accountable for doing so." This wordy attempt to avoid the sting accompanying the bottom line of

Reformed Theology is unacceptable. Piper's assumption, in actuality, positions God to judge the "non-elect" for failing to do the impossible—for failing to believe when they were incapable of believing. In that case, God would be totally unjust and unfit to reign. Piper can't "philosophically demonstrate" his "assumption" to our "satisfaction," for it simply isn't Biblical. Yet, Piper and his fellow Calvinists choose to believe it anyway—which is equivalent to "assuming" that two plus two equals five and professing that all math books teach the same. If you heard a man express such a theory, would you "assume" that he could prove his hypothesis void of contradiction? Absolutely not—that is, if you know that two plus two equals four, no matter who teaches otherwise! Also, a phone call to any institution of higher learning would verify, beyond doubt, the incorrectness of his presupposition. God's Word, in a much deeper sense, verifies the incorrectness of Piper's thinking. Consider the following facts.

Deuteronomy 28:1-2 records God's words to Israel shortly before she crossed the Jordan to enter into Canaan:

> *"Now it shall be, if you will diligently obey the LORD your God,*
> *being careful to do all His commandments which I command you*
> *today, the LORD your God will set you high above all the nations*
> *of the earth. And all these blessings shall come upon you and*
> *overtake you, if you will obey the LORD your God.* (Deuteronomy
> 28:1-2)

Those Jews who chose to obey would receive the innumerable blessings promised in Deuteronomy 28:3-13. These blessings are confirmed again in verses 13 and 14:

> *And the LORD shall make you the head and not the tail, and you*
> *only shall be above, and you shall not be underneath, if you will*
> *listen to the commandments of the LORD your God, which I charge*
> *you today, to observe them carefully, and do not turn aside from*
> *any of the words which I command you today, to the right or to the*
> *left, to go after other gods to serve them.* (Deuteronomy 28:13-14)

Verse 15 states that curses would accompany disobedience:

> *"But it shall come about, if you will not obey the LORD your God,*
> *to observe to do all His commandments and His statutes with*
> *which I charge you today, that all these curses shall come upon*
> *you and overtake you.* (Deuteronomy 28:15)

The curses are listed in verses 16-44 followed by a prophetic warning in verses 45-48:

> *So all these curses shall come on you and pursue you and overtake*
> *you until you are destroyed, because you would not obey the LORD*
> *your God by keeping His commandments and His statutes which*
> *He commanded you. And they shall become a sign and a wonder*
> *on you and your descendants forever. Because you did not serve*
> *the LORD your God with joy and a glad heart, for the abundance*
> *of all things; therefore you shall serve your enemies whom the*
> *LORD shall send against you, in hunger, in thirst, in nakedness,*
> *and in the lack of all things; and He will put an iron yoke on your*
> *neck until He has destroyed you.* (Deuteronomy 28:45-48)

Deuteronomy 28:49-57 continues to describe the consequence of disobedience, followed by a final conditional statement in verse 58:

> *"If you are not careful to observe all the words of this law which*
> *are written in this book, to fear this honored and awesome name,*
> *the LORD your God,* (Deuteronomy 28:58)

Verses 59 through 68 continue explaining the horror that would accompany their sin. What conclusions can be drawn? I will simplify the answer as much as possible, but the following paragraphs may need to be read more than once to comprehend their significance.

God's Word is inundated with conditional statements that promise blessings for obedience and curses for disobedience. However, only those who walk in faith will receive the promised blessings. Those who do not walk in faith will never experience the fulfillment of the promised blessings.

If the repentance and faith required for God's salvation are His gifts to those whom He has chosen to spiritually regenerate (Piper's view), then God would be determining who obeys. This scenario would leave the "non-elect" of Reformed Theology unable to exercise personal repentance and faith, and thus, obedience. If God required obedience from those incapable of obeying, He could not be the Just Ruler of the universe. In an honorable court of law, those punished must have possessed the freedom to obey—the freedom to avoid the crime as well as the consequences. If not, the case would be deemed to have been improperly tried by the court, and the accused would be released of the charge. In other words, no court in America judges the incompetent. Thus, if the non-elect are required to do that which is impossible (Piper's view), the judge Who passes the sentence is Himself unjust. Calvinists (especially Reformed theologians) would argue that God is vindicated by displaying mercy on a few individuals (the elect), especially since all persons are deserving of His wrath. They are right in that all (all human beings) are deserving of God's wrath, but that is not the point of concern. In fact, the Calvinists might have a valid argument should God be incapable of saving all. However, even they agree that God, in the realm of His sovereignty, could have saved all had He chosen to do so. This detail puts the Calvinists in a precarious position—in fact, an impossible one. If God is capable of saving all yet should choose to save only some (the choice as to who will believe being God's choice, not man's), how can He be described in the Scriptures as a God of love? Yet, both 1John 4:8 and 1John 4:16 declare:

> *"...God is love."* (1John 4:8, 16)

Therefore, Calvinism's "T," Total Depravity, damages God's name by making Him, not only unjust, but unloving as well—that is, if you require them to be straightforward regarding their bottom line. They are left to frequently classifying contradiction as mystery, paradox, or tension, and using "logic" rather than Scripture to shield TULIP's inconsistencies.

CHAPTER THIRTEEN

MORE VERSES THAT RELATE TO DEPRAVITY

Matthew 23:37 and Depravity

> *"O Jerusalem, Jerusalem, who kills the prophets and stones those who are sent to her! How often I wanted to gather your children together, the way a hen gathers her chicks under her wings, and you were unwilling.* (Matthew 23:37)

Matthew 23:37 presents a quandary for Reformed Theology. Had man's destiny been established by God from eternity past, Jesus would have been foolish to plead so passionately for every inhabitant of Jerusalem to repent and believe—for the majority rejected his Messiahship. Jesus desired that everyone in Jerusalem choose (while depraved) to come to Him in faith (the Jewish leaders and the common people alike)—a truth that Reformed Theology cannot, under any circumstance, accept.

Calvinists are divided over this verse. In fact, the sharp contrasts that exist within their camp are intriguing.

Dr. Norm Geisler (a moderate Calvinist) in *Chosen But Free* (page 208), states the following regarding Matthew 23:37:

> ...What could be more clear: God wanted all of them, even the unrepentant, to be saved.[50]

Geisler, a moderate Calvinist, views mankind (all persons) as possessing a free will to choose Christ while depraved. (As has been verified in previous discussion,

105

the moderate Calvinists violate their view of free will by perceiving the elect as having been elected to salvation from eternity past. What difference would it make for all mankind to possess a free will if only the elect, chosen to salvation from eternity past, could repent and accept Christ? Such an arrangement assigns God the choice regarding the destiny of the elect long before the elect have opportunity to choose to believe—thus violating moderate Calvinism's free will altogether.)

James White, a Reformed theologian (in his work *The Potter's Freedom*), passionately disagrees with Geisler. White's Reformed view can never allow the non-elect to have a free choice to accept or reject God's gift of salvation. Therefore, instead of viewing the inhabitants of Jerusalem (Matthew 23:37) as possessing the freedom to be unwilling to repent and believe after Christ offered them the opportunity to do so, he perceives the Jewish leaders as *"unwilling"* to allow the inhabitants of the city to gather to hear Christ's message. (Permission was requested to quote White, but permission was denied. Hence, a contextual paraphrase of his conclusions is provided.) White (pages 138-139 of *The Potter's Freedom*) quotes John Gill (another Reformed theologian) for support, taking the following from Gill's *The Cause of God and Truth*:

> That the persons whom Christ would have gathered are not represented as being *unwilling* to be gathered; but their rulers were not willing that they should. The opposition and resistance to the will of Christ, were not made by the people, but by their governors. The common people seemed inclined to attend the ministry of Christ, as appears from the vast crowds which, at different times and places, followed him; but the chief priests and rulers did all they could to hinder the collection of them to him; and their belief in him as the Messiah, by traducing his character, miracles, and doctrines, and by passing an act that whosoever confessed him should be put out of the synagogue; so that the obvious meaning of the text is the same with that of verse 13...and consequently is no proof of men's resisting the operations of the Spirit and grace of God, but of obstructions and discouragements thrown in the way of attendance on the external ministry of the word.[51]

Gill, like White, views Matthew 23:37 as teaching that the Jewish leaders were *"unwilling"* to allow the people to assemble to hear Jesus. After all, should the passage teach that the inhabitants of Jerusalem were *"unwilling"* to repent and believe (the plain meaning of Matthew 23:37), or to "resist the operations of the Spirit and grace of God" (Gill), they would have possessed the capacity to repent and believe. A person can't be unwilling to do what he/she lacks the capacity to will. Thus, the inhabitants of the city whom Jesus desired to "gather" to Himself possessed the capacity to will to repent and believe and be saved—or reject His offer and be damned. God's Word teaches that a majority of the people rejected His offer and died unsaved, although each had the capacity to repent and believe.

The Reformed view of sovereignty depicts God as compelling rulers to conform to His desires, even at the expense of their freedom of choice. Hence, Gill and White, rather than validating the sovereignty required by Reformed Theology, negate it. We know from Romans 13:1 that God establishes all authority. Because Jesus is God (Hebrews 1:8), and One of the three Persons of the Triune Godhead, He would have set in place the men ruling in Jerusalem. Thus, should Matthew 23:37 communicate that the Jewish leaders refused to allow the people to listen to His message, as Gill and White suggest, these leaders would have responded opposite the desires of the Sovereign Who placed them in authority—robbing Jesus of His sovereignty in the process.

Should God be the cause of all things, even sin (as many Reformed theologians believe), and White and Gill be correct in their assumptions regarding Matthew 23:37, Jesus would have been the "cause" behind the Jewish leaders failing to fulfill His desires. What kind of God would this arrangement prove Him to be? Would you view Him as the wise, stable, just, omnipotent, and loving Creator portrayed in the Scriptures? I think not! Should the Reformed view of sovereignty be correct, surely God could have placed men in authority who were eager to fulfill His desires—that is, unless He is playing games with men's souls during their brief stay on earth. Also, Romans 10:21 teaches (indisputably) that God has "*stretched out*" His "*hands to a disobedient and obstinate people*" (the Jews), the most of whom have rejected His offer of salvation. He would never stretch out His hands (offer salvation) to anyone incapable of repenting and believing! Yet, Reformed Theology has Him doing just that—that is, when their doctrine is taken through the full counsel of God's Word!

Norm Geisler (a moderate Calvinist) is in disagreement with Gill's assessment of Matthew 23:37. Gill's words (from Gill's, *The Cause of God and Truth*) are recorded in quotation marks in the following quote from Geisler's *Chosen But Free*, pages 208-209:

> John Gill proposed this is to be understood not of gathering to salvation but only of a gathering to hear him [Jesus] preach and thus to be brought to historical faith "sufficient to preserve them from temporal ruin." Likewise, the will of Christ to gather them "is not to be understood of his divine will...but of his human will, or of his will as a man; which...[is] yet not always the same with it, nor always fulfilled" A clear exposition of the extreme Calvinists' view here is perhaps the best refutation of it, for it forces us to believe that God's concern for the temporal

> conditions of all men is greater than that of His concern for their
> eternal souls.[52]

Gill's "remedy" to the dilemma generated by his interpretation of Matthew 23:37 is to grant Jesus two wills, a "divine will" and a "human will." If Gill should be correct, we must hope that Jesus' "divine will" saves rather than His "human will," since His "human will" is not always fulfilled. Wow! Surely Gill can't be serious.

Great disparity exists within Calvinism, but the extremes to which the Reformed position must yield, in an effort to maintain its definition of total depravity, are inexcusable. They respond so excessively, and in turn, incorrectly, because God's desire that all the inhabitants of Jerusalem repent and believe refutes the "T" of the TULIP of Calvinism (Total Depravity) since the choice to believe was placed in the hands of the depraved listeners. This offer by Jesus (to choose Him in the midst of their depravity) also nullifies (or eradicates) extreme and hyper-Calvinism's (Reformed Theology's) unhealthy view of sovereignty. Their "sovereignty" cannot endure a scenario where Jesus desires a people to come to Him, yet they refuse. How foolish it would have been for Jesus to offer salvation to a people, the majority of whom (according to Reformed Theology) had no opportunity to believe. This predicament causes extreme and hyper-Calvinism to draw such unwarranted conclusions regarding Matthew 23:37.

Dave Hunt in, *What Love Is This?,* pages 461-462, addresses Matthew 23:37 in much depth. Because Hunt is not a Calvinist, his input will be diametrically opposed to White's views. After examining his thoughts, we will study Matthew 23:37 in the context of Matthew 21:23-23:39—a fascinating study indeed.

Hunt begins by referencing a particular dialogue with James White:

> In a radio discussion with James White, I referred to Christ's weeping over Jerusalem. I pointed to His expression of desire ("how often would I") and His lament over Jerusalem's hard-hearted response ("ye would not") as proof of His sincere offer of grace, and of man's right and ability to receive or reject salvation:
>
> > O Jerusalem, Jerusalem, thou that killest the prophets, and stonest them which are sent unto thee, how often would I have gathered thy children together, even as a hen gathereth her chickens under her wings, and ye would not! (Matthew 23:37)
>
> White countered that Christ was not weeping over Jerusalem and that the ones He wanted to gather were Jerusalem's

children, not the religious leaders who rejected Him. "Ye would
not," he insisted, expressed the attitude of the rabbis, not of
Jerusalem's "children" whom He wanted to gather under His
care.

This argument, however, is of no help to White or other
Calvinists who use it. Very few if any of Jerusalem's "children,"
any more than her leaders, ever believed on Christ. Therefore,
even if Christ only meant the children, He was expressing a
desire for the salvation of many who were never saved.

Here is one more example of the way in which Calvinists must
twist Scripture in defending their strange doctrine. In fact, the
expression, "children of Jerusalem" or "children of Israel," etc.,
is used throughout Scripture to indicate "the people" of a city or
country or race—*never* its non-adults. When only the young
children are meant, the context always makes that fact clear, as
"the wives also and the children rejoiced…" (Nehemiah
12:43).[53]

Hunt's following statements confirm that his commitment to the Scriptural view
of Matthew 23:37 is solid. Note the number of verses used in his argument on page
462 of that same work:

The expression, "children of Israel" is found 644 times,
"children of Ammon" 89 times, "children of Benjamin" 36 times,
"children of God" 10 times, and *not once* in those 779
instances is the reference to nonadults! The specific phrase,
"children of Jerusalem," is used in Joel 3:6 for the "inhabitants
of Jerusalem"—exactly as Christ meant in His lament. Among
many similar references to "children" and "Jerusalem" (*none* of
which means its non-adults exclusively) we find:

And in Jerusalem dwelt of the children of Judah,
and of the children of Benjamin, and of the
children of Ephraim, and Manasseh…(1
Chronicles 9:3); the children of Judah and
Jerusalem (2 Chronicles 28:10); And the
children of Israel that were present at Jerusalem
(2 Chronicles 30:21); all the children of the
captivity, that they should gather themselves
together unto Jerusalem (Ezra 10:7); children of
the province…that…came again to Jerusalem

(Nehemiah 7:6); Jerusalem...thy children have
forsaken me...and assembled themselves by
troops in the harlots' houses.... Every one
neighed after his neighbor's wife.... Saith the
Lord: and shall not my soul be avenged on such
a nation as this? (Jeremiah 5:1-9); etc.

There are numerous other similar references, all of which clearly
refer to the *inhabitants* of Jerusalem or some other city or
country and *none* of which refers exclusively to non-adults. In
His great love, Christ is clearly pleading with Israel—as He has
through His prophets for centuries, and as He still pleads with
the world for which He died.[54]

Hunt continues with additional remarks relating to Matthew 23:37 on pages 462-464 of *What Love Is This?:*

Not only is White's argument (which is used by many Calvinists)
both irrational and unbiblical, but even some Calvinist leaders
disagree with it. John MacArthur, Jr., recognizes that Christ is
expressing the same desire for the salvation of all the
inhabitants of Jerusalem that He has expressed for centuries as
the God of Israel through His prophets. He declares that "Jesus
weeps over the city of Jerusalem...we cannot escape the
conclusion that God's benevolent, merciful love is unlimited in
extent.... Luke 19:41-44 gives an even more detailed picture of
Christ's sorrow over the city...." And MacArthur even suggests
that "the city of Jerusalem [represents] the Israelite Nation."

Luther also declared, "In Christ, God comes seeking the
salvation of all men; He offers Himself to all; He weeps over
Jerusalem because Jerusalem rejects Him.... Here God
incarnate says: 'I would, and thou wouldest not.' God
incarnate...was sent for this purpose, to will, say, do, suffer and
offer to all men, all that is necessary for salvation albeit he
offends many who, being abandoned or hardened by God's
secret will of Majesty...do not receive him...."

In a further contradiction of his affirmation at other times of
Limited Atonement, Spurgeon also applied Christ's words both
to all of Jerusalem and to all sinners:

In Christ's name I have wept over you as the
Saviour did, and used his words on his behalf,

110

> "O Jerusalem, Jerusalem, how often would I
> have gathered thy children together as a hen
> gathereth her chickens under her wings, and ye
> would not...." Oh! God does plead
> with...everyone of you, "Repent, and be
> converted for the remission of your sins...." And
> with divine love he woos you...crying, "Come
> unto me...."
>
> "No," says one strong-doctrine man, "God
> never invites all men to himself...." Stop, sir....
> Did you ever read... "My oxen and my fatlings
> are killed, and all things are ready; come unto
> the marriage. And they that were bidden *would
> not come*...." Now if the invitation is...made
> [only] to the man who will accept it, how can that
> parable be true? The fact is...the invitation is
> free.... "*Whosoever will*, let him come...."
>
> Now...some of you [may] say that I
> was...Arminian at the end. I care not. I beg of you
> to...turn unto the Lord with all your hearts.

Spurgeon makes an excellent point. Christ likens the kingdom of God to a supper to which men are invited (Luke 14:15-24). In the parable, there is no question that a bona fide invitation was extended, nor that many if not most of those sincerely invited refused and even scorned the invitation and suffered the Lord's wrath: "For I say unto you, That none of those men which were bidden shall taste of my supper" (v. 24).

The problem for the Calvinist is to explain how God can sincerely invite into His kingdom those for whom Christ did not die, whom He has not elected to salvation, whom He has from a past eternity predestined to eternal torment and who can't accept because He withholds from them the grace they need—then punish them for not responding to His "invitation." How, indeed! And why does He send his servants to "compel" those "in highways and hedges...to come in, that my house may be filled" (v. 23), if regeneration is a sovereign act of God without human response? And if faith is a gift and grace is irresistible, how could the elect refuse the earnest invitation? Spurgeon leaves these questions unanswered, knowing he will be accused of being "Arminian at the end."

> Nor have we found any Calvinist who attempts to answer
> Spurgeon. The only reasonable and biblical response is to
> abandon Calvinism, which Spurgeon would not do, although he
> continued to contradict it in his preaching. And for pointing out
> these contradictions, I am criticized for allegedly misquoting and
> misrepresenting Spurgeon.[55]

Having considered these different views, mainly for the purpose of understanding the magnitude of the disparity within Calvinism, we will address Matthew 23:37 as it relates to its context. In other words, we will address the Scriptural view of this passage:

> *"O Jerusalem, Jerusalem, who kills the prophets and stones those*
> *who are sent to her! How often I wanted to gather your children*
> *together, the way a hen gathers her chicks under her wings, and*
> *you were unwilling.* (Matthew 23:37)

Who made up Jesus' audience? In other words, who was present when Jesus stated these words? To answer this question, we must begin with Matthew 21:23 and work our way forward.

> *And when He had come into the temple, the chief priests and the*
> *elders of the people came to Him as He was teaching, and said,*
> *"By what authority are You doing these things, and who gave You*
> *this authority?"* (Matthew 21:23)

Jesus entered the temple on Tuesday, the 12th of Nisan, 30 AD, before He was crucified on Friday, the 15th of Nisan, 30 AD. He spoke at this location, the temple, from Matthew 21:23 through Matthew 23:39. The chief priests, elders, and Pharisees were in attendance (Matthew 21:23, 45). The Sadducees were present as well (Matthew 22:23), along with the multitudes (Matthew 22:33). In Matthew 22:34-35 and Matthew 22:41, the Pharisees are again mentioned as being present. We can conclude, therefore, that Jesus had a diverse audience when He spoke in the temple that day. This background will greatly assist us as we seek to properly interpret Matthew 23:37.

Jesus spoke more directly to the disciples and the multitudes in Matthew 23:1-12, meaning that the disciples were also present (note verse 1). We can infer as well, based on the previous input, that the scribes and Pharisees were in attendance. In Matthew 23:13-35, however, Jesus spoke more directly to the scribes and Pharisees, with the disciples and multitudes in attendance. We can conclude: When Jesus said, *"O Jerusalem, Jerusalem, who kills the prophets and stones those who are sent to her! How often I wanted to gather your children together, the way a hen gathers her chicks under her wings, and you were unwilling"* (Matthew 23:37), He was not addressing the Jewish leaders only, but was referring to the entire city's inhabitants, many of whom were in attendance among the multitudes. Also, the preceding verse, Matthew 23:36, states:

> *Truly I say to you, all these things shall come upon this generation.* (Matthew 23:36)

In this passage, Jesus transitioned from the scribes and Pharisees (whom He had been criticizing in Matthew 23:13-35) to the entire *"generation"* of Jews living in that day (verse 36). Therefore, arguing that Jesus was addressing the Jewish leaders only when saying, *"O Jerusalem, Jerusalem"* (Matthew 23:37) is improper. This input negates White's assumption that the *"unwilling"* of Matthew 23:37 were the Jewish leaders who, according to White, were *"unwilling"* to allow the *"children"* of Jerusalem to hear Christ's message. White is forced to assume this interpretation because had Jesus offered salvation to all the inhabitants of Jerusalem (which He did), leaving the decision to accept or reject His Messiahship in the hands of the people, total depravity, as defined by Reformed Theology, is proven false. White also realizes that had Jesus offered salvation to all of Jerusalem (which He did), it would confirm that He has always offered salvation to all of mankind. Reformed Theology cannot withstand this truth.

Matthew 23:38-39 offers additional proof that Jesus (in Matthew 23:37) was referring to the entire city of Jerusalem, and not the Jewish leaders only:

> *Behold, your house is being left to you desolate! 39 For I say to you, from now on you shall not see Me until you say, 'Blessed is He who comes in the name of the Lord!'"* (Matthew 23:38-39)

The pronouns *"your"* and *"you"* in verse 38, as well as *"you"* in verse 39, prove that a day will come when the Jewish leaders of Jerusalem along with all its Jewish inhabitants (v.37)—that to which the pronouns *"you"* and *"your"* of verses 38 and 39 make reference—will accept Jesus as Messiah.

Matthew 23:39 ties in well with the fact that Jesus will not return at the Second Coming until every Jew who has survived the Tribulation repents and calls Him back (also read Hosea 5:15). This event will occur due to the Jewish leaders encouraging them to repent and accept Christ as Messiah (Hosea 6:1-3). The entire nation will respond by calling Him back while confessing its sin (Matthew 23:39; Isaiah 53:1-9; 64:1-12; Zechariah 13:7-9; Psalm 79:1-13; 80:1-19), reaping the fruit of spiritual regeneration, or salvation (Romans 11:26):

> *and thus all Israel will be saved...* (Romans 11:26)

Included in this group of repentant Jews will be the inhabitants of Jerusalem, as evidenced by Zechariah 12:10-13:1:

> *"And I will pour out on the house of David and on the inhabitants of Jerusalem, the Spirit of grace and of supplication, so that they will look on Me whom they have pierced; and they will mourn for Him, as one mourns for an only son, and they will weep bitterly over Him, like the bitter weeping over a first-born. 11 In that day there will be great mourning in Jerusalem, like the mourning of Hadadrimmon in the plain of Megiddo. 12 And the land will mourn, every family by itself; the family of the house of David by itself, and their wives by themselves; the family of the house of Nathan by itself, and their wives by themselves; 13 the family of the house of Levi by itself, and their wives by themselves; the family of the Shimeites by itself, and their wives by themselves; 14 all the families that remain, every family by itself, and their wives by themselves. 13:1 In that day a fountain will be opened for the house of David and for the inhabitants of Jerusalem, for sin and for impurity.* (Zechariah 12:10-13:1)

Is it not amazing that Jesus, at His First Coming, due to being God (Hebrews 1:8), and possessing perfect foreknowledge, could prophesy of a day when all the Jews living in Jerusalem will repent and call Him back—due to having believed on Him as Messiah? If in Matthew 23:39 Jesus is making reference to all the Jews who will one day live in Jerusalem, He had to be addressing (in Matthew 23:37) all the Jews who lived in Jerusalem at His First Coming, refuting White and Gill's argument altogether.

Jesus desired that all Jerusalem be saved at His First Coming—every person in the city. He placed the freedom to accept or reject His offer in the hands of those over whom He lamented, even though the majority rejected His offer and walked away. Let's read Matthew 23:37 one more time, with proper context in mind, and try to imagine the pain experienced by the Savior as He agonized over the city:

> *"O Jerusalem, Jerusalem, who kills the prophets and stones those who are sent to her! How often I wanted to gather your children together, the way a hen gathers her chicks under her wings, and you were unwilling.* (Matthew 23:37)

This same Savior died so we might live. Should there be any reason why we cannot enjoy Him this day? None whatsoever!

1Corinthians 1:30 and Depravity

> *But by His doing you are in Christ Jesus, who became to us*
> *wisdom from God, and righteousness and sanctification, and*
> *redemption,* (1Corinthians 1:30)

Reformed theologians use this verse in an attempt to prove that God's choice determines who will be placed *"in Christ Jesus."* They cannot, under any circumstance, allow man to make a choice to believe in his depraved state, as is evidenced by John Piper's quote from his DVD series *TULIP*, Disk 2, Title 7, Chapter 2.

> ... "from Him are you in Christ Jesus." That means He grafted
> you into Christ. The emphasis is not, "from you are you in Christ
> Jesus." "From Him are you in Christ Jesus." We believed in
> order to go into Christ Jesus, but our faith is a gift, and thus, it is
> "from Him that we are in Christ Jesus."[56]

Yes, *"by His doing"* believers *"are in Christ Jesus."* And, *"Salvation is of the Lord"* (Jonah 2:9). Does this mean, however, that God must spiritually regenerate man (in order to bring man out of his depraved state) and give him repentance and faith <u>before</u> man can repent, believe, and be saved? Is this what Paul meant by *"But by His doing you are in Christ Jesus,..."* (1Corinthians 1:30), or did he mean something totally contrary? The answer is simple when all of the Scriptures are examined rather than a select few.

First, a person (during the church age) repents and believes while depraved (John 1:12; 3:15; Acts 2:38; 16:31; Romans 10:9-10; and 2Corinthians 3:16), after which he is placed in Christ through the avenue of the Holy Spirit (1Corinthians 12:13). This sequence lines up perfectly with John 6:37, 39, 44, and 65, where we find that the Father draws all persons and gives each who chooses Christ (while depraved) to the Son. In conjunction with being placed *"in Christ,"* a New Testament believer is spiritually regenerated (*"born again"*—John 3:5-8), receives eternal life (John 3:15; Romans 6:23), and becomes a *"new creation"* (2Corinthians 5:17). Therefore, a person can exercise personal repentance and faith <u>before</u> being spiritually regenerated. Hence God, through the power of the Holy Spirit, places believers *"in Christ"*—and He does so <u>after</u> they put their trust in Christ while in their depraved state. Paul encompasses all of these truths in the statement, *"But by His doing you are in Christ Jesus...."* Simple, isn't it? Again, we see that the believer does the believing, but God, and only God, does the saving—<u>after</u> the depraved exercise repentance and faith while depraved.

If you are a believer, I would like to ask a pertinent question. When you exercised your will (while in your depraved state) and accepted Christ as Savior, did you place yourself in Christ as a result of choosing to repent and believe? Absolutely not!   Reformed Theology, however, must view "freewillers" as believing they can place themselves in Christ through exercising their own personal repentance and faith.   Their view of total depravity would be destroyed if the depraved could choose Christ and not save themselves in the process.   Scripture clearly teaches, on the other hand, that God places the seeker in Christ subsequent to his/her repenting and believing while depraved.

Romans 3:10-12 and Depravity

> ... *"There is none righteous, not even one; 11 there is none who understands, there is none who seeks for God; 12 all have turned aside, together they have become useless; there is none who does good, there is not even one."* (Romans 3:10-12)

Reformed theologians use these verses in an effort to prove that the depraved are incapable of seeking God.   Their theology cannot, under any circumstance, allow the Scriptures to teach that the spiritually unregenerated can repent and believe— even with the help of the Father's drawing (John 6:44) and the Spirit's conviction (John 16:8).   Yet, Paul confirms that although the depraved cannot initiate salvation (Romans 3:11), or achieve it through believing (Romans 4:5), they can exercise personal repentance and faith (2Corinthians 3:16).   Only God initiates salvation, by drawing all mankind to Himself (John 12:32, 6:44) and convicting *"the world"* of *"sin, and righteousness, and judgment"* (John 16:8)—after which He bestows salvation to those who choose to repent and believe.   Thus, although the depraved neither initiate salvation nor achieve it through choosing to turn to God, this turning is required (2Corinthians 3:16) prior to God bestowing righteousness.   Through exercising repentance and faith, the depraved do what is right (what God requires)—only Jehovah imparts righteousness.

On page 114 of *The Potter's Freedom*, James White (a Reformed Theologian) presents a quote from *Chosen But Free* (page 67), written by Dr. Norm Geisler— who believes in the free will promoted by moderate Calvinism.   Presented below is the totality of Geisler's words relating to Romans 3:10-11, of which White records only a portion for the purpose of criticizing Geisler's argument:

> The moderate Calvinist (and Arminian) has no problem with such a rendering of these verses. It is God who *initiates* salvation. "Salvation is of the Lord" (Jonah 2:9 KJV). "We love Him because He first loved us" (1John 4:19 NKJV). We seek Him, then, only because He has first sought us. However, as a result of the convicting work of the Holy Spirit on the whole

> "world" (John 16:8) and "the goodness of God" (Romans 2:4
> NKJV), some people are moved to repent. Likewise, as a result
> of God's grace some seek Him. Hebrews declares that "without
> faith it is impossible to please God, because anyone who comes
> to him must believe that he exists and that he rewards *those*
> *who earnestly seek him"* (Heb. 11:6). God is found by those
> who seek Him, yet when they find Him they discover that He first
> sought them.[57]

According to Reformed Theology (Whites' view), God could never draw a person to Himself (seek someone) without bringing that individual into the kingdom. Should a drawn one fail to enter, God, based on the Reformed view, would be robbed of His sovereignty. White understands correctly that those who believe in free will perceive God as drawing all of mankind to Himself. What he doesn't realize is that God can draw a person to Himself, the person reject His offer as a result of possessing a free will, and God remain sovereign. God can remain sovereign in these conditions by granting every human being, within the realm of His sovereignty, a free will without having been forced to do so. This truth allows the Scriptures to address the salvation of man void of contradiction, unlike the Reformed position, which must consistently yield to "mystery" to mask its error.

Several passages refute the Reformed view of Romans 3:10-12, some of which will be considered shortly. But first we will address the phrases:

"there is none who does good, there is not even one." (Romans 3:12)

Romans 3:12 does not teach that the unregenerate cannot do *"good"* at any time, but rather describes the general state of the depraved. For instance, Jesus said:

And if you do good to those who do good to you, what credit is that
to you? For even sinners do the same. (Luke 6:33)

Jesus viewed the sinner (a depraved individual) as doing *"good"* at times.

Some Reformed theologians, however, use John 15:4-5 in an attempt to equate depravity with an inability to believe. They can't allow the depraved to do "good," even exercise faith. Yet, to believe (exercise faith) is anything but a work (read Romans 3:27-28, 4:4-5, and 9:32). Also, John 15:4-5 says:

Abide in Me, and I in you. As the branch cannot bear fruit of itself,
unless it abides in the vine, so neither can you, unless you abide in
Me. 5 I am the vine, you are the branches; he who abides in Me,
and I in him, he bears much fruit; for apart from Me you can do
nothing. (John 15:4-5)

The following quote is Edwin Palmer's attempt to tie these passages to the Reformed view (*The Five Points of Calvinism*, pages 14-15):

> On another occasion Jesus gave the secret of the Christian life: the indwelling of Christ (John 15). He used the illustration of a grapevine and its branches. In speaking of the inability to do good works, He said: "Just as the branch is not able by itself to bear fruit—unless it abides in the vine—so neither can you unless you abide in me....Apart from me you can do nothing" (John 15:4-5). That's total inability.[58]

Palmer is correct in associating these passages with a person's experience once he/she has been saved. The fact that no good work can be done through a believer unless he/she is yielded to Christ is no indication, however, that depravity equals inability to choose Christ while depraved. Putting Romans 3:11 in context validates this fact:

> *There is none who understands, there is none who seeks for God;*
> (Romans 3:11)

This verse is a general statement regarding the depraved rather than a precise description of every moment of their existence. When taken through the full counsel of God's Word, Romans 3:11 actually teaches that the depraved will never seek God without the Father's drawing (John 6:44) and the Spirit's conviction (John 16:8). Remember, no verse is to be isolated and interpreted as an "island" in itself. All the verses in God's Word are required for proper understanding, that is, if you adopt Paul's method of interpretation (Acts 20:27 KJV):

> *For I have not shunned to declare unto you all the counsel of God.*
> (Acts 20:27 KJV)

Without the aid of *"all the counsel of God,"* Paul himself would be in error by stating:

> *if somehow I might move to jealousy my fellow countrymen and save some of them.* (Romans 11:14)

Surely Paul was not teaching that he possessed the power to save! Such ill-founded instruction would have been nothing less than heresy.

Reformed theologians rely heavily on Romans 3:10-12 to support their perception of total depravity. As we continue, however, several verses will be cited (in addition to those already mentioned) that refute their view. For instance, Paul spoke of his attempt to *"persuade men"* to come to Christ in 2Corinthians 5:11, realizing that a choice was required on their part (in the midst of their depravity) before they could be spiritually regenerated (saved):

> *Therefore knowing the fear of the Lord, we persuade men, but we are made manifest to God; and I hope that we are made manifest also in your consciences.* (2Corinthians 5:11)

In 2Chronicles 15:4 we also find:

> *But in their distress they turned to the LORD God of Israel, and they sought Him, and He let them find Him,* (2Chronicles 15:4)

Man can seek God (in his depravity) before finding Him and receiving spiritual life. *"Seek"* in the following passages confirms that the depraved can pursue the Lord—with the assistance of the Father's drawing (John 6:44) and the Spirit's conviction (John 16:8)—without needing to be spiritually regenerated beforehand. Additional verses could be cited, but for the sake of time and space only a limited number are included. Just these few passages, however, are more than adequate to validate free will.

Psalm 10:4 and Depravity

> *The wicked, through the pride of his countenance, will not seek after God: God is not in all his thoughts.* (Psalm 10:4 KJV)

"Pride," not inability in the midst of their depravity, prevents the *"wicked"* from seeking the Lord. The Scriptures stress that God opposes *"the proud, but gives grace to the humble"* (James 4:6). For this reason the Law was given to the depraved (1Timothy 1:9) so they might repent of their pride and come to Christ (Romans 3:19).

1Chronicles 28:9 and Depravity

> *"As for you, my son Solomon, know the God of your father, and serve Him with a whole heart and a willing mind; for the LORD searches all hearts, and understands every intent of the thoughts. If you seek Him, He will let you find Him; but if you forsake Him, He will reject you forever.* (1Chronicles 28:9)

119

David, the man after God's own heart, told Solomon (his son) that the Lord would allow Solomon to find Him should Solomon *"seek Him."* Therefore, God must be sought before He can be found. In other words, the Lord is found by the depraved who *"seek Him."*

2Chronicles 15:1-4 and Depravity

> *Now the Spirit of God came on Azariah the son of Oded, 2 and he went out to meet Asa and said to him, "Listen to me, Asa, and all Judah and Benjamin: the LORD is with you when you are with Him. And if you seek Him, He will let you find Him; but if you forsake Him, He will forsake you. 3 And for many days Israel was without the true God and without a teaching priest and without law. 4 But in their distress they turned to the LORD God of Israel, and they sought Him, and He let them find Him.* (2Chronicles 15:1-4)

These words were not directed toward Asa alone, but to *"all Judah and Benjamin,"* many of whom were not (at this juncture at least) followers of Jehovah. This example is just one of many where the Lord urges the unregenerate (the depraved) to *"seek"* Him. Seeking precedes finding.

Isaiah 55:6-7 and Depravity

> *Seek the LORD while He may be found; Call upon Him while He is near. 7 Let the wicked forsake his way, And the unrighteous man his thoughts; And let him return to the LORD, And He will have compassion on him; And to our God, For He will abundantly pardon.* (Isaiah 55:6-7)

The *"wicked"* man is to *"forsake his way,"* meaning that the depraved are to make a choice to submit to the Lord before they can be pardoned (saved). They most definitely are to *"Seek"* and *"Call upon"* God prior to being spiritually regenerated.

Jeremiah 29:13 and Depravity

> *And you will seek Me and find Me, when you search for Me with all your heart.* (Jeremiah 29:13)

One must *"seek"* the Lord <u>before</u> finding the Lord and experiencing spiritual regeneration. Thus seeking, <u>prior</u> to spiritual regeneration, precedes finding.

Acts 17:24-28 and Depravity

> *The God who made the world and all things in it, since He is Lord of heaven and earth, does not dwell in temples made with hands; 25 neither is He served by human hands, as though He needed anything, since He Himself gives to all life and breath and all things; 26 and He made from one, every nation of mankind to live on all the face of the earth, having determined their appointed times, and the boundaries of their habitation, 27 that they should seek God, if perhaps they might grope for Him and find Him, though He is not far from each one of us;* (Acts 17:24-28)

Paul, speaking to Greeks (*"Men of Athens"*—v.22), men who were philosophers and fundamentally opposed to Paul's message, uses terminology that confirms that the depraved <u>can</u> *"seek God."* These men would have known nothing of the "elect" of Calvinism, for they were hearing the gospel for the first time. Thus, Paul's antagonistic audience would have never assumed that his use of *"every nation of mankind"* (v.26), *"that they should seek God"* (v.27), *"if perhaps they might grope for Him and find Him"* (v.27), and *"He is not far from each one of us"* (v.27), pointed to the elect alone. The plain meaning of Paul's message is that the depraved are capable of choosing Christ. To *"seek"* and *"grope"* for God occurs in one's state of depravity <u>prior</u> to finding the Lord. Nothing in these passages indicates a need for God to spiritually regenerate the depraved before they can repent and believe.

John Piper, based on his exegesis of 2Chronicles 30:8-12 (verses that were covered earlier in the study), depicts God as making the decision for the seeker before the seeker can seek. Such an arrangement has been proven invalid.

How John 7:37, John 4:10, and John 4:14 Relate to Depravity

> *Now on the last day, the great day of the feast, Jesus stood and*
> *cried out, saying, "If any man is thirsty, let him come to Me and*
> *drink.* (John 7:37)

Jesus offers a *"drink"* of water (salvation) to *"any man"* who *"is thirsty."*
Those who thirst are the depraved who, in the midst of their depravity, recognize
their need for a Savior—confirmed vividly through Jesus' offer of *"living water"*
(salvation) to a depraved Samaritan woman while encouraging her to believe:

> *Jesus answered and said to her, "If you knew the gift of God, and*
> *who it is who says to you, 'Give Me a drink,' you would have asked*
> *Him, and He would have given you living water."* (John 4:10)

"Living water" is equivalent to the salvation (spiritual regeneration) offered to
the depraved, who can receive it simply by choosing (while depraved) to repent and
believe. This verse proves that spiritual regeneration occurs <u>after</u> the depraved
exercise repentance and faith—not before. According to John 4:14, those who
drink of this *"water"* will *"never thirst"*—for it will spring *"up to eternal life":*

> *but whoever drinks of the water that I shall give him shall never*
> *thirst; but the water that I shall give him shall become in him a*
> *well of water springing up to eternal life."* (John 4:14)

We can conclude, therefore, that once the depraved realize they are depraved
(that they are *"thirsty"* and needy—John 7:37), they can choose to ask Christ for
salvation (the *"living water"* of John 4:10) and it will be supplied. Once saved
(spiritually regenerated), the believer will *"never thirst"* again (John 4:14).

Is it any wonder that James White, in *The Potter's Freedom*, fails to mention
John 7:37 and John 4:10? John 4:14 is found only once, and that one time is not in
White's personal commentary, but rather, in one of Norm Geisler's quotes from
Chosen But Free. White shuns these verses because they expose the contradictions
so deeply embedded in the Reformed view of total depravity. One might ask,
"What is it, then, that keeps Calvinists from casting aside Calvinism altogether?"
Edwin Palmer, in *The Five Points of Calvinism"* (pages 85-86), attempts to answer
this question. If you are a thinker, who views truth as non-contradictory in nature,
this passage may stun you. Yet, it displays Reformed Theology's effort to justify
its (according to Palmer) "ridiculous" ideology:

> ...the Calvinist accepts both sides of the antinomy. He realizes
> that what he advocates is ridiculous. It is simply impossible for

man to harmonize these two sets of data. To say on the one hand that God has made certain all that ever happens, and yet to say that man is responsible for what he does? Nonsense! It must be one or the other, but not both. To say that God foreordains the sin of Judas, and yet Judas is to blame? Foolishness! Logically the author of *The Predestined Thief* was right. God cannot foreordain the theft and then blame the thief.

And the Calvinist freely admits that his position is illogical, ridiculous, nonsensical, and foolish. This is in accord with Paul, who said, "The word of the cross is to them that perish foolishness" (1Cor. 1:18). The Greeks seek after wisdom and logic, and to them the Calvinist is irrational. The Calvinist holds to two apparently contradictory positions....[Palmer then references his footnote at the bottom of page 85, which states:] It should be emphasized that the contradiction is only apparent and not real. Man cannot harmonize the two apparently contradictory positions, but God can....[Palmer then continues by saying]...He [the Calvinist] says on the one hand, God has foreordained all things. Then he turns around and says to every man, "Your salvation is up to you. You must believe. It is your duty and responsibility. And if you don't, you cannot blame God. You must blame only yourself. But if you do believe, remember that it was God who worked in you both to believe and do according to His good pleasure" (Phil. 2:12, 13). "If you do press on to lay hold on the goal of life, remember that Christ laid hold on you that you might lay hold on it" (Phil. 3:12). In the face of all logic, the Calvinist says that if man does anything good, God gets all the glory; and if man does anything bad, man gets all the blame. Man can't win.

To many people such a position seems foolish. It is unreasonable. So the Calvinist has to make up his mind: what is his authority? His own human reason or the Word of God?

If he answers, the human reasoning powers, then, like the Arminian and hyper-Calvinist, he will have to exclude one of the two parallel forces. But he cannot do that, for he believes the Bible is God's Word and that it was inspired by the Holy Spirit. He trusts God entirely, knowing that His Word cannot be broken. It is infallible and inerrant.

With this firm belief and a willingness to believe everything in it, he accepts this paradox of divine sovereignty and human responsibility. He cannot reconcile the two; but seeing that the Bible clearly teaches both, he accepts both.[59]

Palmer can't be serious, that is, unless he expects us to cease reasoning altogether. Theology is a study of Who God is. If our theology is "illogical, ridiculous, nonsensical, and foolish," as Palmer labels Reformed Theology's "position," we portray our God as "illogical, ridiculous, nonsensical, and foolish." This conclusion is the only one that can be drawn. Does this properly describe God, or can He be perceived differently? Was God's purpose to write a contradictory arrangement of words and call it the Bible; or did He pen an infallible, non-contradictory letter that can withstand the highest levels of scrutiny, yet remain unscathed? God cannot in any way, shape, or form, contradict Himself; yet the Calvinists begin their defense of their system with God in a state of confusion. A post-modern society, which deems absolutes as obsolete, and contradiction as vogue, could easily accept such an unhealthy view of the Creator of the universe. Remember Isaiah's famous words of Isaiah 1:18:

> *"Come now, and let us reason together," says the LORD,* (Isaiah 1:18)

Individuals cannot *"reason together"* in the midst of contradiction because it renders absolutes unnecessary and meaningless. Truth must be measured by an exact, reliable, consistent, and uncompromised standard. Void of this accountability, "truth" can be whatever one supposes. Therefore, if God's Word is contradictory at all, it is not truth, and God is not God. In fact, if His "infallible" letter to man is inconsistent in the least, He does not exist, never has existed, and will never exist. The magnitude of the matter before us bears this weight. Thus, before you allow someone to draw you into a theological system inundated with irregularity, think long, pray hard, and never accept "mystery" as the answer to the chaos. Deuteronomy 29:29 states that God knows *"secret things"* beyond our capacity to comprehend. However, we cannot, under any circumstance, allow our thinking to be influenced by a compromised system of thought which has classified contradiction as "mystery"—no matter who, regardless of the size of his or her platform, has subscribed to its error. The term *"mystery"* in New Testament Scripture points to that which God is in the process of revealing (read Ephesians 3:3 and Colossians 1:27 for confirmation). Hence, any theological position that classifies inconsistency (contradiction) as "mystery" reveals its lack of understanding of God's truth.

Isaiah 45:22 and Depravity

> *"Turn to Me, and be saved, all the ends of the earth; For I am God, and there is no other.* (Isaiah 45:22)

A choice is to be made *("Turn to Me")* before one can be *"saved."* Thus, one must *"Turn"* to the Lord (while depraved) <u>before</u> spiritual regeneration (salvation) can occur. Nothing is stated in this passage regarding a need for the depraved to be spiritually regenerated before they can turn. In fact, 2Corinthians 3:16 (a verse addressed earlier) has the depraved turning *"to the Lord"* before the *"veil is taken away,"* refuting the Reformed view of total depravity altogether.

John 5:40 and Depravity

and you are unwilling to come to Me, that you may have life. (John 5:40)

Jesus verifies that the unwillingness of the Jews, in the midst of their depravity, kept them from possessing the gift of *"life"* that only Christ can supply. *"Life"* (spiritual regeneration, or salvation) follows making a choice to *"come"* to the Lord while depraved—not life (spiritual regeneration) followed by coming to the Lord— the Reformed view. Reformed Theology also suggests that God's choice (due to their defining total depravity as total inability) determines who will or will not believe. God, however, would have been playing games had He required of these Jews something that only He could supply. The God of the Scriptures, the God of *"love"* (1John 4:8, 16), does not play games with man's destiny. His holiness and justice simply will not allow it!

Acts 7:39 and Depravity

And our fathers were unwilling to be obedient to him, but
repudiated him and in their hearts turned back to Egypt, (Acts
7:39)

Stephen taught that the unwillingness of the Jews, in the midst of their depravity, prevented them from obeying God's commands spoken through Moses. You cannot be *"unwilling to be obedient"* unless you possess the capacity to obey. Thus, the disobedient *"fathers"* mentioned in Stephen's sermon possessed the ability to choose to believe even though depraved.

Hebrews 11:6 and Depravity

And without faith it is impossible to please Him, for he who comes
to God must believe that He is, and that He is a rewarder of those
who seek Him. (Hebrews 11:6)

One must *"believe"* before he/she can come *"to God."* God rewards those who choose to *"seek Him"* through *"faith,"* a *"faith"* that must be exercised prior to spiritual regeneration—as in the case of the depraved Samaritan woman in John 4:10.

Romans 2:4 and Depravity

> *Or do you think lightly of the riches of His kindness and*
> *forbearance and patience, not knowing that the kindness of God*
> *leads you to repentance?* (Romans 2:4)

God's *"kindness,"* not His wrath, *"leads"* man *"to repentance."* Why, therefore, would the lost (depraved) need God's *"kindness"* to lead them *"to repentance"* if the depraved, according to the Reformed view, are incapable of choosing Christ? Also, why would the "elect" need to be led *"to repentance"* through God's *"kindness"* should God be the cause of the "elect" believing? Yet, Romans 2:4, which addresses the moral man who is without Christ, clearly teaches that the *"kindness of God,"* witnessed by the depraved, assists them in seeing their need to repent and believe. Hence, Romans 2:4 negates the Reformed view of total depravity.

Romans 8:1-14 and Depravity, with Special Emphasis on Romans 8:7-8

> *There is therefore now no condemnation for those who are in*
> *Christ Jesus. 2 For the law of the Spirit of life in Christ Jesus has*
> *set you free from the law of sin and of death. 3 For what the Law*
> *could not do, weak as it was through the flesh, God did: sending*
> *His own Son in the likeness of sinful flesh and as an offering for*
> *sin, He condemned sin in the flesh, 4 in order that the requirement*
> *of the Law might be fulfilled in us, who do not walk according to*
> *the flesh, but according to the Spirit. 5 For those who are*
> *according to the flesh set their minds on the things of the flesh, but*
> *those who are according to the Spirit, the things of the Spirit. 6 For*
> *the mind set on the flesh is death, but the mind set on the Spirit is*
> *life and peace, 7 because the mind set on the flesh is hostile toward*
> *God; for it does not subject itself to the law of God, for it is not*
> *even able to do so; 8 and those who are in the flesh cannot please*
> *God. 9 However, you are not in the flesh but in the Spirit, if indeed*
> *the Spirit of God dwells in you. But if anyone does not have the*

Spirit of Christ, he does not belong to Him. 10 And if Christ is in you, though the body is dead because of sin, yet the spirit is alive because of righteousness. 11 But if the Spirit of Him who raised Jesus from the dead dwells in you, He who raised Christ Jesus from the dead will also give life to your mortal bodies through His Spirit who indwells you.

12 So then, brethren, we are under obligation, not to the flesh, to live according to the flesh-- 13 for if you are living according to the flesh, you must die; but if by the Spirit you are putting to death the deeds of the body, you will live. 14 For all who are being led by the Spirit of God, these are sons of God. (Romans 8:1-14)

This section should be extremely encouraging, especially if you have taken our course, *Romans 1-8*. The identity principles ("who we are in Christ") emphasized in that study are essential for proper interpretation. Never have I been more thankful for those truths.

Reformed Theology uses these passages, especially Romans 8:7-8, in an attempt to uphold its definition of total depravity.

because the mind set on the flesh is hostile toward God; for it does not subject itself to the law of God, for it is not even able to do so; 8 and those who are in the flesh cannot please God. (Romans 8:7-8)

James White, based on his words in *The Potter's Freedom*, views Romans 8:5-8 (all four verses) as describing that which occurs among the depraved (lost)—never among those who are saved. Does this agree with the full counsel of God's Word? Let's allow the Scriptures to speak for themselves. (Our course, *Romans 1-8*, addresses in more detail the truths covered here. In fact, the following is only a brief summary of that subject matter.)

God's Word teaches that we were born children *"of wrath"* (Ephesians 2:3) due to the <u>sinful nature</u> (the *"old self"*—Romans 6:6) inherited from Adam. The liberating news is that the sinful nature (Adamic nature, old self, old man, or dead spirit—all synonymous terms) is eradicated when a person during the church age accepts Christ as Savior (Romans 6:6; 7:1-4; and Galatians 2:20). Hence, when we were saved, the sinful nature *("the old self"*—Colossians 3:9) was replaced by the *"new"* creation (2Corinthians 5:17), the *"new self"* (Colossians 3:9-10), who is *"holy"* (Ephesians 1:4), *"sanctified"* (Hebrews 10:10), *"perfected"* (Hebrews 10:14), *"glorified"* (Romans 8:30), *"justified"* (Romans 5:1), *"forgiven"* (Ephesians 4:32; Colossians 2:13; 1John 2:12), *"complete"* (Colossians 2:10), and much more. This truth verifies that the New Testament saint is not dual natured, *"old self"* and *"new self"* (bad dog and good dog, as some teach), but the *"new self"* only.

Some believers would question the validity of this mindset, for it certainly "feels" as if the old self (sinful nature) is alive at times. As we have already confirmed, Romans 6:6, 7:1-4, and Galatians 2:20 teach otherwise. Hence, it is not the old self (who we were before we met Christ) that wars against the new self (who we are now). Rather, it is the *"flesh"* that wars against the new self (new man). Note Paul's words to the <u>believers</u> at Galatia:

> *But I say, walk by the Spirit, and you will not carry out the desire of the flesh. For the flesh sets its desire against the Spirit, and the Spirit against the flesh; for these are in opposition to one another, so that you may not do the things that you please.* (Galatians 5:16-17)

A New Testament believer's struggle is with the *"flesh"*—not the sinful nature. Why is this truth so freeing? The sinful nature is who we used to be—the Adamic nature, old self, old man, dead spirit—all synonymous terms. What then is the *"flesh"*? It certainly isn't the sinful nature (old self, old man, dead spirit, Adamic nature).

While living in our lost state, with the sinful nature alive and well, we performed deeds that the Bible classifies as sinful. Sitting on the throne of our lives, we lived for "me, my, and I" only. In fact, the most natural thing we did as unbelievers was sin. We sinned not only because it was natural, but because *"sin,"* Satan's agent, placed lies in our minds that we bought as the truth. This reality is verified by Romans 7:7-13—where Paul describes how the Law was used to show him his need for a Savior while depraved. The remainder of Romans 7 (verses 14-25) describes Paul's battle with *"sin"* <u>after</u> he became a believer:

> *What shall we say then? Is the Law sin? May it never be! On the contrary, I would not have come to know sin except through the Law; for I would not have known about coveting if the Law had not said, "You shall not covet." 8 But sin, taking opportunity through the commandment, produced in me coveting of every kind; for apart from the Law sin is dead. 9 And I was once alive apart from the Law; but when the commandment came, sin became alive, and I died; 10 and this commandment, which was to result in life, proved to result in death for me; 11 for sin, taking opportunity through the commandment, deceived me, and through it killed me. 12 So then, the Law is holy, and the commandment is holy and righteous and good. 13 Therefore did that which is good become a cause of death for me? May it never be! Rather it was sin, in order that it*

might be shown to be sin by effecting my death through that which is good, that through the commandment sin might become utterly sinful. (Romans 7:7-13)

Vines Expository Dictionary of New Testament Words defines the noun *"sin"* as "an organized power." *"Sin"* (the power of *"sin")* is not a demon, but a power controlled by Satan himself. (Satan is not omnipresent, so he uses *"sin"* as his agent for the purpose of deceiving man.) As a result of buying sin's lies as the truth in our depraved (lost) state (the power of *"sin"* lives in the body, soul, and spirit of an unbeliever), patterns (habits) were formed in the brain (the brain being a piece of meat, or *"flesh")* that programmed us to think, feel, and act in particular ways when exposed to sin's stimulus. As you are well aware, all of these sinful patterns (habits) were not erased when we were made new in Christ. Consequently, when the New Testament believer allows *"sin"* (which lives in the New Testament believer's body only—Romans 7:23) to activate one of these ungodly patterns in the brain (the brain being a piece of flesh), he is allowing the "flesh" to rule. Simple as that! (Consult Diagram 13 in the Reference Section.)

When a New Testament believer allows "sin" to activate one of these ungodly patterns in the brain, he/she is allowing the "flesh" to rule. Simple as that!

James White, based on his comments in *The Potters' Freedom,* fails to understand the difference between the *"sinful nature"* and the *"flesh,"* for he views the phrase, *"the mind set on the flesh"* (Romans 8:7), as pointing to that which is experienced by the lost. This supposition is incorrect. Man is born with a sinful nature, but the term *"flesh"* (used in Romans 8:7) is not equivalent to the sinful nature inherited from Adam. Yet, even the New International Version took the liberty to translate *"flesh"* (NASB) as *"sinful nature"* (NIV) in verses 3, 4, 5, 8, 9, 12 and 13 of Romans 8. The NIV also took the liberty to translate *"sinful flesh"* (NASB) in verse 3 as *"sinful man"* (NIV), and *"the things of the flesh"* (NASB) in verse 5 as *"what that nature desires"* (NIV). Also, in verse 6, the phrase, *"the mind set on the flesh"* (NASB), is translated *"the mind of sinful man"* (NIV). This incorrect rendering does not affect the overall meaning of some of these verses, but in other instances (such as in Romans 8:7) the meaning is altered altogether. This problem will become evident as we continue, for observe below how the NIV renders Romans 8:1-14. Note: I have inserted the NASB rendering in brackets (the proper rendering from the Greek) to reveal how the NIV misrepresents these extremely critical passages. Evidently, those responsible for generating the NIV viewed the New Testament believer as possessing two natures (sinful nature and new self), and therefore took the liberty to replace *"flesh"* with *"sinful nature"* due to assuming that the *"sinful nature"* and *"flesh"* are one and the same. They could not have been more mistaken. Remember, the original Greek (not any particular version or paraphrase of the Bible) has the final say in every case. Presented below is the rendering of Romans 8:1-14 in the New International Version with the corrections in brackets for clarification:

> *Therefore, there is now no condemnation for those who are in Christ Jesus, 2 because through Christ Jesus the law of the Spirit of life set me free from the law of sin and death. 3 For what the law was powerless to do in that it was weakened by the sinful nature* [flesh], *God did by sending his own Son in the likeness of sinful man* [sinful flesh] *to be a sin offering. And so he condemned sin in sinful man* [the flesh], *4 in order that the righteous requirements of the law might be fully met in us, who do not live according to the sinful nature* [the flesh] *but according to the Spirit.*
>
> *5 Those who live according to the sinful nature* [the flesh] *have their minds set on what that nature desires* [on the things of the flesh]; *but those who live in accordance with the Spirit have their minds set on what the Spirit desires. 6 The mind of sinful man* [the mind set on the flesh] *is death, but the mind controlled by the Spirit is life and peace; 7 the sinful mind* [the mind set on the flesh] *is hostile to God. It does not submit to God's law, nor can it do so. 8 Those controlled by the sinful nature* [those who are in the flesh] *cannot please God.*
>
> *9 You, however, are controlled not by the sinful nature* [are not in the flesh] *but by* [in] *the Spirit, if the Spirit of God lives in you. And if anyone does not have the Spirit of Christ, he does not belong to Christ. 10 But if Christ is in you, your body is dead because of sin, yet your spirit is alive because of righteousness. 11 And if the Spirit of him who raised Jesus from the dead is living in you, he who raised Christ from the dead will also give life to your mortal bodies through his Spirit, who lives in you.*
>
> *12 Therefore, brothers, we have an obligation-but it is not to the sinful nature* [the flesh], *to live according to it* [the flesh]. *13 For if you live according to the sinful nature* [the flesh], *you will die; but if by the Spirit you put to death the misdeeds of the body, you will live, 14 because those who are led by the Spirit of God are sons of God.* (Romans 8:1-14 NIV)

Interestingly, the NIV sometimes places a number beside *"sinful nature,"* indicating that the reader is to reference the margin. In such cases the word *"flesh"* is found in the margin. Remarkably, many people who read the Bible disregard the margins. Thus, speak with individuals who use the NIV and they will normally tell you that the sin nature is alive and well in the New Testament believer. Such a conclusion totally misrepresents the original Greek text!

James White (a Reformed Theologian), in *The Potter's Freedom*, views Romans 8:7 as describing the depraved. (Permission was requested to quote White, but the request was denied. Thus, a contextual summation of his views is presented instead.) Yet, when studied in the context of Romans 8:5-6, Paul is describing the disobedient New Testament <u>believer</u>. The fact that the <u>believer</u> can be controlled by the *"flesh"* is verified by Romans 7:25 as well (remember that Romans 7:14-25 describes Paul's struggle with *"sin"* as a <u>believer</u>):

> *Thanks be to God through Jesus Christ our Lord! So then, on the one hand I myself with my mind am serving the law of God, but on the other, with my flesh the law of sin.* (Romans 7:25)

All New Testament believers face this same conflict—the war between the flesh and the new man, the battle that occurs in the <u>mind</u> of all New Testament saints. Several verses in God's Word mention this struggle, such as Romans 7:22-23:

> *For I joyfully concur with the law of God in the inner man, but I see a different law in the members of my body, waging war against the law of my mind, and making me a prisoner of the law of sin which is in my members.* (Romans 7:22-23)

Some people would argue that Romans 7:24 describes an unbeliever and, thus, negates my conclusion:

> *Wretched man that I am! Who will set me free from the body of this death?* (Romans 7:24)

The word *"wretched"* in this case actually means "distressed" or "miserable." Thus, Paul was not saying that he was a wretched person in the sense of being lost, for he knew that Jesus had made him a holy and blameless saint, perfect in His eyes. He was basically communicating that he was distressed (as a believer) over the battle that raged in his mind as a result of the power of sin working through the avenue of his body *("the body of this death")*. He eventually matured and found victory through Christ's indwelling presence:

> *Thanks be to God through Jesus Christ our Lord! So then, on the*
> *one hand I myself with my mind am serving the law of God, but on*
> *the other, with my flesh the law of sin.* (Romans 7:25)

From all indications, White agrees with the New International Version's definition of *"flesh"*—that it is equivalent to the sinful nature. Should this conclusion be valid, White would be correct in viewing Romans 8:4-7 as describing the lost—for only the unsaved possess a sinful nature according to Romans 6:6, 7:1-4, and Galatians 2:20.

The Law is *"holy and righteous and good"* (Romans 7:12). Neither can the Law be kept through one's own power, discipline, or strength. We must understand, however, what occurs when the Holy Spirit takes up residence in a New Testament believer. Paul states that *"the requirement of the Law"* is *"fulfilled"* in those *"who do not walk according to the flesh, but according to the Spirit"* (Romans 8:4). Do you realize what this means for us as holy and blameless saints? The Spirit of God, as we choose to obey, empowers us to walk in a way that agrees with the moral standard of the Law. God, as a result, receives all the credit and glory, and we learn the true meaning of life.

Two phrases in Romans 8:4 must be understood before addressing Romans 8:7-8—the main subject of this lesson. The first phrase is *"walk according to the flesh,"* and the second is "[walk] *according to the Spirit."* Both phrases refer to a particular state of a New Testament <u>believer</u> (these phrases are displayed graphically in Diagrams 13 and 14 in the Reference Section). That to which the latter phrase refers is easily understood, for this situation occurs when we (as New Testament <u>believers</u>) allow the Spirit of God to positively energize the mind—which grants us the wisdom to properly operate the will (Diagram 14). To *"walk according to the flesh,"* on the other hand, points to those times when we (as New Testament <u>believers</u>) allow the power of sin to energize an ungodly habit pattern etched in the brain (Diagram 13). Yes, our habits are stored in the brain (and **the brain is a piece of flesh**—thus the phrase, *"walk according to the flesh"*). We must remember, however, that all of our ungodly habits were <u>not</u> removed when we experienced new birth (salvation) and that new ungodly habits are formed when we walk in disobedience *("according to the flesh").* The great news is that our ungodly habit patterns decrease in size and intensity as we walk *"according to the Spirit."* Yet, their complete removal does not normally occur until physical death.

Paul continues to discuss these two phrases *("according to the flesh"* and *"according to the Spirit")* in Romans 8:5, for he writes:

> *For those who are according to the flesh set their minds on the*
> *things of the flesh, but those who are according to the Spirit, the*
> *things of the Spirit.* (Romans 8:5)

Stated differently, a New Testament believer walks *"according to the flesh"* when he sets his mind on sin's lie sent into the mind through an ungodly habit pattern etched in the brain (the brain being a piece of *"flesh"*), then accepts the lie as truth and responds accordingly (refer to Diagram 13 in the Reference Section). When this situation occurs, the new man commits an act of sin. Paul also states that we walk *"according to the Spirit"* when we set our minds on *"the things of the Spirit"* (refer to Diagram 14 in the Reference Section). In this case, the believer (the new man) is walking in obedience. Sounds pretty simple, doesn't it? It may sound simple, but as we well know, it can certainly be difficult in practice.

To set the mind *"on the flesh"* is *"death"* for the New Testament believer. In other words, to live in a compromised state is *"death"* (a place of misery and unrest) for the saint of God; *"the mind set on the Spirit is life and peace"* (Romans 8:6). Paul then puts the icing on the cake in Romans 8:7:

> *because the mind set on the flesh is hostile toward God; for it does*
> *not subject itself to the law of God, for it is not even able to do so;*
> (Romans 8:7)

Yes, a New Testament believer who sets his mind *"on the flesh"* will sometimes behave much like an unbeliever, but in most cases will repent and come home. If not, he will be overwhelmingly miserable, as was David in the midst of his sin (read Psalm 51).

Romans 8:7 describes what sometimes occurs with New Testament believers—not what transpires with the depraved, as White incorrectly assumes. We again witness the unbiblical conclusions drawn by Reformed Theology in an attempt to protect its unjustifiable view of the "T" of the TULIP, Total Depravity.

Paul next describes what it means to be *"in the flesh"* versus *"in the Spirit"*:

> *and those who are <u>in the flesh</u> cannot please God. However, you*
> *are not <u>in the flesh</u> but <u>in the Spirit</u>, if indeed the Spirit of God*
> *dwells in you. But if anyone does not have the Spirit of Christ, he*
> *does not belong to Him.* (Romans 8:8-9)

The apostle first states that a person who is *"in the flesh"* cannot please God (Romans 8:8). This fact verifies that to be *"in the flesh"* is to be lost. Romans 7:5-6 confirms the same truth:

> *For while we were <u>in the flesh</u>, the sinful passions, which were*
> *aroused by the Law, were at work in the members of our body to*
> *bear fruit for death. But now we have been released from the Law,*
> *having died to that by which we were bound, so that we serve in*

newness of the Spirit and not in oldness of the letter. (Romans 7:5-6)

James White, remaining true to the Reformed position in *The Potter's Freedom*, suggests that Romans 8:8 totally disproves "free willism." Does it? Quite the contrary! This verse is <u>not</u> teaching that a person cannot believe while depraved, rather that the depraved cannot live in a manner that is pleasing to God on an ongoing basis—described as walking *"according to the Spirit"* in Romans 8:4-5, a lifestyle characterized by the Spirit's leading. White, by missing the context of Romans 8:8, through improperly interpreting the verses that precede it, presents an argument that is a-contextual and false. (Remember: Permission was requested to quote White, but the request was denied. Thus, a contextual summation of his views has been presented instead.)

Paul continues by stating (in Romans 8:9) that a person is *"in the Spirit"*—and not *"in the flesh"*—*"if indeed the Spirit of God dwells in you."*

> *However, you are not in the flesh but in the Spirit, if indeed the*
> *Spirit of God dwells in you. But if anyone does not have the Spirit*
> *of Christ, he does not belong to Him.* (Romans 8:9)

Stated differently, to be *"in the flesh"* (vv.8-9) is to be lost, while being *"in the Spirit"* (v.9) means that one has been indwelt by the *"Spirit of God"* and is, therefore, saved/justified. Paul continues (v.9) by saying *"if anyone does not have the Spirit of Christ, he does not belong to Him."* This verse confirms once again that to be *"in the flesh"* (vv.8-9) means to be lost and without Christ. Can you see the difference between being *"in the flesh"* (Romans 8:8-9) and walking *"according to the flesh"* (Romans 8:4-5)? The phrase, *"in the flesh,"* refers to a person who does not know Christ; walking *"according to the flesh"* refers to a New Testament believer who has allowed the power of sin to energize one of his/her ungodly habit patterns in the brain, the brain being a piece of *"flesh."*

Other passages in Romans validate our findings, such as Romans 8:12-13:

> *So then, brethren, we are under obligation, not to the flesh, to live*
> *according to the flesh—13 for if you are living according to the*
> *flesh, you must die; but if by the Spirit you are putting to death the*
> *deeds of the body, you will live.* (Romans 8:12-13)

Paul teaches that a New Testament believer (note the word *"brethren"* in verse 12) can live *"according to the flesh."* He confirms this same truth while writing to believers in Galatia:

But I say, walk by the Spirit, and you will not carry out the desire
of the flesh. For the flesh sets its desire against the Spirit, and the
Spirit against the flesh; for these are in opposition to one another,
so that you may not do the things that you please. (Galatians 5:16-
17)

These verses verify once again that Paul was addressing believers in Romans 8:7 rather than the depraved. A review of Romans 8:7 allows us to see the correlation:

because the mind set on the flesh is hostile toward God; for it does
not subject itself to the law of God, for it is not even able to do so;
(Romans 8:7)

Consequently, for the New Testament believer, *"living according to the flesh"* (Romans 8:13) is the same as setting the mind *"on the flesh"* (Romans 8:7).

Romans 6:12-14 shows that the New Testament believer can allow *"sin"* to control his behavior:

Therefore do not let sin reign in your mortal body that you should
obey its lusts, 13 and do not go on presenting the members of your
body to sin as instruments of unrighteousness; but present
yourselves to God as those alive from the dead, and your members
as instruments of righteousness to God. 14 For sin shall not be
master over you, for you are not under law, but under grace.
(Romans 6:12-14)

Because the book of Romans was written to *"brethren"* (Romans 1:13), the word *"your"* in Romans 6:12 confirms that Paul is describing what can occur in the life of a New Testament believer. Thus, when we allow *"sin"* to control, that which Paul warns against in Romans 6:12-14, we are *"living according to the flesh"* (Romans 8:13), which is one and the same with setting the mind *"on the flesh"* (Romans 8:7).

Paul, again writing to believers in Romans 6:15-19, states that the New Testament believer becomes the slave of *"sin"* when he/she chooses to walk in disobedience.

What then? Shall we sin because we are not under law but under
grace? May it never be! 16 Do you not know that when you present
yourselves to someone as slaves for obedience, you are slaves of
the one whom you obey, either of sin resulting in death, or of
obedience resulting in righteousness? 17 But thanks be to God that
though you were slaves of sin, you became obedient from the heart

> *to that form of teaching to which you were committed, 18 and*
> *having been freed from sin, you became slaves of righteousness. 19*
> *I am speaking in human terms because of the weakness of your*
> *flesh. For just as you presented your members as slaves to impurity*
> *and to lawlessness, resulting in further lawlessness, so now present*
> *your members as slaves to righteousness, resulting in*
> *sanctification.* (Romans 6:15-19)

These verses are additional confirmation that Romans 8:7, instead of describing the depraved (as White suggests), describes a New Testament believer who has chosen to disobey.

Conclusion

> *because the mind set on the flesh is hostile toward God; for it does*
> *not subject itself to the law of God, for it is not even able to do so;*
> (Romans 8:7)

Romans 8:7 describes a New Testament believer who is walking in disobedience, who is walking with his *"mind set on the flesh."* Such a mind *"is hostile toward God,"* making the believer appear, in some cases, as though he is an unbeliever (as was the case with King David in 2Samuel 11).

> *and those who are in the flesh cannot please God.* (Romans 8:8)

Romans 8:8, by using *"in the flesh,"* especially when coupled with what Romans 8:9 states regarding the phrase, confirms that *"in the flesh"* describes the lost (depraved). Does this confirmation mean that Romans 8:8 validates Reformed Theology's definition of total depravity—that the depraved are incapable of choosing Christ? Not at all, for Reformed Theology's definition of total depravity violates the relationship between Romans 8:8 and the verses that both precede (vv.4-7) and follow it (vv.9-17). In essence, the contextual view of Romans 8:8 reveals that the depraved cannot live a lifestyle characterized by walking *"according to the Spirit"* (Romans 8:4), the lifestyle of a New Testament believer. New birth (salvation) is necessary for this transformation to occur, a transformation that ensues subsequent to the depraved exercising personal repentance and faith. Romans 8:8, therefore, does not teach that the depraved are incapable of choosing Christ.

CHAPTER FOURTEEN

FAITH AND DEPRAVITY

MANY BELIEVERS ASK: Is the faith exercised prior to salvation God's gift, or does it originate with man (the depraved)? We will begin answering this question by examining Ephesians 2:8-9.

How Ephesians 2:8-9 Relates to Faith and Depravity

For by grace you have been saved through faith; and that not of yourselves, it is the gift of God; not as a result of works, that no one should boast. (Ephesians 2:8-9)

Paul emphasizes that salvation is most definitely by God's *"grace"* (also read Romans 3:24 and Titus 3:7)—reiterating what he recorded earlier in Ephesians 2:5 (*"by grace you have been saved"*). He also affirms that God's salvation is *"through faith"* (also confirmed by Habakkuk 2:4, Romans 1:17, Galatians 3:11, Philippians 3:9, Hebrews 10:38, Hebrews 11:1-2, and Hebrews 11:6).

The word *"that"* in the phrase, *"and that not of yourselves"* (Ephesian 2:8), is the source of much debate. Both sides of the argument will be addressed, not to vilify those in disagreement with my position, but to present the facts regarding what is at stake. Remember, this study addresses God's heart, the most splendid topic to grace the mind of man. In fact, a proper view of Who God is supersedes all issues of life. Too much is at stake, therefore, to approach this subject passively or haphazardly. For this reason we will dig deeply in our pursuit of the truth regarding this extremely critical theological matter.

The Reformed view of Ephesians 2:8-9, due to perceiving the depraved as incapable of believing, normally envisions *"that"* (Ephesians 2:8) as referring to *"faith"* (v.8). They picture God as spiritually regenerating man and granting him repentance and faith before he can repent, believe, and be saved. R.C. Sproul, a proponent of this mindset, writes in *Grace Unknown*, pages 156-157:

> Considerable debate has ensued regarding the meaning of the first sentence. What is the antecedent for the word *that: grace, saved, or faith*? The rules of Greek syntax and grammar demand that the antecedent of *that* be the word *faith*. Paul is declaring what every Reformed person affirms, that faith is a gift from God. Faith is not something we conjure up by our own effort, or the result of the willing of the flesh. Faith is a result of the Spirit's sovereign work of regeneration. It is no accident that this statement concludes a passage that begins with Paul's declaration that we have been "quickened" or "made alive" while we were in a state of spiritual death.[60]

Is Sproul correct in his assessment? After all, others view this passage totally differently due to recognizing that the terms *"faith"* and *"grace"* are both feminine in gender, and *"that"* is neuter. Consequently, they view *"that"* as referring to *"saved"* rather than *"faith."* The following quote from Dave Hunt's, *What Love Is This?,* pages 452-453, expresses well the disparity that exists between "free-will" and the Reformed view (extreme and hyper-Calvinism):

> ... That faith is a gift is a major foundational principal of Calvinism. The favorite passage offered as proof is Ephesians 2:8-10. Mathison says, "Saving faith is a gift of God, a result of the regenerating work of the Holy Spirit." Storms claims, "Numerous texts assert that such [saving] faith is God's own gracious gift (see especially Ephesians 2:8-9...)." Clark declares:
>
>> A dead man cannot...exercise faith in Jesus Christ. Faith is an activity of spiritual life, and without the life there can be no activity. Furthermore, faith...does not come by any independent decision. The Scripture is explicit, plain, and unmistakable: "For by grace are ye saved through faith, and that not of yourselves, it is the gift of God" (Ephesians 2:8). Look at the words again, "It is the gift of God." If God does not give a man faith, no amount of will power and decision can manufacture it for him.
>
> On the contrary, the subject of the preceding seven verses is salvation, not faith. Verse 8 then declares concerning salvation,

"by grace are ye saved...it [obviously salvation] is the gift of God." It is not saving faith, but being saved that is God's gift. We are repeatedly told that eternal life is "the gift of God" (Romans 6:23; see also John 4:10; Romans 5:18; Hebrews 6:4; etc.). No less definitive, as Calvin admitted and then tried to deny, is the statement that "faith comes by hearing and hearing by the Word of God." There is no biblical basis for suggesting that God gives saving faith to a select group and withholds it from others.

Furthermore, the construction of the Greek in Ephesians 2:8–10 makes it impossible for faith to be the gift. Such is the verdict of many Greek authorities, including Alford, F. F. Bruce, A. T. Robertson, W. E. Vine, Scofield, and others. Vance notes that "A witness to the truth of Scripture against the Calvinist 'faith-gift' interpretation can be found in the Greek grammarians." He lists W. Robertson Nicoll, Kenneth S. Wuest, Marvin R. Vincent, and others.

Among the reasons the experts cite is the fact that the word faith is a feminine noun, while the demonstrative pronoun that ("and that not of yourselves, it is the gift") is neuter and thus could not refer to faith. Nor will the grammar, as W. G. MacDonald says, "permit 'faith' to be the antecedent of 'it.'" Of course, "it is" is not in the Greek but was added for clarity by the KJV translators and thus is italicized. Nor does it require a knowledge of Greek, but simply paying attention to the entire context of Ephesians 2:8–10, to realize that salvation, not faith, is "the gift of God"—as all of Scripture testifies.

A number of other Greek authorities could be cited to that effect. Though a Calvinist, F. F. Bruce explains, "The fact that the demonstrative pronoun 'that' is neuter in Greek (touto), whereas 'faith' is a feminine noun (pistis), combines with other considerations to suggest that it is the whole concept of salvation by grace through faith that is described as the gift of God. This, incidentally, was Calvin's interpretation." Calvin himself acknowledged, "But they commonly misinterpret this text, and restrict the word 'gift' to faith alone. But Paul...does not mean that faith is the gift of God, but that salvation is given to us by God...." Thus White and other zealous Calvinists who today insist that faith is the gift are contradicting not only the Greek construction but John Calvin himself.[61]

Let's examine more closely Calvin's quote (mentioned above by Hunt) regarding Ephesians 2:8— taken from Calvin's *Commentary on the Epistle to the Ephesians,* in *the Comprehensive John Calvin Collection* (Ages Digital Library, 1998).

> Many persons restrict the word gift to faith alone. But Paul is
> only repeating in other words the former sentiment. His
> meaning is, not that faith is the gift of God, but that salvation is
> given to us by God, or, that we obtain it by the gift of God.[62]

Realizing that Calvin's words contradict the Reformed position, James White (a Reformed theologian) attempts to prove (in *The Potter's Freedom*) that Calvin was teaching the opposite—that the faith exercised prior to salvation is God's gift to those who believe. White's argument, though wordy and assertive, is not convincing. (Permission was requested to quote his argument, but permission was denied.)

R.C. Sproul (a Reformed theologian), in *Chosen by God*, page 119, regarding Ephesians 2:8 writes:

> Paul concludes that it is a matter of grace and not a matter of
> works. His sterling summary is, "For by grace you have been
> saved through faith, and that not of yourselves, it is the gift of
> God." This passage should seal the matter forever. The faith by
> which we are saved is a gift. When the apostle says it is not of
> ourselves, he does not mean that it is not our faith. Again, God
> does not do the believing for us. It is our own faith but it does
> not originate with us. It is given to us. The gift is not earned or
> deserved. It is a gift of sheer grace.[63]

John Piper (also a devotee to the Reformed position), in his DVD series *TULIP, Disk 1, Title 6, Chapter 2, states*:

> Faith and repentance are a gift of God....For by grace you have
> been saved through faith, that not of yourselves, it is the gift of
> God, not a result of works, so that no one may boast. God is
> very eager to strip us from boasting. So salvation and faith here
> are called the gift of God.[64]

However, Sir Robert Anderson, in *The Gospel and its Ministry*, thirteenth edition revised, page 54 footnote, views *"that"* (Ephesians 2:8) as pointing to *"salvation"*:

> "The gift of God" here is salvation by grace through faith. Not
> the faith itself.... The matter is sometimes represented as
> though God gave faith to the sinner first, and then, on the
> sinner's bringing Him the faith, went on and gave him salvation!

> Just as though a baker, refusing to supply empty-handed
> applicants, should first dispense to each the price of a loaf, and
> then, in return for the money from his own till, serve out the
> bread! To answer fully such a vagary as this would be to rewrite
> the following chapter. Suffice it, therefore, to point out that to
> read the text as though faith were the gift, is to destroy not only
> the meaning of verse 9, but the force of the whole passage.[65]

What, therefore, is Ephesians 2:9?

not as a result of works, that no one should boast. (Ephesians 2:9)

This passage proves, beyond doubt, that *"salvation,"* not *"faith,"* is the *"gift"* addressed in Ephesians 2:8. For one to suggest that faith is *"not as a result of works"* makes no sense, although faith not being a work is rock-solid truth (as verified shortly). Faith being *"a result of works"* is found nowhere in the Scriptures. However, to argue that salvation is not of works is exactly what Paul teaches, not only in Ephesians, but elsewhere as well. Read Romans 3:27-28, for example, realizing that *"justified"* points to salvation:

Where then is boasting? It is excluded. By what kind of law? Of works? No, but by a law of faith. For we maintain that a man is justified by faith apart from works of the Law. (Romans 3:27-28)

Paul's message in Romans 3:27-28 is that salvation is not *"Of works"*—that God bestows salvation once the depraved exercise *"faith"* (along with repentance, of course). Paul also confirms that *"boasting"* is *"excluded"* among those who exercise personal *"faith"* in Christ while depraved. Thus, faith is not a work, for Paul contrasts *"faith"* with *"works"* on many occasions in the Scriptures. Consequently, choosing to exercise personal *"faith"* (in the midst of one's depravity) can never be viewed as a meritorious deed. Paul teaches the same truth in Romans 4:5, contrasting *"work"* to believing:

But to the one who does not work, but believes in Him who justifies the ungodly, his faith is reckoned as righteousness, (Romans 4:5)

Paul again contrasts *"faith"* to *"works"* in Romans 9:30-33:

What shall we say then? That Gentiles, who did not pursue righteousness, attained righteousness, even the righteousness which is by faith; 31 but Israel, pursuing a law of righteousness, did not arrive at that law. 32 Why? Because they did not pursue it

*by faith, but as though it were by works. They stumbled over the
stumbling stone, 33 just as it is written, "Behold, I lay in Zion a
stone of stumbling and a rock of offense, and he who believes in
Him will not be disappointed."* (Romans 9:30-33)

Once more we see that salvation *("righteousness")* is not of *"works"* but is the
gift granted to those who exercise personal *"faith"* while depraved. The same
principle appears in Paul's words to the church at Galatia:

*nevertheless knowing that a man is not justified by the works of the
Law but through faith in Christ Jesus, even we have believed in
Christ Jesus, that we may be justified by faith in Christ, and not by
the works of the Law; since by the works of the Law shall no flesh
be justified.* (Galatians 2:16)

*This is the only thing I want to find out from you: did you receive
the Spirit by the works of the Law, or by hearing with faith?*
(Galatians 3:2)

The following passages also confirm that salvation (not faith) is God's *"gift"* to
the hungry seeker (underline for emphasis only):

*Jesus answered and said to her, "If you knew the <u>gift of God</u>, and
who it is who says to you, 'Give Me a drink,' you would have asked
Him, and He would have given you living water."* (John 4:10-11)

*But the <u>free gift</u> is not like the transgression. For if by the
transgression of the one the many died, much more did the grace of
God and the <u>gift</u> by the grace of the one Man, Jesus Christ, abound
to the many. 16 And the <u>gift</u> is not like that which came through the
one who sinned; for on the one hand the judgment arose from one
transgression resulting in condemnation, but on the other hand the
<u>free gift</u> arose from many transgressions resulting in justification.
17 For if by the transgression of the one, death reigned through the
one, much more those who receive the abundance of grace and of
the <u>gift of righteousness</u> will reign in life through the One, Jesus
Christ.* (Romans 5:15-17)

*For the wages of sin is death, but the <u>free gift of God is eternal life</u>
in Christ Jesus our Lord.* (Romans 6:23)

And the witness is this, that God has <u>given us eternal life</u>, and this *life is in His Son.* (1John 5:11)

Although salvation is a free gift, it must be received by the depraved who recognize their need for a Savior. The following verses are highly problematic for those who reject free will:

> *Come to Me, all who are weary and heavy-laden, and I will give you rest.* (Matthew 11:28)

> *Jesus answered and said to her, "If you knew the gift of God, and who it is who says to you, 'Give Me a drink,' you would have asked Him, and He would have given you living water."* (John 4:10-11)

> *Now on the last day, the great day of the feast, Jesus stood and cried out, saying, "If any man is thirsty, let him come to Me and drink.* (John 7:37)

> *And the Spirit and the bride say, "Come." And let the one who hears say, "Come." And let the one who is thirsty come; let the one who wishes take the water of life without cost.* (Revelation 22:17)

We understand well that Reformed theologians (due to their definition of depravity) view spiritual regeneration as preceding faith. We proved earlier, however, that spiritual regeneration is equivalent to salvation (review the notes associated with John 3:3-6). This fact refutes Reformed Theology because no one can be saved prior to exercising personal faith. Such a scenario would cause the believer to be saved twice, forcing Christ to die a second time (an impossibility according to Hebrews 6:4-6; 9:28; 10:10). Keep this truth in mind as we proceed.

To receive the gift of salvation (spiritual regeneration), the depraved must first believe (exercise personal faith). Therefore, faith precedes salvation (spiritual regeneration) rather than follows it, as confirmed by the following passages. (Only a portion of the hoard of verses that validate this truth are presented.)

> *He who has believed...shall be saved;...* (Mark 16:16)

> *And those beside the road are those who have heard; then the devil comes and takes away the word from their heart, so that they may not believe and be saved.* (Luke 8:12)

> *Of Him all the prophets bear witness that through His name everyone who believes in Him receives forgiveness of sins."* (Acts 10:43)

And they said, "Believe in the Lord Jesus, and you shall be saved, you and your household." (Acts 16:31)

For I am not ashamed of the gospel, for it is the power of God for salvation to everyone who believes, to the Jew first and also to the Greek. (Romans 1:16)

But now apart from the Law the righteousness of God has been manifested, being witnessed by the Law and the Prophets, even the righteousness of God through faith in Jesus Christ for all those who believe; ... (Romans 3:21-22)

for "Whoever will call upon the name of the Lord will be saved." (Romans 10:13)

For you are all sons of God through faith in Christ Jesus. (Galatians 3:26)

...as an example for those who would believe in Him for eternal life. (1 Timothy 1:16)

And without faith it is impossible to please Him, for he who comes to God must believe that He is, and that He is a rewarder of those who seek Him. (Hebrews 11:6)

The following passages confirm that the faith exercised prior to salvation is the seeker's faith—not God's gift to the seeker. Note the words *"your faith"* in the verses listed below:

... "Be it done to you according to your faith." (Matthew 9:29)

And He said to the woman, "Your faith has saved you; go in peace." (Luke 7:50)

...your faith has made you well." (Luke 17:19)

your faith is being proclaimed throughout the whole world. (Romans 1:8)

that your faith should not rest on the wisdom of men, but on the power of God. (1 Corinthians 2:5) and if Christ has not been raised, then our preaching is vain, your faith also is vain. (1Corinthians 15:14)

since we heard of your faith in Christ Jesus... (Colossians 1:4)

...but also in every place your faith toward God has gone forth... (1Thessalonians 1:8)

R.C. Sproul, a Reformed theologian, disagrees with these findings due to viewing the faith exercised in the previous verses as originating with God—but becoming the possession of the elect in conjunction with their being spiritually regenerated. Reformed Theology cannot allow the depraved to exercise personal faith prior to spiritual regeneration. As a result, Reformed Theology (extreme and hyper-Calvinism) must view those who believe in free will (who believe that the depraved can exercise faith) as teaching a works-based salvation. Sproul writes, in *Grace Unknown*, pages 155-156:

> ...Why do some respond favorably to the Holy Spirit rather than refusing the wooing? If we say the answer lies in the intensity of the wooing (namely, that the Spirit entices some more strongly than others), then we are back to the problem of sovereign selection. If we say instead that some respond favorably to the wooing because of something found in them, then we root our salvation ultimately in a human work. Does one respond to the wooing positively due to greater intelligence or greater virtue? If so, then we have something to boast about.
>
> When I pose this question to my Arminian friends, they readily see the dilemma and seek to avoid it by saying: "Certainly it is not a matter of intelligence or of any inherent superior virtue in those who respond positively. They respond this way because they see their need for Christ more clearly." With this reply they dig themselves deeper into the pit. The answer only postpones the problem one step.
>
> Why do some people see their need for Christ more clearly than do others? Have they received greater illumination from the Holy Spirit? Are they more intelligent? Are they less prejudiced toward Christ and more open to his call, which is itself a virtue? No matter how one delays it, sooner or later we must face the question of greater or lesser inherent virtue.
>
> Following Paul's lead in Ephesians, Reformed theology teaches that faith itself is a gift given to the elect. God himself creates the faith in the believer's heart. God fulfills the

> necessary condition for salvation, and he does so without
> condition. Again we look to Paul's words: "For by grace you
> have been saved through faith, and that not of yourselves; *it is*
> the gift of God, not of works, lest anyone should boast. For we
> are His workmanship, created in Christ Jesus for good works,
> which God prepared beforehand that we should walk in them."
> (Eph. 2:8-10)[66]

Is Sproul correct? Are virtue and merit associated with receiving a free gift? If so, those who believe in free will are grossly misguided. However, consider what Samuel Fisk records in his work, *Divine Sovereignty and Human Freedom*, pages 25-29:

> ...the employment of that free will which man does make use of
> is nothing meritorious, it is nothing wherein to glory or boast, it
> is nothing to his personal credit.
>   ...The reason why it is emphasized that faith has no merit, is
> so that, when it is urged that man must give heed to exercising
> faith, no objection can rightly be raised. That is, it cannot be
> claimed that salvation thereby ceases to be wholly of grace or
> that it is of human achievement, for the faith man exercises is
> entirely nonmeritorious, nothing which gives him the slightest
> ground for any claim on God. Faith, as will be seen, is the mere
> channel, not the ground of man's salvation. The ground or
> basis of salvation from sin, of course, is the divine provision in
> the finished work of Christ; the means or instrument of making
> effective that heavenly boon is an unworthy person casting
> himself on God's mercy and accepting it all for himself. This he
> must do, and he alone can do.
>   ...That man must receive salvation by faith and that his so
> doing would still not make it a matter of human achievement or
> of worthiness on his part, is evident in these quotations about
> the necessity of exercising faith, the freeness thereof, and the
> nonmeritorious nature of that faith.
>   Dr. Griffith Thomas said: "There is no credit or merit in the act
> of believing, for trust in another is absolutely incompatible with
> self-righteousness and dependence on our own powers.... Faith
> is an essential principle of human life, without which there can
> be no salvation.... There is absolutely no virtue or merit in faith.
> Trust is man's answer to God's truth. Faith is the condition, not
> the ground of salvation." (*Epistle to the Romans*, Vol. 1, pp.
> 154, 165)

Similarly, Dr. E. Y. Mullins wrote: "We are not saved by works, but by grace through faith as the condition. Faith, then, according to the New Testament, is never regarded as a meritorious work.... Saving faith is an active as well as a passive principle. Looked at from one standpoint, faith is simply opening the hand to receive. It is simply surrender of the will.... Faith on man's part is not a work of merit possessing purchasing power, but the condition of salvation. Only by faith, apart from meritorious deeds, could man be saved." (*The Christian Religion in its Doctrinal Expression*, pp. 373, 375-376)

Dr. Leander S. Keyser, whom H. A. Ironside characterized as "a great theologian," said on this: "Faith has been made, in Scripture, the channel through which justification comes to man for the very reason that it will exclude all human merit, and make man's salvation a pure work of God's grace.... From the very nature of faith it can have no merit. Faith is simply the act of the soul by which it accepts God's gift of salvation. There surely can be no merit in a poor, unworthy, guilty sinner accepting the grace which God gratuitously offers him. The fact is, the necessity of simply accepting the gratuity, without the ability to do anything to make him deserving, accentuates and enhances his unworthiness." (*Election and Conversion*, pp. 26-27)

Bishop H. C. G. Moule expressed himself on this in the following words: "Let us note that Faith, seen to be reliance, is obviously a thing as different as possible from merit. No one in common life thinks of a well-placed reliance as meritorious. It is right, but not righteous.... The man who, discovering himself, in the old-fashioned way...to be a guilty sinner, whose 'mouth is shut' before God, relies upon Christ as his all for pardon and peace, certainly does not merit anything for closing with his own salvation. He deserves nothing by the act of accepting all." (*The Fundamentals*, Vol. II, p. 116)...

This same truth was recognized by C.H. Spurgeon, who said, "A knowledge of the truth teaches us that faith is the simple act of trusting, that it is not an action of which man may boast; it is not an action of the nature of a work, so as to be a fruit of the law." (*Treasury of the New Testament*, Vol. III, p. 784)

...Dr. Albertus Pieters was a scholar and writer of the Reformed Church in America, a decidedly Calvinistic group, yet even he had a very strong testimony in this area: "We are not to think that since we are saved by faith, therefore faith is something meritorious. Faith is like the act of a beggar in stretching out the hand to receive my gift. He does not earn anything by that, not a cent; it is merely the acceptance of a free, unearned alms.... So there is no power in faith to save; the power is in Christ and His atoning work, but we cannot receive it without the touch of faith.... We know also that we are free and responsible beings, rejecting Christ, if we reject Him, because we have no love for holiness; and accepting Him, if we accept Him, of our own free will, without being in any way forced to do so." (*Facts and Mysteries of the Christian Faith*, third edition, pp. 167, 185)

Another one from the Reformed Church in America was Dr. David James Burrell, whose published works were widely accepted. He said, "it does not devolve upon me to reconcile the divine sovereignty with the freedom of the human will.... I am persuaded that there is an omniscient God; and I am equally sure that I have a sovereign will. The important fact is this: if I am ever saved, it will be the exercise of personal faith; yet will I join with the innumerable company of the redeemed in ascribing all the glory to God." (*Old Time Religion*, pp. 336-337)

In this connection Dr. H. C. Thiessen quoted Dr. Hodge, of similar theological position to the two just quoted: "A positive response to prevenient [antecedent] grace is not 'merit.' Even Hodge said: "There is no merit in the asking or in the willingness, which is the ground of the gift. It remains a gratuitous favor; but it is, nonetheless, suspended upon the asking.'" (*Lectures in Systematic Theology*, p. 157)[67]

Those quoted above would disagree with the idea that the faith exercised prior to salvation must be God's gift to man. In fact, their theology lines up well with what we discovered in Ephesians 2:8-9: That *"saved"* (or salvation), rather than *"faith,"* is the antecedent of *"that."* Stated in simplified terminology, Paul was teaching in Ephesians 2:8-9 that salvation is not of *"ourselves."* He most definitely was not advocating that the faith exercised prior to salvation is God's gift to the elect (the Reformed view).

To choose Christ through personal faith (while depraved) does not mean that we approach God based on anything good we have done. All that is required is a humble heart that recognizes its need for salvation. Some would ask, "Is not humility a virtue?" God doesn't think so or He would have omitted James 4:6:

... *"God is opposed to the proud, but gives grace to the humble."*
(James 4:6)

Humility and pride are opposites—never compatible. You can't be prideful and humble at the same time, for the prideful love to boast. Hence, to see one's need for a Savior, through a broken and humble heart, would never cause one to approach God on the basis of personal merit or virtue. Yes, man is to humble himself before God (Psalm 138:6; Proverbs 3:34; Matthew 23:12; 1Peter 5:5), but never with the mindset that his humility grants him the right to boast. If so, he has never known what it means to be humble. Thus, Sproul's previous argument, listed below, is irrelevant:

> Why do some people see their need for Christ more clearly than do others? Have they received greater illumination from the Holy Spirit? Are they more intelligent? Are they less prejudiced toward Christ and more open to his call, which is itself a virtue? No matter how one delays it, sooner or later we must face the question of greater or lesser inherent virtue.[68]

Sproul makes such assertions for a specific reason. Should the depraved be capable of exercising personal faith (a fact proven in the Scriptures), total depravity, as defined by Reformed Theology, could not stand. However, let's assume for a moment that Sproul is correct—that man in his depravity cannot humble himself and exercise faith. Irresistible Grace (the "I" of the TULIP) would then be necessary to bring the elect to Christ. But forced grace (grace is "Irresistible" in Reformed Theology) is no longer grace, for free will belonging to the depraved (who can exercise personal repentance and faith should they see their need for salvation) is required for grace to remain grace.

Paul's words in Ephesians 2:9 forever settle how Ephesians 2:8 is to be perceived. Should the phrase, *"and that not of yourselves"* (Ephesians 2:8), point to *"faith"* rather than *"saved"* (the Reformed view), for Paul to teach that *"faith"* (v.8) is not *"a result of works"* (v.9) would be irrational. Not once in God's Word do we find anything that would suggest such a notion. However, over and over again the Scriptures stress that salvation is <u>not</u> *"a result of works"*—that God grants salvation to those who exercise personal repentance and faith while depraved. Consequently, *"that not of yourselves"* (Ephesians 2:8), must point to *"saved"* (v.8) rather than *"faith"* (v.8).

How Romans 12:3 Relates to Faith and Depravity

For through the grace given to me I say to every man among you not to think more highly of himself than he ought to think; but to think so as to have sound judgment, as God has allotted to each a measure of faith. (Romans 12:3)

The Scriptures have a great deal more to say regarding *"faith."* We have already discovered that the *"faith"* (Ephesians 2:8-9) exercised prior to salvation originates within the heart of the depraved (Acts 16:31; and Romans 10:8-10) This faith is not God's gift, but springs forth from the depraved who desire to be saved. I exercised personal repentance and faith when I said in my depravity, "God help, I need a Savior" (repentance is examined when we complete our study of *"faith"*). Thus, the faith exercised prior to salvation was not a gift from the Father. However, it (personal faith) could not have been exercised without the assistance of the Father's drawing (John 6:44) and the Spirit's conviction (John 16:8)—review the notes associated with Romans 3:10-13 for additional input. The *"faith"* addressed in Ephesians 2:8-9, therefore, is not God's gift. Salvation is the gift (Ephesians 2:8-9) once faith has been exercised by the depraved.

However, according to Romans 12:3, *"a measure of faith"* is *"allotted"* by God once personal faith has been implemented:

> *For through the grace given to me I say to every man among you*
> *not to think more highly of himself than he ought to think; but to*
> *think so as to have sound judgment, as God has allotted to each a*
> *measure of faith.* (Romans 12:3)

This *"faith"* cannot be the same faith exercised prior to salvation. If so, Paul's words in Romans 12:3 contradict his words in Ephesians 2:8-9—for we have already confirmed that the *"faith"* of Ephesians 2:8-9 is not God's gift. How can this teaching be reconciled void of contradiction? We will confirm that the gift of *"faith"* *"allotted"* (granted by God) in Romans 12:3 is the faith required to function within the area of the New Testament believer's spiritual gifting, not the personal faith exercised by the depraved prior to spiritual regeneration (salvation).

According to 1Peter 4:10, Romans 12, 1Corinthians 12 and 14, and Ephesians 4, every believer (during the church age) receives a spiritual gift. This spiritual gift is received in conjunction with being placed into Christ's body through the avenue of the Holy Spirit (1Corinthians 12:13; Ephesians 1:3)—after having exercised personal repentance and faith while depraved. Consequently, the *"faith"* addressed in Romans 12:3 is of utmost importance if the New Testament believer is to function properly within the area of his/her gifting. This gift of faith is not the personal faith of Ephesians 2:8-9, but the faith that God grants to those who have previously repented and believed. In fact, once the depraved exercise their own personal repentance and faith, they are baptized into Christ's body through the avenue of the Holy Spirit (1Corinthians 12:13), are born again (John 3:3-6), become new creations (2Corinthians 5:17), and become part of the body of Christ (Ephesians 5:30). Thus, in association with being placed in Christ, God gives *"faith"* (Romans 12:3) to every member of Christ's body, the church, so each gifted member within the body might function as efficiently and powerfully as possible. This *"faith"* is God's gift (Romans 12:3), unlike the *"faith"* of Ephesians 2:8-9, which belongs to the depraved prior to spiritual regeneration (salvation).

The *Wycliffe Bible Commentary*, Electronic Database. Copyright (c) 1962 by Moody Press, records the following regarding Romans 12:3:

> Paul is not here speaking of "saving faith"... "Saving faith" would be no standard for correct self-judgment. Only pride would say: "See how much saving faith I have." But it is a humbling experience to say: "Here is the faith I have for carrying out this or that particular task for God." This can only lead to the prayer, "Lord, increase our faith" (see Luke 17:5). In the account of the heroes of faith in Heb 11, we see that the measure of faith given corresponds to the task to be accomplished.[69]

The *"faith"* of Ephesians 2:8-9, exercised by the depraved (once they see their need for a Savior), must not be confused with God's gift of *"faith"* (Romans 12:3) given to those who have previously chosen to repent and believe. Yes, God gives believers *"faith"* (Romans 12:3), but it is the faith needed to function within the area of a particular spiritual gifting. We can draw this conclusion because Paul is addressing spiritual gifts in Romans 12. This *"faith"* cannot be equated with the personal faith exercised by the depraved when they choose to believe. Those who fail to make this distinction find themselves entangled in a wealth of insurmountable theological abnormalities. Why would God plead with the unregenerate to exercise faith (all of whom will not be saved) if He (God) should be the source of the faith required prior to salvation? Such a scenario would portray God as playing games with men's souls. Yet, John Piper (a Reformed theologian) records the following in his DVD series, *TULIP*, CD 1, Title 6, Chapter 2:

> Faith and repentance are a gift of God...."For by grace you have been saved through faith, that not of yourselves, it is the gift of God, not as a result of works, so that no one may boast." [Ephesians 2:8-9] God is very eager to strip us from boasting. So salvation and faith here are called the gift of God. Romans 12:3—"Through the grace given to me, I say to everyone among you, not to think of himself more highly than he ought to think, but to think so as to have sound judgment, as God has allotted to each the measure of faith."[70]

Piper makes no distinction between the *"faith"* of Ephesians 2:8-9 and the *"faith"* of Romans 12:3; in his mind both are gifts and one and the same. Reformed Theology cannot acknowledge that the depraved could exercise personal faith, for such an arrangement destroys the TULIP. We have discovered, however, that the *"faith"* of Ephesians 2:8-9 is personal *"faith"* exercised by the depraved—while the *"faith"* of Romans 12:3 is God's gift, granted in proportion to the spiritual gift received by those who have previously chosen (while depraved) to repent and believe. As verified earlier, exercising personal faith while depraved grants no one the right to boast:

> *Where then is boasting? It is excluded. By what kind of law? Of*
> *works? No, but by a law of faith.* (Romans 3:27)

This truth refutes Piper's argument in his previous quote, where he states:

> God is very eager to strip us from boasting. So salvation and
> faith here are called the gift of God.[71]

If exercising personal faith excludes *"boasting"* (Romans 3:27), how could anyone boast before God after having chosen while depraved to believe? Boasting would be impossible! Therefore, the depraved can exercise personal faith without viewing their choice as a meritorious deed, negating Piper's argument altogether.

Also, *"faith"* can be *"enlarged"* (2Thessalonians 1:3) as church saints grow in their understanding of the truth:

> *We ought always to give thanks to God for you, brethren, as is only*
> *fitting, because your faith is greatly enlarged, and the love of each*
> *one of you toward one another grows ever greater;*
> (2Thessalonians 1:3)

Paul was encouraged by the *"faith"* of the believers at Rome:

> *First, I thank my God through Jesus Christ for you all, because*
> *your faith is being proclaimed throughout the whole world.*
> (Romans 1:8)

"God has allotted to each a measure of faith" (Romans 12:3), the *"measure of faith"* that corresponds to one's unique spiritual gifting. This faith is not the personal faith exercised by the depraved, as has already been established. Is this faith all that is required for the gift to function efficiently? Not at all!

The believer's spiritual gift is not only imparted through the avenue of God's grace but empowered through His grace as well. Consider the following passages:

> *And since we have gifts that differ according to the grace given to*
> *us,...* (Romans 12:6)

*...but I labored even more than all of them, yet not I, but the grace
of God with me.* (1Corinthians 15:10).

*But to each one of us grace was given according to the measure of
Christ's gift.* (Ephesians 4:7)

Paul realized that God's grace not only granted him his spiritual gift but also
energized him as he served in the area of his gifting. To boast would have been
impossible!

The Lord energizes us as well in the area of our own unique gifting which we
received through His grace. This spiritual gift was bestowed by God in conjunction
with our new birth, a birth that resulted from being placed *"in Christ"* (John 3:3-6;
2Corinthians 5:17) through the avenue of the *"Spirit"* (1Corinthians 12:13) <u>after</u> we
chose (while depraved) to repent and believe. Consider Paul's words from
Ephesians 1:3:

*Blessed be the God and Father of our Lord Jesus Christ, who has
blessed us with every spiritual blessing in the heavenly places in
Christ,* (Ephesians 1:3)

Yes, *"every spiritual blessing"* is granted to each New Testament believer in
conjunction with being placed *"in Christ."* Consequently, God gives all church
saints a spiritual gift in association with being spiritually regenerated (saved), a
regeneration that occurs subsequent to exercising personal repentance and faith
while depraved.

A deeper look at Ephesians 4:7 would blend in well with the present subject
matter:

*But to each one of us grace was given according to the measure of
Christ's gift.* (Ephesians 4:7)

Paul begins Ephesians 4:7 with *"But to each one,"* because, in Ephesians 4:7-16,
he mentions some of the spiritual gifts granted to the body of Christ. *"Each"* New
Testament believer has been given *"grace"* (Ephesians 4:7)—the Greek word for
"grace" in this case being *charis*. This *"grace"* is imparted *"according to the
measure of Christ's gift"* (Ephesians 4:7). The Greek word for *"gift"* (Ephesians
4:7) is *dorea*, pointing to the freeness of the gift. Thus, this *"grace"* (*charis*) is
without cost. The purpose of this *"grace"* is to energize the spiritual gifts given to
the church, the *charisma* gifts, listed in Romans 12:6-8, 1Corinthians 12:4-30, and
referenced in 1Peter 4:10—along with the gifts mentioned in Ephesians 4:7-11.
This *"grace"* (Ephesians 4:7) empowers New Testament believers as they
"employ" their *"gift"* (singular—1Peter 4:10) to God's glory. Hence, the *"grace"*

153

(*charis*) addressed in Ephesians 4:7 is *"given according to the measure of Christ's gift"* (Ephesians 4:7) and is more than sufficient to energize one's gift. Any spiritual gift is received through the working of God's *"grace"* (Romans 12:6). Consequently, through grace, the New Testament believer's spiritual gift is both received and energized to God's glory.

The grace that Paul references in Ephesians 4:7 is different from the grace the believer must appropriate in the midst of personal difficulties. The grace needed for times of adversity is unlimited, while the grace required to function within an area of gifting is fixed according to the particular gift received (Ephesians 4:7). Ephesians 1:2 confirms what is addressed here:

> *Grace to you and peace from God our Father and the Lord Jesus Christ.* (Ephesians 1:2)

"Grace to you and peace from God our Father and the Lord Jesus Christ," is one of Paul's favorite statements. He uses these same words in Romans 1:7, 1Corinthians 1:3, 2Corinthians 1:2, Galatians 1:3; Philippians 1:2, Colossians 1:2, 1Thessalonians 1:1, 2Thessalonians 1:2, 1Timothy 1:2, 2Timothy 1:2, Titus 1:4, and Philemon 3.

> *Grace to you and peace...* (Ephesians 1:2a)

"Grace" can be defined as "unmerited favor" as well as "the power to do God's will." Paul realized that God's grace directed toward the New Testament believer, at the point of spiritual regeneration as well as throughout his earthly pilgrimage, is necessary for abundant living. The grace received when one first submits to Christ (while depraved) results in new life, whereas the grace provided on a daily basis grants the power to do God's will. In other words, we make the choice to obey; and God, through His grace, supplies the power that sustains us in the midst of our obedience. Paul writes:

> *And God is able to make all grace abound to you, that always*
> *having all sufficiency in everything, you may have an abundance*
> *for every good deed.* (2Corinthians 9:8)

Abundant grace is available for every need that crosses the believer's path. *"Peace,"* which results from accepting God's grace, is a *"fruit of the Spirit"* (Galatians 5:22).

Thus in Ephesians 1:2, Paul gives additional input regarding God's grace, a popular topic with the passionate apostle. He teaches that God's grace is accessible to believers as they face the trials certain to come their way. When this grace is accepted, peace results. When it is rejected, turmoil and confusion are certain to follow. God's *"grace is sufficient"* (when accepted) for any circumstance of life (2Corinthians 12:9). Consequently, Paul urged Timothy to *"be strong in the grace that is in Christ Jesus"* (2Timothy 2:1). The writer of Hebrews also reveals where and how *"grace"* is found—through boldly approaching God's *"throne"* (Hebrews 4:16). Peter also states that this *"grace"* is *"multiplied"* to the believer as his *"knowledge"* of the Godhead is enhanced (2Peter 1:2), and that the believer is to *"grow in the grace and knowledge of our Lord and Savior Jesus Christ"* (2Peter 3:18).

Now to the last half of Ephesians 1:2:

> *...from God our Father and the Lord Jesus Christ.* (Ephesians 1:2b)

This verse confirms that the Godhead is the Source of all grace. Thus, the grace we receive during times of adversity is from God.

Conclusion

The depraved exercise personal repentance (Acts 2:38) and faith (Ephesians 2:8-9). Once a depraved individual during the church age (which began in Acts 2) exercises this repentance and faith, his old man (Adamic nature, old self, sinful nature, dead spirit—all synonymous) is placed in Christ through the avenue of the Holy Spirit (1Corinthians 12:13) and crucified (Romans 6:6; 7:1-4; Galatians 2:20)—totally eradicated. The new man is instantaneously born (2Corinthians 5:17). In conjunction with being placed in Christ, God gives the New Testament believer a spiritual gift (1Peter 4:10; Romans 12; 1Corinthians 12 and 14; and Ephesians 4). He also gives ample faith to function in the area of the gifting (Romans 12:3). God's grace both grants and empowers the gift (Romans 12:6; 1Corinthians 15:10; Ephesians 4:7) to His glory.

No boasting can be involved. How can one boast after realizing that: (1) God's grace grants us a spiritual gift (2) God, not man, determines which gift we receive (3) God supplies the faith to walk in our particular area of gifting (4) God's grace supplies the strength to walk in the gifting (5) The grace that supplies this strength can be rejected, causing the gift to lie dormant? Our responsibility, therefore, is to accept God's grace on a moment-by-moment basis, through which He empowers our gift to His glory!

What an amazing plan! The writer of Hebrews recorded:

> *There remains therefore a Sabbath rest for the people of God. For the one who has entered His rest has himself also rested from his works, as God did from His.* (Hebrews 4:9-10)

Thus, we can rest, for the indwelling Christ will energize us beyond measure:

> *Now I rejoice in my sufferings for your sake, and in my flesh I do my share on behalf of His body (which is the church) in filling up that which is lacking in Christ's afflictions. 25 Of this church I was made a minister according to the stewardship from God bestowed on me for your benefit, that I might fully carry out the preaching of the word of God, 26 that is, the mystery which has been hidden from the past ages and generations; but has now been manifested to His saints, 27 to whom God willed to make known what is the riches of the glory of this mystery among the Gentiles, which is Christ in you, the hope of glory. 28 And we proclaim Him, admonishing every man and teaching every man with all wisdom, that we may present every man complete in Christ. 29 And for this purpose also I labor, striving according to His power, which mightily works within me.* (Colossians 1:24-29—emphasis added)

To Him be the glory!

A difference exists between the personal *"faith"* exercised by the depraved prior to spiritual regeneration (Ephesians 2:8-9) and the *"measure"* of *"faith"* bestowed (by God) to each New Testament believer (to function within a particular spiritual gifting) once he is placed in Christ (Romans 12:3).

Additional Verses Implemented by Reformed Theology Regarding Faith

As has already been established, John Piper (a Reformed theologian) teaches that the faith exercised prior to salvation is God's gift—otherwise faith (in his mind) would be a work, especially if exercised by the depraved. He fails to recognize the wealth of verses that discredit his argument, namely Romans 3:27:

> *Where then is boasting? It is excluded. By what kind of law? Of works? No, but by a law of faith.* (Romans 3:27)

This passage by no means supports Piper's view, for personal *"faith"* (exercised while depraved) is no grounds for *"boasting."* In fact, *"boasting"* is totally *"excluded"* (made null and void) when the depraved choose to believe. According to Romans 4:5 and 9:32, to choose to believe in one's lost (depraved) condition has never been, nor ever will be, categorized in the Scriptures as a meritorious deed.

156

Colossians 1:3-4, 2Thessalonians 1:3, and Faith

Reformed theologians such as James White (in *The Potter's Freedom*) use Colossians 1:3-4 and 2Thessalonians 1:3 in an attempt to prove that the faith exercised prior to salvation finds its origin in God—never man:

> *We give thanks to God, the Father of our Lord Jesus Christ,*
> *praying always for you, since we heard of your faith in Christ*
> *Jesus and the love which you have for all the saints;* (Colossians
> 1:3-4)

> *We ought always to give thanks to God for you, brethren, as is only*
> *fitting, because your faith is greatly enlarged, and the love of each*
> *one of you toward one another grows ever greater;*
> (2Thessalonians 1:3)

White argues that if faith is generated by the depraved, why should God be thanked when it is exercised? He concludes that God can be thanked only if faith finds its origin in Him alone—and is a gift? (Again, permission was requested to quote directly from *The Potter's Freedom*, but the request was denied. Thus, this contextual paraphrase must suffice.)

White is mistaken in the details of his argument. God can be thanked (Colossians 1:3-4; 2Thessalonians 1:3) because God's drawing (John 6:44; 12:32), which is upon every human being, is ever-present when personal faith is exercised by the depraved who choose to believe. Yes, the depraved exercise their own faith, but God's drawing is there to assist. Neither could personal "*faith*" be implemented by the depraved apart from God opening "*a door*" for it to occur:

> *And when they had arrived and gathered the church together, they*
> *began to report all things that God had done with them and how*
> *He had opened a door of faith to the Gentiles.* (Acts 14:27)

God "*opened a door of faith to the Gentiles.*" In other words, God gives all Gentiles (all people in fact) the <u>opportunity</u> to exercise personal "*faith*" in Christ while depraved. He does not cause Gentiles to believe (as Reformed Theology supposes) but rather gives Gentiles everywhere <u>opportunity</u> to employ faith. Thus, God spiritually regenerates those who exercise personal faith while depraved. Therefore, for God to open "*a door of faith to the Gentiles*" (Acts 14:27) does not mean that all Gentiles are saved (Universalism)—or that only the "elect" Gentiles (chosen by God to salvation from eternity past) will be saved (Calvinism). It does mean, however, that God will save any Gentile who chooses to employ personal faith in his depraved state. Paul thanked Him for the faith that had been exercised by the Gentile believers at Colossae, (Colossians 1:3-4); for had He not *"opened a door"* (Acts 14:27—given opportunity) for such faith to be implemented, they would never have chosen, in their depravity, to believe.

In Acts 12:10 we find the same Greek word used for *"opened"* as is used in Acts 14:27:

> *And when they had passed the first and second guard, they came to the iron gate that leads into the city, which <u>opened</u> for them by itself; and they went out and went along one street; and immediately the angel departed from him.* (Acts 12:10—emphasis added)

The gate had been *"opened"* for Peter and the angel, but by no means were they required to pass through. They passed through because they chose to pass through, not because they were coerced to do so. The same Greek word is used for *"opened"* in Acts 16:25-28, but Paul and Silas did not exit the jail:

> *But about midnight Paul and Silas were praying and singing hymns of praise to God, and the prisoners were listening to them; and suddenly there came a great earthquake, so that the foundations of the prison house were shaken; and immediately all the doors were opened, and everyone's chains were unfastened. And when the jailer had been roused out of sleep and had seen the prison doors <u>opened</u>, he drew his sword and was about to kill himself, supposing that the prisoners had escaped. But Paul cried out with a loud voice, saying, "Do yourself no harm, for we are all here!"* (Acts 16:25-18—emphasis added)

1Corinthians 16:9 and 2Corinthians 2:12 confirm this same truth: even though God opened a door of service to Paul, he could have turned the other way, as did Jonah when initially commissioned to go to Nineveh (Jonah 1:1-3). Consequently, the phrase, *"opened a door of faith to the Gentiles"* (Acts 14:27), points to God granting every Gentile the option of believing or remaining in his state of depravity.

Another essential truth is that a New Testament believer (once saved) cannot be *"transformed"* in the area of his spiritual maturity apart from God's assistance. 2Corinthians 3:18:

> *But we all, with unveiled face beholding as in a mirror the glory of the Lord, are being transformed into the same image from glory to glory, just as from the Lord, the Spirit.* (2Corinthians 3:18)

Also, as one chooses to gaze at God, through prayerfully reading His Word, His flawless attributes are revealed to an ever-increasing degree, resulting in an expanded "*faith*":

> *For I am not ashamed of the gospel, for it is the power of God for*
> *salvation to everyone who believes, to the Jew first and also to the*
> *Greek. For in it the righteousness of God is revealed from faith to*
> *faith; as it is written, "But the righteous man shall live by faith."*
> (Romans 1:16-17)

The believer's "*faith*" is enhanced *("from faith to faith")* as he spends quality time in God's presence. This increased faith, in fact all spiritual "*growth*," "*is from God:*"

> *...from whom the entire body, being supplied and held together by*
> *the joints and ligaments, grows with a growth which is from God.*
> (Colossians 2:19)

Paul, therefore, could thank God for the "*greatly enlarged...faith*" of the Thessalonians (2Thessalonians 1:3) without viewing God as the source of the faith they exercised prior to spiritual regeneration—while in the midst of their depravity.

Philippians 1:29 and Faith

Philippians 1:29 is yet another passage used by Reformed theologians (James White in *The Potter's Freedom*) in an attempt to prove that the faith exercised prior to salvation is God's gift:

> *For to you it has been granted for Christ's sake, not only to believe*
> *in Him, but also to suffer for His sake,* (Philippians 1:29)

White perceives Philippians 1:29 as proving that the depraved are incapable of exercising personal faith; that faith must be God's gift to the elect prior to salvation—that it must be "*granted*" to the elect. The Scriptures teach, however, that the depraved are amply capable of exercising their own faith prior to being saved (John 3:15; 12:46; Acts 16:31; 26:18; and Romans 10:9-10). The Scriptures teach as well that the depraved exercising faith can occur due to God having "*granted*" the depraved the freedom to choose to believe (as will be confirmed to a greater degree shortly).

CHAPTER FIFTEEN

REPENTANCE AND DEPRAVITY

The Contextual View of Repentance in 2Timothy 2:24-26

John Piper (a Reformed theologian), in his DVD series *TULIP*, Disk 1, Title 7, Chapter 2, regarding faith and repentance, states:

> Faith is a gift, or repentance is a gift....We are brought to the place where grace gives us faith, gives us repentance.[72]

Piper not only believes that faith in all cases is God's gift (including the *"faith"* of Ephesians 2:8-9), but repentance as well. Paul's teaching in 2Timothy 2:24-26 has led some to conclude that he too, was a Reformed theologian, but was he, and did his words verify Piper's conclusion?

> *And the Lord's bond-servant must not be quarrelsome, but be kind to all, able to teach, patient when wronged, 25 with gentleness correcting those who are in opposition, if perhaps God may grant them repentance leading to the knowledge of the truth, 26 and they may come to their senses and escape from the snare of the devil, having been held captive by him to do his will.* (2Timothy 2:24-26)

The key phrase is *"if perhaps God may grant them repentance leading to the knowledge of the truth"* (v.25). Did Paul perceive the repentance required prior to salvation to be God's gift to the elect? John Piper believes so, based on his DVD series *TULIP*, Disk 1, Title 6, Chapter 2:

> Faith and repentance are a gift of God.... 2Timothy 2:24, this

161

> one had a huge effect on me when I saw it years ago, because it combined what we usually separate, namely human effort to change somebody and divine decisive effort to change them.... "if perhaps God may grant them," here's the gift, "may grant them repentance leading to a knowledge of the truth and they may come to their senses and escape from the snare of the devil, having been held captive by him to do his will.".... this verse teaches that ... whether somebody repents depends on whether God grants them repentance. Repentance is a gift.[73]

Piper concludes from the word *"grant"* in 2Timothy 2:25 (he states the incorrect Scripture address by saying "2Timothy 2:24" in his previous quote) that *"repentance"* is God's gift to the elect. Was this Paul's meaning? We will allow other passages that contain the word *"grant"* (or *"granted"*), taken from the Greek root *didomi*, to assist us in our decision. The first verse is Acts 5:31:

> *He is the one whom God exalted to His right hand as a Prince and*
> *a Savior, to grant repentance to Israel, and forgiveness of sins.*
> (Acts 5:31)

As has already been established, Reformed Theology stresses that God must grant (give) faith and repentance to the elect <u>before</u> they can repent and believe. Does this idea line up with the full counsel of God's Word? *"Peter and the apostles"* (Acts 5:29) stated that both *"repentance"* and *"forgiveness"* have been granted to *"Israel"* (Acts 5:31). The word *"Israel"* points to everyone of Jewish descent, not just believers. The apostles were speaking to the leaders of the Jews, most of whom had rejected Jesus' Messiahship. Had the apostles been speaking of Jewish believers only, and not the entire Jewish nation, they would have made a distinction in this instance.

Suddenly, our study becomes even more compelling, especially if you desire to interpret Acts 5:31 based on all of the Scriptures rather than a select few. First, *"repentance"* is a gift in the sense that *"forgiveness"* is a gift. Second, if the Reformed view is correct, the apostles were teaching that the entire Jewish nation had been given *"repentance"* and *"forgiveness."* If the apostle were teaching this totality, every Jew would be saved, which the Scriptures vehemently deny. Third, Romans 9:27 stresses that only a *"remnant"* of *"Israel"* will be *"saved."* Fourth, since only a *"remnant"* of *"Israel"* will be *"saved"* (Romans 9:27), the apostles could not be teaching, in Acts 5:31, that God had given the gift of *"repentance"* and *"forgiveness"* to every Jew. If so, the whole nation would be spiritually regenerated, contradicting Romans 9:27 (along with a hoard of additional verses—such as Romans 2:17-3:8). The apostles were simply teaching that God had granted to all the Jews the <u>opportunity</u> to repent while depraved. They were also teaching that God had granted to all the Jews the opportunity to receive His forgiveness through exercising personal repentance and faith while depraved. Acts 5:31 can be viewed no other way and be void of contradiction.

Can you understand how easily (by interpreting Acts 5:31 out of context) a follower of Reformed Theology could transition into Universalism, a system of thought that views all persons as children of God? After all, the "L" of the TULIP, Limited Atonement, suggests only two options: (1) Jesus died for the elect alone and only the elect will be saved (2) Jesus died for all and all will be saved.

Conclusion

God grants *"repentance"* in the sense that He offers all mankind the opportunity to repent.

The Contextual View of Repentance in Acts 11:18

Luke addresses "R*epentance"* in Acts 11:18, using *"granted,"* while Paul uses *"grant"* (2Timothy 2:25)—both words from the Greek root *didomi*:

> *And when they heard this, they quieted down, and glorified God, saying, "Well then, God has granted to the Gentiles also the repentance that leads to life."* (Acts 11:18)

As was verified earlier, a great disparity exists between God giving *"repentance"* as a gift (the Reformed view) versus God granting the opportunity for mankind to repent. If the *"repentance"* in Acts 11:18 points to the gift of *"repentance"* that is supposedly given to the elect of Reformed Theology, one can "logically" conclude that all Gentiles have received *"repentance"* and are, therefore, part of the elect. Again we see how easily a follower of Reformed Theology could fall into Universalism. However, do all Gentiles mentioned in the Scriptures believe? Certainly not! Have we known Gentiles who have rejected Christ and died void of repentance and faith? Of course we have! Thus, this verse discredits what many Calvinists assume regarding the term *"repentance."* In Acts 11:18, Peter is simply teaching that God has *"granted to the Gentiles"* the opportunity to repent. He is in no way advocating that the *"repentance"* required prior to salvation is God's gift to the elect. Note: The preceding was written realizing that both personal repentance and personal faith are required prior to spiritual regeneration (salvation), not personal repentance alone—although personal repentance and personal faith can be viewed as two parts of the same action. Scripture clearly states that salvation includes both rejecting evil (personal repentance) and embracing that which is good (personal faith). This subject will be addressed in greater depth later in our study.

Also, note that *"repentance...leads to life"* (Acts 11:18). This truth negates the Reformed view: God must spiritually regenerate the elect (grant them spiritual life) before He gives them the repentance and faith required prior to salvation. Peter states, *"repentance that leads to life"* (Acts 11:18)—not life that leads to repentance. The Reformed view reverses the scriptural order. *"Repentance"* precedes spiritual regeneration and new birth (Acts 11:18)—not the other way around.

Conclusion

The phrase, *"God has granted to the Gentiles also the repentance that leads to life"* (Acts 11:18), proves that God has *"granted"* to all Gentiles during the church age the opportunity to repent in the midst of their depravity and, in turn, receive God's eternal *"life."* (Faith, of course, is also required from the depraved prior to salvation but is not the topic of discussion in Acts 11:18.)

CHAPTER SIXTEEN

A MORE THOROUGH EXPLANATION OF PREVIOUS STATEMENTS

IN PREVIOUS MATERIALS, the original *Romans 1-8* and *Hebrews* courses (generated over twenty years prior to this series), I made statements similar to: "When I came to Christ, I basically said, 'God help, I need a Savior,' and He saved me. He gave me faith and granted me repentance."

When I said, "God help," I, in my depravity, exercised personal faith (my own faith) by looking to God as my Redeemer. I also exercised personal repentance (my own repentance) in my depravity by saying, "I need a Savior." Of course, believers continue to repent for their misdeeds after receiving salvation (justification), but that form of repentance is not the subject being addressed.

I have also stated in earlier materials that God gave (allotted) me faith and granted me repentance. My meaning was: The *"faith"* God *"allotted"* (gave) me (Romans 12:3—NASB) was not my own, personal faith which I exercised in my depravity, but the *"measure of faith"* needed to function in the area of my spiritual gifting. This *"measure of faith"* (Romans 12:3) was *"allotted"* (given) to me once I was placed in Christ subsequent to that moment when I exercised personal repentance and personal faith while depraved. Also, by stating that God granted me *"repentance"* (Acts 11:18; 2Timothy 2:25), I meant that God accepted, or honored, my personal repentance (implemented in my depravity) due to having granted me the opportunity to repent. After all, He grants every person who lives the opportunity to repent (Acts 5:31; 11:18).

Conclusion

God grants everyone the opportunity to exercise personal repentance and faith while depraved, although many people live as though this opportunity is nonexistent. Once the depraved during the church age (which began in Acts 2) repent and exercise faith, God places them into Christ. They have done that which He requires prior to granting new life. Once they are *"in Christ"* (2Corinthians 5:17), God saves and blesses them with *"every spiritual blessing"* (Ephesians 1:3)—one of the blessings being the *"measure of faith"* (Romans 12:3) needed to function in their particular spiritual gifting. If anything I have written or taught in previous studies seems to differ with what I have communicated here, know that this explanation portrays the meaning that I intended for the reader or listener to understand. The current theological climate requires that I define those events more precisely.

CHAPTER SEVENTEEN

ADDITIONAL VERSES THAT RELATE TO REPENTANCE AND FAITH

Philippians 1:29 Revisited

The word *"granted"* in Scripture can point to God granting the depraved the opportunity to exercise their own repentance and faith. Let's address Philippians 1:29 once again with this thought in mind:

> *For to you it has been granted for Christ's sake, not only to believe in Him, but also to suffer for His sake,* (Philippians 1:29)

A factor that allows *"granted"* (Philippians 1:29) to point to opportunity is found in the phrase, *"to suffer for His sake."* God grants believers the opportunity *"to suffer,"* but suffering can be purposely avoided during seasons of doubt and despair—the very situation the writer of Hebrews warns against in that powerful epistle (Hebrews 2:1, 3; 10:35-36; 12:3-5, 12-13; 13:13). The recipients of the book of Hebrews had been *"granted"* the opportunity to suffer but were contemplating relinquishing that opportunity due to the impending persecution from the unbelieving Jews. They later repented of their sin and were restored to fellowship, risking their lives for the cause of the gospel.

James White's conclusions regarding Philippians 1:29 (conclusions we addressed earlier from *The Potter's Freedom*) are ill founded. Our discoveries will greatly benefit our understanding of John 6:65 (a foundational verse for Reformed Theology) when we study *God's Heart as it Relates to Election-Atonement-Grace-Perseverance,* the fourth (and final) book of this series. Considerable research is required for proper context, but free will easily prevails.

167

> *And He was saying, "For this reason I have said to you, that no*
> *one can come to Me, unless it has been granted him from the*
> *Father."* (John 6:65)

Determining the contextual view of Jesus' words will be included in book four of this series.

The Contextual View of Faith in Philippians 3:8-9

Reformed Theology also uses Philippians 3:8-9 in an attempt to prove that God supplies the faith required prior to ones' salvation:

> *More than that, I count all things to be loss in view of the*
> *surpassing value of knowing Christ Jesus my Lord, for whom I*
> *have suffered the loss of all things, and count them but rubbish in*
> *order that I may gain Christ, and may be found in Him, not having*
> *a righteousness of my own derived from the Law, but that which is*
> *through faith in Christ, the righteousness which comes from God*
> *on the basis of faith,* (Philippians 3:8-9)

"*Faith*" in this instance is not God's gift. The *"righteousness which comes from God on the basis of faith"* is His gift. Thus, the depraved exercise personal "*faith*" prior to receiving God's gift of "*righteousness.*"

The Contextual View of Faith in 1Peter 1:21

Reformed Theology also relies heavily upon 1Peter 1:21:

> *who through Him are believers in God, who raised Him from the*
> *dead and gave Him glory, so that your faith and hope are in God.*
> (1Peter 1:21)

James White, in *The Potter's Freedom*, suggests that the words "*through Him*" prove that the faith exercised prior to salvation is God's gift to the elect. Is White correct? The full counsel of God's Word negates such an argument.

Jesus leaves no doubt that we *"are believers"*... "*through Him,*" for He said:

> ... *"I am the way, and the truth, and the life; no one comes to the*
> *Father, but <u>through Me</u>.* (John 14:6)

Christ is teaching that no one can come to the Father but *"through"* Him (John 14:6)—through believing on Him as Savior. This passage in no way teaches that the faith God requires prior to bestowing salvation is His gift, as White suggests. Paul's words to the Galatians tie in here as well:

> *For you are all sons of God through faith in Christ Jesus.*
> (Galatians 3:26)

Jesus stated:

> ... *"He who believes in Me does not believe in Me, but in Him who sent Me.* (John 12:44)

The phrase, *"through Him are believers"* (1Peter 1:21), does not suggest, therefore, that the faith exercised prior to salvation is God's gift to the elect. Rather, it proves that apart from Christ (and what He accomplished through the cross) no one would have opportunity to believe. Jesus paid the price for sin, which paved the way for salvation to be offered to all descendants of Adam (John 3:16; 1Timothy 4:10; and 1John 2:2). Hence, 1Peter 1:21 leaves ample room for the depraved to exercise personal faith, and for God to follow by imparting eternal salvation.

The Contextual View of Faith in 2Peter 1:1

> *Simon Peter, a bond-servant and apostle of Jesus Christ, to those who have received a faith of the same kind as ours, by the righteousness of our God and Savior, Jesus Christ:* (2Peter 1:1)

The phrase that will be given special attention is *"...who have received a faith of the same kind as ours...."* John MacArthur (a follower of Reformed Theology) discusses this passage in *The MacArthur Study Bible*:

> Even though faith and belief express the human side of salvation, God still must grant that faith....So, not only do they have faith because God gives it to them, they are saved only because God imputes righteousness to them.[74]

MacArthur, being a Reformed theologian, perceives 2Peter 1:1 as teaching that God must give faith to the "elect" before they can believe. Does this passage teach such an idea?

Peter was writing to Jews who had *"received a faith"* like his (2Peter 1:1). For proper interpretation, one must know that First and Second Peter were written to the same group of Jewish believers (read 2Peter 3:1). A significant span of time transpired, however, between the two epistles, for in 1Peter 2:2, Peter encourages his readers to desire the *"milk of the word"*—whereas in Second Peter, as he approaches the end of his life (2Peter 1:14), he recognizes that they *"have been established in the truth"* (2Peter 1:12).

Remarkably, Jude, another New Testament epistle, follows the same general outline of Second Peter. The similarities can be seen by comparing: (1) 2Peter 1:1 with Jude 1a and 3b (2) 2Peter 2:1 with Jude 4 (3) 2Peter 2:4 with Jude 6 (4) 2Peter 2:6 with Jude 7 (5) 2Peter 2:10 with Jude 8 (6) 2Peter 2:11 with Jude 9 (7) 2Peter 2:12 with Jude 10 (8) 2Peter 2:15 with Jude 11 (9) 2Peter 2:17 with Jude 12-13 (10) 2Peter 2:18 with Jude 16 (11) 2Peter 3:2 with Jude 17 (12) 2Peter 3:3 with Jude 18. As these verses are paired with one another, notice the similar terminology:

> *Simon Peter, a bond-servant and apostle of Jesus Christ, to those who have received a faith of the same kind as ours, by the righteousness of our God and Savior, Jesus Christ:* (2Peter 1:1)

> *Jude, a bond-servant of Jesus Christ,...* (Jude 1a)

> *...I felt the necessity to write to you appealing that you contend earnestly for the faith which was once for all delivered to the saints.* (Jude 3b)

> *But false prophets also arose among the people, just as there will also be false teachers among you, who will secretly introduce destructive heresies, even denying the Master who bought them, bringing swift destruction upon themselves.* (2Peter 2:1)

> *For certain persons have crept in unnoticed, those who were long beforehand marked out for this condemnation, ungodly persons who turn the grace of our God into licentiousness and deny our only Master and Lord, Jesus Christ.* (Jude 4)

> *For if God did not spare angels when they sinned, but cast them into hell and committed them to pits of darkness, reserved for judgment;* (2Peter 2:4)

> *And angels who did not keep their own domain, but abandoned their proper abode, He has kept in eternal bonds under darkness*

for the judgment of the great day. (Jude 6)

and if He condemned the cities of Sodom and Gomorrah to destruction by reducing them to ashes, having made them an example to those who would live ungodly thereafter; (2Peter 2:6)

Just as Sodom and Gomorrah and the cities around them, since they in the same way as these indulged in gross immorality and went after strange flesh, are exhibited as an example, in undergoing the punishment of eternal fire. (Jude 7)

and especially those who indulge the flesh in its corrupt desires and despise authority. Daring, self-willed, they do not tremble when they revile angelic majesties, (2Peter 2:10)

Yet in the same manner these men, also by dreaming, defile the flesh, and reject authority, and revile angelic majesties. (Jude 8)

whereas angels who are greater in might and power do not bring a reviling judgment against them before the Lord. (2Peter 2:11)

But Michael the archangel, when he disputed with the devil and argued about the body of Moses, did not dare pronounce against him a railing judgment, but said, "The Lord rebuke you." (Jude 9)

But these, like unreasoning animals, born as creatures of instinct to be captured and killed, reviling where they have no knowledge, will in the destruction of those creatures also be destroyed, (2Peter 2:12)

But these men revile the things which they do not understand; and the things which they know by instinct, like unreasoning animals, by these things they are destroyed. (Jude 10)

forsaking the right way they have gone astray, having followed the way of Balaam, the son of Beor, who loved the wages of unrighteousness, (2Peter 2:15)

Woe to them! For they have gone the way of Cain, and for pay they have rushed headlong into the error of Balaam, and perished in the rebellion of Korah. (Jude 11)

These are springs without water, and mists driven by a storm, for whom the black darkness has been reserved. (2Peter 2:17)

These men are those who are hidden reefs in your love feasts when they feast with you without fear, caring for themselves; clouds without water, carried along by winds; autumn trees without fruit, doubly dead, uprooted; 13 wild waves of the sea, casting up their own shame like foam; wandering stars, for whom the black darkness has been reserved forever. (Jude 12-13)

For speaking out arrogant words of vanity they entice by fleshly desires, by sensuality, those who barely escape from the ones who live in error, (2Peter 2:18)

These are grumblers, finding fault, following after their own lusts; they speak arrogantly, flattering people for the sake of gaining an advantage. (Jude 16)

that you should remember the words spoken beforehand by the holy prophets and the commandment of the Lord and Savior spoken by your apostles. (2Peter 3:2)

But you, beloved, ought to remember the words that were spoken beforehand by the apostles of our Lord Jesus Christ, (Jude 17)

Know this first of all, that in the last days mockers will come with their mocking, following after their own lusts, (2Peter 3:3)

that they were saying to you, "In the last time there shall be mockers, following after their own ungodly lusts." (Jude 18)

Is it not amazing how much Jude parallels Second Peter? We can know that Jude was written subsequent to Second Peter, for the false teachers that Peter warned against (*"there will also be"* in 2Peter 2:1 is future tense) had arrived by the time Jude penned his letter (Jude 8, 10, 12, 16, and 19 contain the present tense). We can conclude, therefore, that Jude was led by God's Spirit to follow the general outline of Second Peter as he wrote (evidently) to these same Jewish believers.

With all of this said, we can draw some solid conclusions regarding 2Peter 1:1, especially in light of what Jude records in Jude 3.

> *Simon Peter, a bond-servant and apostle of Jesus Christ, to those who have received a faith of the same kind as ours, by the righteousness of our God and Savior, Jesus Christ:* (2 Peter 1:1)

> *Beloved, while I was making every effort to write you about our common salvation, I felt the necessity to write to you appealing that you contend earnestly for the faith which was once for all delivered to the saints.* (Jude 3)

Jude *"felt the necessity to write"* a letter of exhortation regarding *"the faith which was once for all delivered to the saints," "the faith"* being the overall body of truth (doctrine) taught in the Scriptures. He penned this epistle due to the false teachers who were spreading error among his readers. Thus, *"the faith"* (Jude 3) does not indicate that God gives faith to the elect so they might receive *"salvation"* (the Reformed view), but rather points to the overall body of truth (doctrine) known as *"the faith"* mentioned on numerous occasions in the Scriptures. The following verses confirm this fact:

> *And the word of God kept on spreading; and the number of the disciples continued to increase greatly in Jerusalem, and a great many of the priests were becoming obedient to the faith.* (Acts 6:7)

> *But Elymas the magician (for thus his name is translated) was opposing them, seeking to turn the proconsul away from the faith.* (Acts 13:8-9)

> *...encouraging them to continue in the faith,...* (Acts 14:22)

> *So the churches were being strengthened in the faith,...* (Acts 16:5)

> *...stand firm in the faith...* (1Corinthians 16:13)

> *Test yourselves to see if you are in the faith;* (2Corinthians 13:5)

> *"He who once persecuted us is now preaching the faith which he once tried to destroy."* (Galatians 1:23)

...being shut up to the faith which was later to be revealed.
(Galatians 3:23)

*until we all attain to the unity of the faith, and of the knowledge of
the Son of God, to a mature man, to the measure of the stature
which belongs to the fullness of Christ.* (Ephesians 4:13)

...striving together for the faith of the gospel; (Philippians 1:27)

...some will fall away from the faith... (1Timothy 4:1)

*In pointing out these things to the brethren, you will be a good
servant of Christ Jesus, constantly nourished on the words of the
faith and of the sound doctrine which you have been following.*
(1Timothy 4:6)

*But if anyone does not provide for his own, and especially for those
of his household, he has denied the faith, and is worse than an
unbeliever.* (1Timothy 5:8-9)

*For the love of money is a root of all sorts of evil, and some by
longing for it have wandered away from the faith, and pierced
themselves with many a pang.* (1Timothy 6:10)

which some have professed and thus gone astray from the faith.
(1Timothy 6:21)

*I have fought the good fight, I have finished the course, I have kept
the faith;* (2Timothy 4:7)

*This testimony is true. For this cause reprove them severely that
they may be sound in the faith,* (Titus 1:13)

Considering that Jude, using *"the faith"* in Jude 3, was making a parallel statement to Peter's *"a faith of the same kind as ours"* in 2Peter 1:1, both *"a faith"* (2Peter 1:1) and *"the faith"* (Jude 3) point to the overall body of truth (doctrine) recorded in the Scriptures. Hence, neither verse supports the Reformed view—that faith is God's gift to the spiritually regenerated prior to their believing for salvation. Thus, to perceive Peter as teaching that he and his readers had received the same body of truth (taught in the Scriptures) is the most feasible interpretation.

Yet, John MacArthur, in *The MacArthur Study Bible*, fails to make this connection. He views 2Peter 1:1 as teaching that God gives faith to the elect so they can believe for salvation (as mentioned in his previous quote) yet views *"the faith"* in Jude 3 as "...the whole body of revealed salvation truth contained in the

Scriptures."

God led Jude to follow Peter's basic outline, addressing the same subject matter as Peter in a majority of his letter. Consequently, Jude's *"the faith"* (Jude 3) is equivalent to Peter's *"a faith"* (2Peter 1:1)—not two different subjects, as MacArthur incorrectly supposes.

Peter wrote, *"who have received a faith of the same kind as ours"* (2Peter 1:1). When considering how 2Peter 1:1 and Jude 3 parallel one another, Peter's readers, as well as Peter himself, had received *"the same"* overall body of truth (*"the same kind"*) recorded in the Scriptures.

Are you seeing, to even a greater degree, the thrill associated with taking your thoughts through the full counsel of God's Word? It truly is an adventure second to none.

The Contextual View of Repentance in Acts 17:30

> *Therefore having overlooked the times of ignorance, God is now*
> *declaring to men that all everywhere should repent,* (Acts 17:30)

Norm Geisler (a moderate Calvinist) discusses this passage (and several similar passages) in *Systematic Theology, Volume 3, Sin/Salvation,* page 487:

> Nowhere does the Bible teach that saving faith is a special gift
> of God to only a select few. Further, everywhere God's Word
> assumes that anyone who wills to be saved can exercise saving
> faith. Every scriptural passage that calls upon unbelievers to
> believe or repent for salvation implies this truth.[75]

I agree with Dr. Geisler's words, for the Bible clearly teaches that all people (in the midst of their depravity) are given opportunity to exercise personal repentance and faith prior to spiritual regeneration (salvation). Moderate Calvinists, however, even though believing that man possesses a free will and can exercise repentance and faith while depraved, teach that only those elected to salvation from eternity past will believe—eliminating free will altogether. Thus, the moderate Calvinists believe a contradiction.

The Contextual View of Faith in Hebrews 12:1-2

Reformed Theology (due to its distorted view of the depravity of man) also relies heavily on Hebrews 12:1-2 in its attempt to make faith God's gift to the elect prior to salvation.

175

> *Therefore, since we have so great a cloud of witnesses surrounding*
> *us, let us also lay aside every encumbrance, and the sin which so*
> *easily entangles us, and let us run with endurance the race that is*
> *set before us, 2 fixing our eyes on Jesus, the author and perfecter*
> *of faith, who for the joy set before Him endured the cross,*
> *despising the shame, and has sat down at the right hand of the*
> *throne of God.* (Hebrews 12:1-2)

One prominent Reformed theologian argues that the word *"author"* (*archegon*) means "origin, source, beginning, and then by extension, author." He then states that *"perfecter"* (*teleiotes*) refers to one who completes and perfects. Using these suppositions, he erroneously concludes that Jesus is the origin and source of the faith exercised by the "elect" prior to their being saved. In his mind, this faith is a divine faith, not a "mere" human faith generated by the depraved. What he does not mention is intriguing. Follow closely.

The word *"author"* (*archegon* in Greek), in some editions of the NASB, has a reference in the margin. The word *"leader"* is in the margin, indicating that this rendering is viable for the Greek term *archegon*. In fact, the three other occurrences of *archegon* in the Scriptures are rendered *"Prince"* on two occasions (Acts 3:15; 5:31—KJV) and *"captain"* in the other (Hebrews 2:10—KJV). *Vine's Expository Dictionary* is in agreement:

> archegos... primarily signifies one who takes a lead in, or
> provides the first occasion of, anything.... In Heb 12:2 where
> Christ is called the "Author and Perfecter of faith," He is
> represented as the One who takes precedence in faith and is
> thus the perfect exemplar of it. The pronoun "our" does not
> correspond to anything in the original, and may well be omitted.
> Christ in the days of His flesh trod undeviatingly the path of
> faith, and as the Perfecter has brought it to a perfect end in His
> own person. Thus He is the leader of all others who tread that
> path.[76]

These words fit the context of Hebrews 12:2 flawlessly, especially since Jesus truly was and is the *"leader...of faith"* (Hebrews 12:2), the greatest example that has (or ever will) grace the earth. The writer of Hebrews then wrote:

> *For consider Him who has endured such hostility by sinners*
> *against Himself, so that you may not grow weary and lose heart.*
> (Hebrews 12:3)

The recipients of this epistle were to emulate their *"leader"* (Hebrews 12:2) as they faced the trials of their day. If they followed Jesus' example, by living by the life of another (John 14:10), they would *"not grow weary and lose heart"* (Hebrews 12:3).   The encouraging news is that the recipients of Hebrews heeded the instruction of its writer.   As a result, not one of them died when Titus, a Roman general, destroyed Jerusalem and King Herod's temple in AD 70.   According to Josephus, a Jewish historian of that day, the total number of prisoners taken was 97,000—while 1.1 million people died during the battle, most of whom were Jews. The epistle to the Hebrews greatly influenced the believing Jews to abandon Jerusalem and the Law, and no Hebrew Christian died when the city fell. (Our course on Hebrews addresses this intriguing season of Jewish history in greater depth.)

The context of Hebrews 12:2 seems to make the word *"leader,"* rather than *"author,"* the better fit.   In fact, the RSV uses *"pioneer."*   This passage is absolutely not teaching that the faith exercised prior to salvation is God's gift to the elect (the Reformed view).   Jesus is the *"leader...of faith,"* the *"pioneer...of faith"*—not the supplier of the faith required prior to being made new (saved/justified).

Jesus is not only the *"leader...of faith,"* but the *"perfecter of faith"* as well (Hebrews 12:2).   Once the depraved choose to repent and believe and God makes them *"new"* (2Corinthians 5:17), their *"faith is greatly enlarged"* (2Thessalonians 1:3) as they grow *"from faith to faith"* (Romans 1:16-17) in their knowledge of Christ.   Their intimacy with the One Who is their *"life"* (2Corinthians 3:18; Colossians 3:4) increases as well.

A quote from R.C. Sproul's, *Faith Alone*, page 26, is fitting to examine at this time. Our present study allows the informed student to refute his argument:

> All who are regenerated are changed. Reformed theology views regeneration as the immediate supernatural work of the Holy Spirit that effects the change of the soul's disposition. Before regeneration the sinner is in the grips of original sin, by which he is totally disinclined toward God. He is in willing bondage to sin and has no desire for Christ. Faith is a fruit of regeneration. The believer is a changed person. He is still a sinner but is in a process of spiritual reversal that has, by the efficacious work of the Holy Spirit, already begun.[77]

Sproul believes that "Faith is a fruit of regeneration."   Thus, he views faith (the faith exercised prior to salvation) as God's gift to the "elect" once they are spiritually regenerated.   In other words, Sproul believes that God spiritually regenerates the "elect" and follows by granting them faith so they can believe and be saved.   However, the Scriptures teach that spiritual regeneration and salvation/justification are one and the same, and that faith is exercised by the depraved prior to salvation/spiritual regeneration (read John 1:12, 3:15, Acts 16:31, and Romans 10:9-10).

Sproul also classifies a person who has been spiritually regenerated (according to his definition of spiritual regeneration—that salvation is subsequent to spiritual regeneration) as a "sinner." The Scriptures teach, however, that the spiritually regenerated are not only saved/justified, but also *"holy"* (Ephesians 1:4), *"complete"* (Colossians 2:10), *"righteous"* (2Corinthians 5:21), *"glorified"* (Romans 8:30), *"saints"* of God (1Corinthians 1:2)—and a great deal more.

My question is simple, yet problematic for Reformed Theology. If spiritual regeneration (being born again—John 3:3-6 teaches that being *"born again"* is equivalent to salvation) does nothing more than transform the "elect" into sinners (Sproul's view), when do the "elect" become holy and blameless saints? Is it after physical death? If so, the cross was insufficient in carrying out God's plan of salvation. The Scriptures teach that New Testament believers are *"sanctified"* (made holy) in their souls and spirits the moment they are spiritually regenerated (born again—saved/justified). The Scriptures also teach that this sanctification can occur through only one avenue—*"through the offering of the body of Jesus Christ once for all."*

> By this will we have been sanctified through the offering of the
> body of Jesus Christ once for all. (Hebrews 10:10)

Hebrews 10:14 confirms this same truth:

> For by one offering He has perfected for all time those who are
> sanctified. (NASB)

> because by one sacrifice he has made perfect forever those who are
> being made holy. (NIV)

These passages prove that New Testament believers are *"sanctified"* and *"made perfect"* (Hebrews 10:10, 14) in soul and spirit (in their person) the moment they are spiritually regenerated (saved/justified), while their behavior is *"being made holy"* (Hebrews 10:14 NIV) on an ongoing basis. Therefore, the spiritually regenerated (saved/justified) saint is anything but a lowly "sinner." (Our courses, *Hebrews* and *Romans 1-8*, cover much more on this subject.)

Conclusion

Jesus is the "leader" and "pioneer" of *"faith"* (Hebrews 12:2), not the supplier of the faith required prior to salvation.

CHAPTER EIGHTEEN

A WORKS-BASED SALVATION – FREE WILL OR REFORMED THEOLOGY

REFORMED THEOLOGY (extreme and hyper Calvinism), believing that the faith exercised prior to salvation/justification is God's gift to the spiritually regenerated who are not yet saved/justified, views those who adhere to "free will" as teaching a works-based salvation. Norm Geisler, a moderate Calvinist (and, therefore, no proponent of Reformed Theology), in *Systematic Theology, Volume 3, Sin/Salvation*, (pages 488-489) writes:

> J.I. Packer and O.R. Johnston have said that "Reformed theology condemned Arminianism as being in principle a return to Rome (because in effect it turned faith into a meritorious work). R.C. Sproul seems to agree:
>
>> The Arminian acknowledges that faith is something a person does. It is a work, though not a meritorious one. Is it a good work? Certainly it is not a bad work. It is good for a person to trust in Christ and in Christ alone for his or her salvation....[Thus] the Arminian finds it difficult to escape the conclusion that ultimately his salvation rests on some righteous act of the will he has performed. He has "in effect" merited the merit of Christ, which differs only slightly from the view of Rome. (CG, 25-26)[78]

Geisler counters by saying:

This is an inaccurate description of Arminianism. As earlier
cited, Jacob Arminius long ago replied to this charge:

> A rich man bestows, on a poor and famished beggar,
> alms by which he may be able to maintain himself and
> his family. Does it cease to be a pure gift, because the
> beggar extends his hand to receive it? Can it be said
> with propriety that "the alms depend partly on the
> liberality of the Donor, and partly on the liberty of the
> Receiver, though the latter would not have possessed
> the alms unless he had received it by stretching out his
> hand?"... If these assertions cannot be truly made about
> a beggar who receives alms, how much less can they be
> made about the gift of faith, for the receiving of which
> far more acts of Divine Grace are required! (WJA,
> 2.52.27)[79]

A great gulf exists between the Reformed view and Arminianism; even though I am a follower of neither, I find their differences intriguing. In fact, I have very much enjoyed reading their arguments while researching this subject matter.

I am not "Arminian" for several reasons, one of which is its view of election. Arminians view unregenerate man as responsible for exercising repentance and faith prior to salvation/justification. No problem here. However, they perceive God as having looked into the future from eternity past, and after seeing who would believe, electing them to salvation from eternity past by means of an eternal decree. In our study of *God's Heart as it Relates to Foreknowledge-Predestination*, we addressed why this mindset is not in agreement with the Scriptures. (Reference Diagram 2 for additional input)

I am not a follower of Reformed Theology for several reasons, one of which is its view of faith. Reformed Theology views faith as God's gift to the "elect" subsequent to spiritual regeneration. Yet, according to John 3:1-15, spiritual regeneration (being "born again") is equivalent to salvation/justification. Thus, the Reformed view has salvation/justification preceding the faith exercised for salvation. Such reasoning is nonsensical. In fact, it is exactly opposite of what Paul taught in Romans 5:1:

> *Therefore having been justified by faith, we have peace with God*
> *through our Lord Jesus Christ,* (Romans 5:1)

Faith (believing) always precedes justification (spiritual regeneration). Hence, Reformed Theology reverses the Scriptural order.

How Arminianism and Calvinism <u>Generally</u> View Faith's Relationship to Depravity

<u>Arminianism</u>— The faith exercised prior to salvation originates with unregenerate man (the depraved), and is dependent upon man's choice—but does not occur without the Spirit's conviction (John 16:8) and the Father's drawing (John 6:44). This faith, therefore, is <u>not</u> God's gift. Faith will be exercised by the elect only, and no elect person will die without exercising it.

<u>Moderate Calvinism</u>— The faith exercised prior to salvation originates with unregenerate man (the depraved), and is dependent upon man's choice—but does not occur without the Spirit's conviction (John 16:8) and the Father's drawing (John 6:44). This faith, therefore, is <u>not</u> God's gift. Faith will be exercised by the elect only, and no elect person will die without exercising it.

<u>Extreme Calvinism</u>— The faith exercised prior to salvation <u>is</u> God's gift to the spiritually regenerated because the depraved are incapable of believing. Thus, God must spiritually regenerate the elect and give them faith before they can believe and be saved.

<u>Hyper-Calvinism</u>— The faith exercised prior to salvation <u>is</u> God's gift to the spiritually regenerated because the depraved are incapable of believing. Thus, God must spiritually regenerate the elect and give them faith before they can believe and be saved.

<u>The Scriptural View</u>— The faith exercised prior to salvation originates with man while in his depraved state. This faith is dependent on man's choice (in the midst of his depravity), but does not occur without the Spirit's conviction (John 16:8) and the Father's drawing (John 6:44). Thus, the faith exercised prior to salvation (addressed in Ephesians 2:8-9) is <u>not</u> God's gift. In conjunction with being placed in Christ and made new (after repentance and faith are exercised while depraved), the New Testament believer is given "*a measure of faith*" (Romans 12:3) to function within the area of his/her spiritual gifting.

We, by no means, have exhausted our study of "faith" and how it relates to depravity, but at least some of the more debated verses associated with the subject have been observed. As the course progresses, additional passages will be examined that confirm our findings. The faith exercised by the depraved prior to salvation is not a work. Later, in the fourth book of this series titled *God's Heart as it Relates to Election-Atonement-Grace-Perseverance*, we will discover that the elect of Reformed Theology must perform good deeds in an attempt to validate their election. Yes, the "P" of the TULIP (Perseverance of the Saints) is legalism at its best!

The Hill

CHAPTER NINETEEN

A SHORT BUT ENCOURAGING DETOUR

MY DESIRE IS THAT WE VIEW GOD PROPERLY, and in turn, be able to defend what we believe regarding His heart. Hence, we need to take a short detour and address a subject that is somewhat intimidating on the surface, but "user friendly" in the end. Therefore, don't allow the terminology associated with its beginning stages to threaten you. In fact, you will likely find this portion of the study extremely encouraging since it takes the truths from *God's Heart as it Relates to Foreknowledge-Predestination* as well as *God's Heart as it Relates to Sovereignty-Free Will,* and weaves them flawlessly into our present study, *God's Heart as it Relates to Depravity.*

As we continue, keep in mind what we discovered in *God's Heart as it Relates to Foreknowledge-Predestination* regarding God's decrees. They are *"eternal"* (Jeremiah 5:22), meaning that they (every one of them) have always existed in God's heart. As a result, God's decrees cannot be sequential—one after the other.

This fact ties in more with our study of "Depravity" than one might imagine, especially since extreme and hyper-Calvinists (Reformed theologians) believe that unregenerate man is so depraved that God was required to elect the elect to salvation by means of an eternal decree. This erroneous view of election stems from their improper view of depravity, which will not, under any circumstance, allow for the depraved to choose to believe. Thus, according to the Reformed view, God must make that choice for the elect before they are born. Yet, Reformed Theology has concluded that God's "eternal" decrees were issued sequentially—according to a certain order.

Arminians and moderate Calvinists believe that God's eternal decrees were issued sequentially as well, even though they view man as capable of choosing Christ while depraved.

My question is: "Can an order be associated with God's eternal decrees and all the decrees remain eternal?" In other words, if "eternal" means no beginning and no end, can one eternal decree precede another eternal decree and all the decrees remain eternal? We will discover that this situation is impossible, yet Arminianism and all forms of Calvinism adopt this view. Norm Geisler, a moderate Calvinist, discusses the subject in *Systematic Theology, Volume 3, Sin/Salvation*, pages 184-185:

The Order of God's Decrees

Whereas there is general agreement on the *origin* of salvation, theologians have long debated the *order* of God's salvific decrees. The fact of God's election is clear in Scripture; it is the progression of His choices relating to election that is the subject of much dialogue.

The main discussion on the order of God's decrees has followed along the lines indicated by the chart below, the primary question being whether God decreed to elect before or after He decreed to permit the Fall (Lat: *lapsus*).

The chart begins with the most Calvinistic on the left and proceeds to the Arminian (i.e., Wesleyan) view on the right. Various terms on the chart will be subsequently defined and explained.

THE ORDER OF GOD'S DECREES

Hyper Supralapsarianism	Strong (Extreme) Infralapsarianism	Moderate Supralapsarianism	Arminian Wesleyanism
(1) Decree to elect some and reprobate others	(1) Decree to create all	(1) Decree to create all	(1) Decree to create all
(2) Decree to create both the elect and the non-elect	(2) Decree to permit the Fall	(2) Decree to permit the Fall	(2) Decree to permit the Fall
(3) Decree to permit the Fall	(3) Decree to elect some and pass others by	(3) Decree to provide salvation for all	(3) Decree to provide salvation for all
(4) Decree to provide salvation only for the elect	(4) Decree to provide salvation only for the elect	(4) Decree to elect those who believe and pass by those who do not	(4) Decree to elect based on the foreseen faith of believers
(5) Decree to apply salvation only to the elect	(5) Decree to apply salvation only to the elect	(5) Decree to apply salvation only to believers (who cannot lose it)	(5) Decree to apply salvation only to believers (who can lose it)

The term *supralapsarian* is from the Latin *supra* (*above*) and *lapsus* (*fall*), meaning that God's decree of election (predestination) is considered by supralapsarians to be *above*, or logically prior to, His decree to permit the Fall. Since *infra* means "below," the infralapsarians consider God's decree of election to be beneath, or logically after, His decree to permit the Fall. The sublapsarians...are similar to the infralapsarians, except they place God's order to provide salvation before His order to elect....Wesleyans adhere to the same basic order as infralapsarians, except they hold that God's election is *based on His foreknowledge* rather than simply *in accord with it*. Hence, for Wesleyans (Arminians), God's decree is conditional instead of unconditional (which is maintained by the three Calvinistic views).

Supralapsarians are *hyper*-Calvinists, being double-predestinarians. Infralapsarians are *strong* [extreme] Calvinists but are not double-predestinarians. Sublapsarians...are

185

> *moderate* Calvinists, holding to unlimited atonement. Again, Wesleyans are Arminians, insisting that election is conditional, not unconditional. Wesleyans also do not believe in eternal security, while adherents to the other views do.[80]

Dr. Geisler, understanding that viewing God's decrees as sequential is contradictory, attempts to reconcile the contradiction on pages 185-186 of *Systematic Theology, Volume 3, Sin/Salvation*:

> ## The Sequence of God's Decrees
>
> One of the primary problems with this discussion is the way it has been framed, namely, on the assumption that there is an order in the decrees of God. In view of God's attributes, one thing is clear: Whatever order there may be in God's choices, it is not chronological, since an eternal Being has no chronological sequence. God is both simple and eternal, and, as such, He does not think or act sequentially.
>
> *There Is No Chronological Order in God's Decrees*
>
> Being eternal (nontemporal), God does not have any time-related sequence in His thoughts or decisions. Whatever things He has thought and whatever actions He has done, He has thought and done simultaneously, from all eternity.
>
> *There Is No Logical Order in God's Decrees*
>
> Is there a logical order, though, to God's decrees? Not for Him. God does not think sequentially (i.e., discursively, having one thought after another). He knows all things immediately and intuitively in Himself, since He is simple, eternal, and immutable in His Being. As such, all that He knows and chooses is known and performed immediately and intuitively, from all eternity.
>
> *There Is an Operational Order in God's Decrees*
>
> Of course, there is an operational order in the execution of God's decrees. God eternally willed things to happen in a certain temporal sequence (one after another), just as a doctor wills in advance the patient's cure by prescribing, for instance, the ingestion of a pill a day for a week. Hence, God willed, for

> example, that Creation would occur before the Fall, and that
> salvation would be provided after the Fall.
>   It makes no sense to speak of God having a logical order in
> His mind, as though one of His thoughts followed after another.
> All thoughts are known by God in one eternal contuition (i.e., co-
> intuition). As a simple Being, He therefore knows all things
> simply, which is why the Bible speaks of election as being *"in
> accordance with"* His will (Eph. 1:5; cf. 1Peter 1:2) and not
> based on or independent of other attributes. *All* of God's
> attributes, thoughts, and decisions are eternal in accord with
> one another, and none is logically dependent on or independent
> of another. If it were, there would be a contradictory logical
> sequence in a God who has no multiplicity, not even in His
> thoughts.[81]

Dr. Geisler tells much about his views of God's nature in this series of quotes. However, he fails to reconcile the fact that God's foreknowledge must precede the election of a New Testament believer.

> *Elect according to the foreknowledge of God...* 1Peter 1:2 (KJV)

The phrase *"according to"* (1Peter 1:2) is used 790 times in the New American Standard Bible, and 725 in the King James. On occasion, it is found more than once in a verse. The action or entity that follows the words *"according to"* (such as God's *"foreknowledge"* in 1Peter 1:2) must occur (or exist) before the action or entity that precedes the words *"according to"* (such as *"elect"* in 1Peter 1:2). In other words:

If **A** is according to **B**

Then **B** precedes **A**

This principle applies in every instance where *"according to"* is used in the Scriptures. Consequently, God's *"foreknowledge"* must precede His election of the *"Elect"*—that is, if we are to remain true to the full counsel of His Word. For this reason, some people have attempted to redefine *"foreknowledge"* as "foreordination" (a subject discussed in depth in *God's Heart as it Relates to Foreknowledge-Predestination*). After all, if *"foreknowledge"* is allowed to retain its meaning ("to know beforehand"), election, as defined by the Calvinists, cannot stand. God cannot foreknow what has always existed!

This inconsistency presents a huge problem for not only Calvinism but Arminianism as well. If the Scriptures require God's foreknowledge to precede election (1Peter 1:2 KJV), and election should come about by means of God's eternal decree (as Arminians and Calvinists believe), then eternity would have a beginning, which would nullify eternity entirely. (Diagram 2, "Why God's Foreknowledge Cannot Precede His Eternal Decrees," located in the Reference Section, addresses this subject in graphic form.) This contradiction results from incorrectly viewing God as having chosen the elect to salvation from eternity past (by means of an eternal decree) rather than correctly perceiving Him as choosing (electing) New Testament believers to a special office once they are in Christ— after they exercise personal repentance and faith while depraved. Let's now simplify this wonderful truth.

Election (the New Testament believer's chosenness) occurs after the depraved exercise personal repentance and faith, as outlined below:

1. The depraved choose Christ by exercising personal repentance and faith.

2. After exercising personal repentance and faith, the depraved are placed into Christ through the avenue of the "*Spirit*" (1Corinthians 12:13), "*crucified*" (Romans 6:6; Galatians 2:20), and made "*new*" (2Corinthians 5:17).

3. As a result of the New Testament believer being in Christ, in the "*chosen [elect] one*" of God (Isaiah 42:1), Jesus Himself, he is automatically chosen, or elected (Ephesians 1:4), to a special office within Christ's body (given a special spiritual gift—1Peter 4:10).

4. Because Jesus possesses eternal life, with no beginning or end, the New Testament believer receives this type of life in conjunction with being made new—and is perceived by the Father as having always been in Christ.

5. Because the Father views the church saint as having always been in Christ, all New Testament believers are perceived by the Father as having been "*in Him before the foundation of the world*" (Ephesians 1:4) once they are made new after repenting and believing while depraved.

For a graphic assessment of this full counsel view, go to Diagram 8 ("Scriptural Election/Chosenness and Predestination") in the Reference Section. Based on this interpretation, the New Testament believer can be chosen in Christ in conjunction with being placed in Christ ("*in Him*"—Ephesians 1:4), after having exercised personal faith (and repentance) while depraved—yet be viewed by the Father as having been chosen in Christ "*before the foundation of the world.*" This arrangement, therefore, allows New Testament believers to be saved due to a decision they make while depraved rather than a decision God made from eternity past. The depraved choose to repent and believe—God does the saving. This unshakable truth verifies that the New Testament saint is chosen (elected) to a special office in the body of Christ in conjunction with being placed in Christ <u>after</u> repenting and believing while depraved—rather than having been chosen (elected) to salvation from eternity past by means of an eternal decree (as Arminianism and all forms of Calvinism suppose). This scenario allows God's foreknowledge to precede the election (chosenness) of the New Testament believer, just as the Scriptures prescribe (1Peter 1:1-2)—refer to Diagram 2 in the Reference Section, "Why God's Foreknowledge Cannot Precede His Eternal Decrees." The notes associated with Ephesians 1:4 in our previous *God's Heart* studies (*Foreknowledge-Predestination* and *Sovereignty-Free Will*) add more input regarding this fascinating subject.

Conclusion

Unregenerate man is <u>not</u> so spiritually depraved that he cannot choose Christ. Thus, the depraved <u>can</u> choose to repent and believe. Therefore, God is <u>not</u> required to elect the "elect" (the chosen) to salvation from eternity past by means of an eternal decree. Rather, the New Testament believers' chosenness (election) has to do with the special office (or position) that God gives all church saints in Christ—<u>after</u> they have exercised personal repentance and faith while depraved. Hence, after believing (and repenting) while depraved, we became new creations as a result of the *"Spirit"* (1Corinthians 12:13) placing us in Jesus Himself (2Corinthians 5:17). Once in Him (in God's *"chosen one"*—Isaiah 42:1 NASB), we were chosen (elected) to a special office within Christ's body. God now sees us as having been *"in Him,"* in Christ, from eternity past (*before the foundation of the world"*—Ephesians 1:4) due to the type of life, eternal life, we received in His Son. Consequently, <u>God saves (justifies) all New Testament believers in Christ due to a decision they make while depraved, not due to a decision He made from eternity past.</u> This order of events prevents the need for God's eternal decrees to be viewed as sequential, an erroneous idea adopted by Calvinism and Arminianism alike.

All of the confusion within Calvinism stems from its extreme view of depravity. In fact, Edwin Palmer in, *The Five Points of Calvinism*, page 19, states that depravity is:

> ...the most central issue between the Arminian and the Calvinist, what Martin Luther even said was the hinge on which the whole Reformation turned."[82]

Thus, refute the Reformed view of total depravity and you eliminate Reformed Theology (extreme and hyper-Calvinism) altogether. Yet, Calvin himself refuted it in the following quotes from *Institutes*:

> *Institutes*: Book 2; Chapter 2, Section 18— I deny not, indeed, that in the writings of philosophers we meet occasionally with shrewd and apposite remarks on the nature of God, though they invariably savour somewhat of giddy imagination. As observed above, <u>the Lord has bestowed on them some slight perception of his Godhead</u> that they might not plead ignorance as an excuse for their impiety, and has, at times, instigated them to deliver some truths, the confession of which should be their own condemnation. Still, though seeing, they saw not. Their discernment was not such as to direct them to the truth, far less to enable them to attain it, but resembled that of the bewildered traveler, who sees the flash of lightning glance far and wide for a moment, and then vanish into the darkness of the night, before he can advance a single step.[83]

> *Institutes*: Book 2; Chapter 2, Section 22— "When the Gentiles, which have not the law, do by nature the things contained in the law, these, having not the law, are a law unto themselves: which show the work of the law written in their hearts, their conscience also bearing witness, and their thoughts the meantime accusing or else excusing one another." (Rom 2: 14, 15) If the Gentiles have the righteousness of the law naturally engraven on their minds, <u>we certainly cannot say that they are altogether blind</u> as to the rule of life. Nothing, indeed is more common, than for man to be sufficiently instructed in a right course of conduct by natural law, of which the Apostle here speaks.[84]

Based on these statements, Calvin (without realizing it) denied Reformed Theology's "T" of the TULIP, Total Depravity—that the depraved are spiritual corpses. Yet, in other writings he upheld the "T" with persistent fervor, contradicting the previous quotes. So which is it? Are the depraved totally blind, a spiritual corpse (the Reformed view), or has God granted them a measure of sight? Calvin failed to communicate his answer void of contradiction, even though he vehemently criticized those who view the depraved as capable of choosing to repent and believe.

The question that must be answered in regard to the Reformed view of total depravity is: If God gives the depraved "some slight perception of his godhead" (according to Calvin), what kept Him from giving them enough to choose to repent and believe? Reformed Theology's answer to this question is dreadful: <u>He needed something on which to display His wrath so the elect can possess a greater appreciation of His grace.</u> Thus, in the Reformed mind, God is capable of saving all (due to His sovereignty), yet chooses to save only some, so His wrath against the non-elect (who are never given opportunity to believe) might encourage the elect. Is this your perception of the God of the Scriptures?

As a result of the time invested in this study, God has given us some very special tools by which to interpret the Scriptures. Let's use these tools to dig deeper into our study of His heart by addressing additional verses that grant the depraved the freedom to believe. These same tools will be used to dismantle Reformed Theology's "T" (Total Depravity) by addressing some of their favorite passages.

CHAPTER TWENTY

ADDITIONAL PASSAGES USED BY CALVINISTS REGARDING TOTAL DEPRAVITY

John 1:5, John 1:11 and Depravity

And the light shines in the darkness, and the darkness did not comprehend it. (John 1:5)

He came to His own, and those who were His own did not receive Him. (John 1:11)

Edwin Palmer, a Reformed theologian, on page 15 of *The Five Points of Calvinism* addresses John 1:11 in regards to John 1:5:

> During the ministry of Jesus, the Jews rejected Him. "He came to his own and his own did not receive him" (John 1:11). The trouble was not in the presentation of the truth. The Truth was there. Jesus was the Son of God incarnate. The Light shone in the darkness, but the darkness <u>could not</u> comprehend it. [85]

A vast difference exists between *"did not"* (John 1:5) and "could not" (Palmer's rendering). Yes, a great disparity exists between, *"and the darkness did not comprehend it"* (John 1:5) and "the darkness <u>could not</u> comprehend it" (Palmer's quote). The two statements are nowhere near equivalent. Interestingly, Palmer makes the switch without commenting on the fact that he did so. Yet, the NASB,

193

ASV, RSV, KJV, NKJV, NASB Updated, even the NIV and Living Bible, never use "could not." Even my Greek interlinear translates: *"it not comprehended."* Those who remained in *"darkness"* (John 1:5) at Jesus' First Coming did so due to refusing to believe, not because they could not believe.

1Corinthians 12:3 and Depravity

> *Therefore I make known to you, that no one speaking by the Spirit of God says, "Jesus is accursed"; and no one can say, "Jesus is Lord," except by the Holy Spirit.* (1Corinthians 12:3)

This verse warns against listening to false instruction. However, Reformed theologians such as Steele, Thomas, and Quinn use it in an attempt to justify their definition of total depravity and irresistible grace, for example, in *The Five Points of Calvinism*, on pages 54-55:

> The doctrine of irresistible or efficacious grace is set forth in the Westminster Confession of Faith in these words: "All those whom God hath predestined unto life, and those only, He is pleased, in His appointed and accepted time, effectually to call, by His Word and Spirit, out of that state of sin and death [depravity], in which they are by nature, to grace and salvation, by Jesus Christ; enlightening their minds spiritually and savingly to understand the things of God, taking away their heart of stone, and giving unto them an heart of flesh; renewing their wills, and by His almighty power; determining them to that which is good, and effectually drawing them to Jesus Christ: yet so, as they come most freely, being made willing by His grace."[86]

On page 53 of this same work, Steele, Thomas, and Quinn record: (As you read, note how their exaggerated view of depravity affects their understanding of "regeneration.")

> The inward change wrought in the elect sinner [the change that results from Reformed theology's spiritual "regeneration"] enables him to understand and believe spiritual truth; in the spiritual realm, he is given the seeing eye and the hearing ear. The Spirit creates within him a new heart or a new nature. This is accomplished through regeneration or the new birth by which the sinner is made a child of God and is given spiritual life. His will is renewed thorough this process, so that the sinner

> spontaneously comes to Christ of his own free choice. Because
> he is given a new nature so that he loves righteousness, and
> because his mind is enlightened so that he understands and
> believes the biblical gospel, the renewed sinner freely and
> willingly turns to Christ as Lord and Savior. Thus, the once dead
> sinner is drawn to Christ by the inward, supernatural call of the
> Spirit, who through regeneration makes him alive and creates
> faith and repentance within him.[87]

According to Steele, Thomas, and Quinn, "regeneration" results in a sinner receiving "a new heart or a new nature." This "regeneration" (according to their opinion) also causes that individual to be "made a child of God," after which he is drawn by the Father and given repentance, faith, and a new will. A "choice" is then made to repent and believe, and he is finally saved.

Wow! Such an interpretation, if correct, would mean that "regeneration" is separate from salvation (justification)—which is the Reformed view. Yet, the Scriptures teach that regeneration, new birth, and salvation are all one and the same. In fact, a person becomes a new "creation" (receives salvation, experiences new birth) through only one avenue—being placed *"in Christ"* (2Corinthians 5:17) subsequent to repenting and exercising faith while depraved (Galatians 3:26). The fact that scripture disallows the notion that a person becomes a new creation <u>before</u> he is saved (justified) is problematic for the Reformed theologian. Because scriptural "regeneration" is the same as becoming a new "creation" (becoming God's child and receiving salvation), what need would exist for God to grant repentance and faith to those spiritually regenerated, since they are already saved. In other words, why would they need to be saved if they are already God's children? Such an arrangement would make no sense.

Reformed Theology's extreme view of sovereignty, that God must be the cause of all things, creates a great deal of confusion. They realize that for their type of sovereignty to exist, it would be impossible for unregenerate man (the depraved) to make a choice to exercise personal repentance and faith. Thus, in their minds at least, the choice had to be God's alone from eternity past. Hence, total depravity is defined by Reformed Theology as "total inability." However, the contextual view of 1Corinthians 12:3 communicates something entirely different, as explained, very simply below.

Paul warned the Corinthians, who were previously *led astray* when they were *pagans* (1Corinthians 12:2), to be aware of the difference between true and false teachers—what is of God and what is not of God.

> *Therefore I make known to you, that no one speaking by the Spirit*
> *of God says, "Jesus is accursed"; and no one can say, "Jesus is*
> *Lord," except by the Holy Spirit.* (1Corinthians 12:3)

The teachers who taught that *"Jesus is accursed"* were not under the influence of *"the Spirit of God."* They were to be avoided. Those who taught that *"Jesus is Lord"* did so only through *"the Holy Spirit."* The words of these Spirit-led teachers were to be accepted by the Corinthian believers. As was mentioned earlier, this verse is easily interpreted (void of contradiction) when viewed in proper context.

Genesis 6:3 and Depravity

> *Then the LORD said, "My Spirit shall not strive with man*
> *forever,...* (Genesis 6:3)

God's Spirit was striving with unregenerate man even in the days of Noah. Scripture teaches, therefore, that God's Spirit strives with the depraved, bidding them to exercise personal repentance and faith. Why would God strive with individuals who lack the ability to repent and believe—which would be the case should Reformed Theology's definition of total depravity be valid? Dave Hunt (who is not a Calvinist), in *What Love Is This?*, page 141, writes:

> The Calvinist insists that being spiritually dead in sin means that man can no more hear the gospel or respond to God than if he were physically dead. Yet in the very context of the first expose of man's wicked heart, which the Calvinist offers as proof of Total Depravity, we hear God saying, "My spirit shall not always strive with man" (Genesis 6:3).
> How can there be a real "striving" if man is dead in sin and therefore cannot even hear, much less be persuaded? Why would the Spirit of God *strive* with a *corpse*? And how could God be sincerely striving to convince those to believe for whom Christ did not die, and from whom He withholds the faith to believe? The entire teaching of Calvinism denies *sincerity* on God's part in seemingly offering salvation to those He has no intention of saving.[88]

Man's freedom to repent and believe while depraved is the only answer to God's striving with mankind—every person and not just some. Because the depraved (all the depraved and not just a select few) possess the capacity to repent and believe, God is free to sincerely strive with man and retain His sovereignty, even in those cases where man rejects His free offer of salvation. God, in His sovereignty, granted man a free will, without someone holding Him at gunpoint while choosing to do so. Therefore, should the depraved possess no capacity to repent and believe, as Reformed Theology espouses, God's striving would be insincere with those who reject His offer, flawing His character in the process. Such a scenario would not only prove Him foolish, but also lacking in sovereignty.

God's Spirit strives with man from Genesis through Revelation. Jesus says of the Holy Spirit, in John 16:8:

> *And He, when He comes, will convict the world concerning sin,*
> *and righteousness, and judgment;* (John 16:8)

"World" means "the inhabited earth," pointing to all persons and not just some. The Spirit convicts the *"world"* of *"sin, and righteousness, and judgment,"* meaning that every person has opportunity to repent and exercise personal faith while depraved. Even the unbelieving (and unregenerate) Jewish leaders were convicted by Jesus' words according to John 8:9:

> *And when they heard it, they began to go out one by one, beginning*
> *with the older ones, and He was left alone, and the woman, where*
> *she was, in the midst.* (John 8:9)

Yes, the Spirit of God convicts all persons of their need for a Savior. God requires, however, that the depraved exercise personal repentance and faith <u>prior to</u> becoming part of His family. If they refuse His offer, He retains His sovereignty (due to having granted them a free will), yet takes no *"pleasure"* in their callous response:

> *Do I have any pleasure in the death of the wicked,"* declares the
> *Lord GOD, "rather than that he should turn from his ways and*
> *live?* (Ezekiel 18:23)

Romans 10:9-10 dovetails with what we have addressed thus far.

Romans 10:9-10 and Depravity

> *that if you confess with your mouth Jesus as Lord, and believe in*
> *your heart that God raised Him from the dead, you shall be saved;*
> *10 for with the heart man believes, resulting in righteousness, and*
> *with the mouth he confesses, resulting in salvation.* (Romans 10:9-
> 10)

This passage not only confirms that exercising personal faith in one's depravity precedes *"salvation"* but also disputes Reformed Theology's supposition that God must give a person faith in order for salvation to occur. No need exists for the depraved to be spiritually regenerated (and given faith—by God) before they can believe—as Reformed Theology supposes; neither does God grant the necessary faith. The Greek verb for *"confess,"* *homologeo* and the Greek verb for *"believe,"* *pisteuo* are both in the active voice which indicates that the subject is performing the action. Thus, *you,* the subject of Romans 10:9-10, meaning anyone in a depraved state, is the source of the action, the action being confessing and believing. If God were supplying the faith and regenerating an individual in his depravity before he could confess and believe as Reformed Theology presumes, then *homologeo, "confess"* and *pisteuo, "believe"* would be in the passive voice, which would show that an outside source, someone other than the subject of the sentence, would be supplying the action. Thus God is not the progenitor of the faith needed for salvation.

The order of events in these two verses demonstrates the chronological sequence of salvation: if you confess and believe, you shall be saved. No mention of any necessary, preceding regeneration by God is included. Therefore, prior spiritual regeneration before a depraved individual can confess and believe is not part of the process.

John MacArthur (a Reformed theologian), in *The MacArthur Study Bible*, gives the following commentary on Romans 10:9. The fact that he does not address such a significant sequence of events, *"confess...and believe...you shall be saved,"* is most interesting.

> Confess...Jesus as Lord. Not a simple acknowledgement that He is God and the Lord of the universe, since even demons acknowledge that to be true (Jas 2:19). This is the deep personal conviction, without reservation, that Jesus is that person's own master or sovereign. This phrase includes repenting from sin, trusting in Jesus for salvation, and submitting to Him as Lord. This is the volitional element of faith (see note on 1:16).[89]

MacArthur sounds like, on the surface at least, that he could be a "freewiller"— the label some Reformed theologians place on those who believe that the depraved can exercise personal repentance and faith. MacArthur fails to mention that his view of total depravity requires the Lord to spiritually regenerate the depraved (along with grant them repentance and faith) before they can choose to repent, believe, and be saved. Interestingly, his commentary on Romans 1:16, covered previously in this study, states:

> ...True saving faith is supernatural, a gracious gift of God that
> He produces in the heart (see note on Eph 2:8)....[90]

MacArthur may have referenced this note, requiring the reader to turn back to Romans 1:16 (instead of stating them outright in his commentary on Romans 10:9) because Romans 10:9 proves (beyond doubt) that the depraved are capable of exercising faith <u>prior</u> to being spiritually regenerated—refuting his argument altogether. Let's follow MacArthur's trail and observe his commentary on Ephesians 2:8, to which he referred in his previous quote:

> ...Although men are required to believe for salvation, even that
> faith is part of the gift of God which saves and cannot be
> exercised by one's own power.[91]

Again, we see that MacArthur perceives "faith" (the faith that God requires before bestowing salvation) as God's gift to the elect, even though we have proven that the confessing and believing originate with the depraved individual doing the confessing and believing. In addition, MacArthur, a Reformed theologian, views this faith as being received <u>after</u> God brings the elect out of their depravity through spiritual regeneration. Why does MacArthur not state this belief outright in his commentary on Romans 10:9? Romans 10:9-10 refutes his argument! After all, should God be required to spiritually regenerate the depraved and grant them repentance and faith <u>before</u> they can repent, believe, and be saved, Reformed Theology's spiritual regeneration would leave man unsaved (in their minds at least), since God requires that repentance and faith precede justification (salvation—Romans 5:1). How, therefore, can a person be born again before he repents, believes, and is saved, when John 3:1-14 teaches that being born again is equivalent to receiving salvation? Such is impossible! (For more input, review the notes associated with John 3:3-6—addressed in Chapter Nine.)

My point is this: God cannot spiritually regenerate a person and that person remain unsaved. Is it any wonder that Reformed Theology has never reconciled this major imperfection within their system of reasoning?

We have proven that God is <u>not</u> required to spiritually regenerate the depraved, and grant them repentance and faith, before they can repent, believe, and be saved and that the faith required for salvation originates with the depraved, not with God. If either of the suppositions posed by Reformed Theology were valid, Paul would likely have included them in Romans 10. Yet, we find not the slightest trace of either in Romans 10 or any of Paul's writings.

Wayne Grudem avoids Romans 10:9-10 in the Scripture index of his work: *Bible Doctrine, Essential Teachings of the Christian Faith.* However, on page 301 he writes about "regeneration," confirming that he also has failed to resolve Reformed Theology's contradictions relating to regeneration:

> ...Scripture indicates that regeneration must come before we can respond to effective calling with saving faith....As the gospel comes to us, God speaks through it to summon us to himself (effectual calling) and to give us new spiritual life (regeneration) so that we are enabled to respond in faith....regeneration is God the Father and God the Holy Spirit working powerfully in us to make us alive.[92]

Grudem fails to recognize the flaw in his argument or site any scriptural support. How can a person be made "alive" (spiritually) by God <u>prior</u> to exercising repentance and faith for the purpose of coming alive through God's salvation? Such a scenario would have man saved <u>twice</u>—a total impossibility.

We find a wealth of truth in Romans 10:9-10, some of which is listed below. What extraordinary news the Lord has given us in His Word regarding how man can be saved:

1. *"Heart"* is the inner being of a person, which points to the <u>mind</u>, the mind being part of the soul. From within the mind faith springs forth. In other words, you believe with your mind.

2. No one can be saved without believing.

3. The faith required for salvation originates with the depraved. In other words, the confessing and believing are done by the depraved, not by God for the depraved.

4. For salvation to occur, you must *"confess with your mouth"* and *"believe in your heart."*

5. One must *"confess....Jesus as Lord"* to be saved, in other words, believe that Jesus is Deity.

6. Believing in the resurrection of Jesus Christ is essential for salvation— *"believe in your heart that God raised Him from the dead."*

7. More is involved in the personal faith exercised by the depraved than understanding the truth associated with salvation. Faith is an act of the will whereby the truth is accepted and acted upon.

8.   Man <u>can</u> exercise faith while depraved.

Let's take the scriptural tools we now possess and allow them, with the assistance of the Holy Spirit, to rightly divide Acts 16:14.

Acts 16:14 and Depravity

> *And a certain woman named Lydia, from the city of Thyatira, a seller of purple fabrics, a worshiper of God, was listening; and the Lord opened her heart to respond to the things spoken by Paul.* (Acts 16:14)

Reformed theologians rely heavily on this passage as they attempt to substantiate their definition of total depravity.   Edwin Palmer, a Reformed theologian, in *The Five Points of Calvinism*, page 15, states:

> Not only is man unable to do the good by himself, he is not even able to understand the good. He is as blind as Cyclops with his one eye burned out. Lydia, for example, heard Paul preach Christ at the riverside of Philippi. Only after the Lord opened her heart was she able to give heed to what was said by Paul (Acts 16:14). Until then, her understanding was darkened, to use Paul's description of the Ephesian Gentiles (Eph. 4:18). Or, to use another Pauline illustration, a veil over her heart prevented her from seeing the truth (2Cor. 3:12-18). But when God operated on her spiritual heart, she could respond to Paul's preaching.[93]

Palmer's argument is easily defused through using the same verses (2Corinthians 3:12-18) that he references while attempting to prove his case.   Palmer's interpretation of Acts 16:14 is out of context due to Paul's words in 2Corinthians 3:16:

> *but whenever a man turns to the Lord, the veil is taken away.* (2Corinthians 3:16).

Paul believed that man *"turns"* (makes a choice to turn to the Lord while depraved) <u>before</u> *"the veil is taken away"*—refuting Palmer's argument (and Reformed Theology) altogether. In other words, *"the veil is taken away"* <u>after</u> the depraved exercise repentance and faith—disproving the idea that spiritual regeneration is required <u>before</u> man can repent and believe. This sequence makes

Lydia's experience in Acts 16:14 remarkably intriguing, for two interpretations are commonly associated with the passage. Yet, a third interpretation (that I deem totally compatible with the full counsel of God's Word) exists as well.

1. The first view has already been addressed though Palmer's quote, which depicts Lydia depraved (lost) when initially hearing Paul's message—with God opening her depraved heart (through spiritual regeneration) and granting her repentance and faith. In this scenario, spiritual regeneration precedes repentance and faith—the exact opposite of what Acts 16:31 requires.

2. In the second view Lydia is depraved (lost) prior to Paul's visit, yet makes a choice to believe Paul's message in her depraved state—after which she is saved. This view was mine for some time, but I think an even better way to perceive Lydia's experience exists and is listed next.

3. In the third view Lydia is a believer (having exercised repentance and faith in the midst of her depravity) prior to Paul's visit. After all, she was *"a worshipper of God"* before hearing his message, much as Cornelius *"feared God"* (Acts 10:2) before hearing Peter's message in Acts 10:34-43. Thus the phrase, *"the Lord opened her heart to respond,"* means that God allowed her to understand what she was hearing due to her previous choice (in her depravity) to repent and believe. This sequence of events occurs over and over in the Scriptures, for God is pleased to supply additional revelation to passionate believers (Simeon and Annan in Luke 2:25-38). Lydia, through Paul's message, was hearing (evidently for the first time) a fuller revelation of the gospel, that she had previously believed through the Old Testament Scriptures. Certainly, the Old Testament spoke of a suffering Savior (Genesis 3:15; Psalm 22; and Isaiah 53). But the apostles (including Paul in Acts 9) had seen the Savior, which resulted in an enhanced understanding of the gospel that the Old Testament writers failed to possess (read 1Peter 1:10-12 for confirmation).

Acts 16:14 does not teach that the Lord opened Lydia's heart to believe so she could be saved. Rather, it states that *"the Lord opened her heart to respond to the things spoken by Paul."* (A similar incident occurred in Luke 24:45 where Jesus *"opened"* the *"minds"* of His disciples who were already believers: *"Then He opened their minds to understand the Scriptures."*) Can we even begin to imagine the degree to which Paul's words comforted Lydia who already passionately loved Jehovah? Also note (in Acts 16:15) that Lydia chose to be water *"baptized,"* which was part of her response referenced in Acts 16:14. Even though water baptism follows salvation, Lydia's baptism in no way signifies that she was saved while hearing Paul's message— we have already observed that she followed Jehovah prior to Paul's visit. How, then, can this account be properly reconciled? Because water baptism is a picture of what has already occurred in the realm of the Spirit (when one is saved from the penalty of sin), it is non-contradictory (and proper) to conclude that Lydia's salvation transpired prior to Paul's arrival.

With the above in mind, lets again read Acts 16:14:

> *And a certain woman named Lydia, from the city of Thyatira, a*
> *seller of purple fabrics, a worshiper of God, was listening; and the*
> *Lord opened her heart to respond to the things spoken by Paul.*
> (Acts 16:14)

The following quotes confirm that the first two views are prominent within Christendom. Let's first read Norm Geisler's words from *Systematic Theology, Volume 3, Sin/Salvation*, page 479—Geisler being a moderate Calvinist who seems to agree with the second view:

> One need not deny that God moves upon the hearts of
> unbelievers to persuade and prompt them to faith; what we
> deny is that God does this coercively (by irresistible grace) and
> that He only does it on some persons (the elect). The Holy Spirit
> is convicting "the world of sin, and of righteousness, and of
> judgment" (John 16:8), but God does not force anyone to
> believe in Him (cf. Matt. 23:37; John 5:40). While the Lord
> opened Lydia's heart to believe, Luke does not say that He did
> so against her will.[94]

Yet, Wayne Grudem (a Reformed theologian), in *Bible Doctrine, Essential Teachings of the Christian Faith*, page 303, agrees with the first view:

> This inward act of regeneration is described beautifully when
> Luke says of Lydia, *"The Lord opened her heart* to give heed to
> what was said by Paul" (Acts 16:14). First the Lord opened her
> heart, then she was able to give heed to Paul's preaching and to
> respond in faith.[95]

Grudem's order unquestionably violates Paul's order of 2Corinthians 3:16, where Paul teaches that man turns <u>prior</u> to spiritual regeneration:

> *but whenever a man turns to the Lord, the veil is taken away.*
> (2Corinthians 3:16).

Grudem avoids 2Corinthians 3:16 in the Scripture index of his previously cited work perhaps because it disproves his theory that spiritual regeneration must precede the repentance and faith exercised prior to salvation. Once again we observe the value of the full counsel of God's Word. The Scriptures are to be interpreted based on the whole body of truth included in God's letter to man— never on a few verses, taken out of context, for the purpose of upholding one's preconceived notions regarding Who God is and how He relates to man. Considering what we have discovered, let's evaluate Grudem's assessment of what occurs during spiritual regeneration, which in his mind, transpires prior to man's repenting, believing, and receiving salvation. This quote is taken from pages 301-302 of Grudem's *Bible Doctrine, Essential Teachings of the Christian Faith:*

> Exactly what happens in regeneration is mysterious to us. We know that somehow we who were spiritually dead (Eph. 2:1) have been made alive to God and in a very real sense we have been "born again" (John 3:3, 7; Eph. 2:5; Col. 2:13). But we don't understand how this happens or what exactly God does to us to give us this new spiritual life. Jesus says, "The wind blows where it wills, and you hear the sound of it, but you do not know whence it comes or whither it goes; so it is with everyone who is born of the Spirit" (John 3:8).[96]

Grudem equates spiritual regeneration with being "born again," for he continues by writing:

> Scripture views regeneration as something that affects us as whole persons. Of course, our "spirits are alive" to God after regeneration (Rom. 8:10), but that is simply because we as *whole persons* are affected by regeneration. It is not just that our spirits were dead before—we were dead to God in trespasses and sins (see Eph. 2:1). And it is incorrect to say that all that happens in regeneration is that our spirits are made alive (as some would teach), for *every part of us* is affected by regeneration: "If any one is in Christ, he is a new creation; the old has passed away, behold, the new has come" (2Corinthians 5:17).[97]

Grudem teaches that Reformed Theology's spiritual regeneration results in the spirit of the person coming "alive," making that individual a *"new creation"..."in Christ"* (2Corinthians 5:17). This idea is impossible! To be placed *"in Christ"* (2Corinthians 5:17) means that one is saved (*"justified"*—Romans 5:1) and part of God's family—not spiritually regenerated so one can then receive God's gifts of repentance and faith, repent, believe, and be saved. To be *"in Christ"* means that one is a spiritually blessed child of God, not a spiritually regenerated individual who will subsequently repent, believe, and receive salvation. The following verses verify this truth:

> *... through the redemption which is <u>in Christ</u> Jesus;* (Romans 3:24)

> *... the free gift of God is eternal life <u>in Christ</u> Jesus our Lord.* (Romans 6:23)

> *... to those who have been sanctified <u>in Christ</u> Jesus...* (1Corinthians 1:2)

> *I thank my God always concerning you, for the grace of God which was given you <u>in Christ</u> Jesus,* (1Corinthians 1:4)

> *Blessed be the God and Father of our Lord Jesus Christ, who has blessed us with every spiritual blessing in the heavenly places <u>in Christ</u>,* (Ephesians 1:3)

> *and raised us up with Him, and seated us with Him in the heavenly places, <u>in Christ</u> Jesus,* (Ephesians 2:6)

> *...to all the saints <u>in Christ</u> Jesus who are in Philippi...* (Philippians 1:1)

> *...that they also may obtain the salvation which is <u>in Christ</u> Jesus...* (2Timothy 2:10)

These verses are only a partial listing of the passages that could have been cited, but they give ample proof that to be *"in Christ"* means that one is saved—not spiritually regenerated to be saved later. Yet, Grudem continues with his argument:

> Because regeneration is a work of God within us in which he gives us new life, it is right to conclude that it is an *instantaneous event.* It happens only once. At one moment we are spiritually dead, and then at the next moment we have new spiritual life from God. Nevertheless, we do not always know exactly when this instantaneous change occurs. Especially for children growing up in a Christian home, or for people who attend an evangelical church or Bible study over a period of

time and grow gradually in their understanding of the gospel, there may not be a dramatic crisis with a radical change of behavior from "hardened sinner" to "holy saint," but there will be an instantaneous change nonetheless, when God through the Holy Spirit, in an unseen, invisible way, awakens spiritual life within. The change will *become evident* over time in patterns of behavior and desires that are pleasing to God.

In other cases (in fact, probably most cases when adults become Christians), regeneration takes place at a clearly recognizable time at which the person realizes that previously he or she was separated from God and spiritually dead, but immediately afterward there was clearly new spiritual life within. The results can usually be seen at once—a heartfelt trusting in Christ for salvation, an assurance of sins forgiven, a desire to read the Bible and pray (and a sense that these are meaningful spiritual activities), a delight in worship, a desire for Christian fellowship, a sincere desire to be obedient to God's Word in Scripture, and a desire to tell others about Christ.... (emphasis added)[98]

Grudem believes that "a heartfelt trusting in Christ for salvation" occurs after spiritual "regeneration" (read the underlined portion of the previous quote). Thus, he believes that spiritual regeneration precedes justification (salvation). When exposed to the full counsel of God's Word, this arrangement would have the elect saved twice—a total impossibility. Note: We will discover later that the elect are actually saved three times according to the Reformed view, that is when their theology is taken through the Scriptures from cover to cover.

R.C. Sproul, a Reformed theologian, on page 72 of *"Chosen by God,"* shows that he is in the same camp with Grudem:

The Reformed view of predestination teaches that before a person can choose Christ his heart must be changed [spiritually regenerated]. He must be born again....One does not first believe, then become reborn, and then be ushered into the kingdom....If a person who is still in the flesh, who is not yet reborn by the power of the Holy Spirit, can incline or dispose himself to Christ, what good is rebirth? This is the fatal flaw of non-Reformed views. They fail to take seriously man's moral inability, the moral impotency of the flesh.[99]

According to Sproul, God was required to predestine Reformed Theology's elect to salvation from eternity past due to the depraved lacking the ability to exercise faith—to believe for themselves (review Diagram 11 in the Reference Section). Reformed Theology also views God as not only spiritually regenerating the depraved and giving them repentance and faith before they are saved, but refraining from granting the non-elect the freedom to believe. Yet, this same system of thought teaches that God judges the non-elect for not believing. Can God, in your mind, possess such an unjust heart? At the same time, they convey that God, within the realm of His sovereignty, could have chosen (elected) all had He been so inclined. Does this view properly describe the God of *"love"* (1John 4:8, 16) Who gave us His infallible Word?

Warning: Remain alert throughout the remainder of this section addressing Acts 16:14. If you understand the depth of theology discussed here, you are well on your way to defending depravity from the side of free will.

As was mentioned earlier in this study, Reformed Theology views God as having elected (chosen) only some to salvation, so the "elect" will have a greater appreciation of His grace through observing His wrath displayed against the non-elect. These statements are verified by John Piper, a Reformed theologian, in *"Are there Two Wills in God"*—taken from Dave Hunt's *What Love Is This*, Page 374:

> ...my answer to the question about what restrains God's will to save all people is his supreme commitment to uphold and display the full range of his glory through the sovereign demonstration of his wrath and mercy for the enjoyment of his elect and believing people from every tribe and tongue and nation.[100]

Does this description properly portray the God of the Scriptures? If so, He is not only unloving, but totally unjust—discarding His sovereignty in the process.

Considering what we have gleaned, the answer to R.C. Sproul's previous question of should the benefit of the new birth ("rebirth") occur subsequent to the depraved exercising faith, is quite simple. Follow closely.

God granted the depraved the freedom to believe without anyone (or anything) forcing Him to do so. He responded in this manner, because *"God is love"* (1John 4:8, 16). So granting man a free will to exercise repentance and faith while depraved means that God can be trusted to consistently respond according to His nature. In other words, Who God is, being *"love,"* allowed Him to grant the depraved the freedom to repent and believe—for love cannot exist void of the freedom of choice. Therefore, if the depraved refuse His loving offer of salvation, it does nothing to diminish His sovereignty; God granted the right of choice in the first place. With these truths in mind, let's return to Sproul's question submitted in his preceding quote:

> If a person who is still in the flesh, who is not yet reborn by the

power of the Holy Spirit, can incline or dispose himself to Christ, what good is rebirth?

We have answered this question (void of contradiction) in our previous comments, for the spiritual regeneration ("rebirth") that results from man exercising personal repentance and faith while depraved makes room for God to retain both His sovereignty and His love. Hence, much "good" is associated with this view of "rebirth." Sproul's problem is failing to understand that a choice to repent and believe (while depraved) does not save the depraved. God does the saving through spiritually regenerating those who choose (in their depravity) to come to Christ. Thus, much benefit results from the spiritual regeneration <u>following</u> that moment when the depraved choose to exercise personal repentance and faith. As a result, I view Sproul's question as nonsensical.

John Piper (a Reformed theologian) is quoted by Dave Hunt (who is not a Calvinist) on page 310 of *What Love Is This?* Piper's perception of the "new birth" dovetails with Grudem and Sproul's common view:

We do not think that faith precedes and causes new birth. Faith is the evidence that God has begotten us anew.[101]

Like Grudem and Sproul, Piper believes: (1) that "new birth" occurs <u>before</u> faith is exercised (2) that "faith is the evidence that God has begotten us anew." Wow! This view assumes that the spiritually regenerated of Reformed Theology are part of God's family <u>before</u> they exercise faith—that is, if you define "new birth" and "begotten...anew" based on all the Scriptures rather than a select few interpreted outside their context. Piper's view totally contradicts Mark 16:16, Romans 5:1, Acts 16:31, John 1:12, John 11:25, Romans 10:9, 1Corinthians 1:21, Ephesians 1:13, and Hebrews 10:39. Dave Hunt, in *What Love Is This?,* page 362, records yet another quote from Piper that addresses this same issue:

...be born of God. Then, with the new nature of God, he immediately receives Christ.[102]

Piper reverses the Biblical order by teaching spiritual regeneration followed by faith and salvation rather than faith followed by spiritual regeneration (salvation). Thus, a theological impasse accompanies the Reformed view: <u>Why would the spiritually regenerated of Reformed Theology need to exercise faith prior to salvation (and subsequent to spiritual regeneration) when the Biblical view of spiritual regeneration is the equivalent of salvation/justification—granting man a new nature?</u> (Do not continue until you thoroughly understand the previous sentence.) According to the Biblical view, man receives a "new nature"—becomes a *"new"* creation (2Corinthians 5:17), receives *"eternal life"* (Romans 6:23), receives salvation—when he is placed *"in Christ"* (2Corinthians 5:17) through the power of the Holy "Spirit" (1Corinthians 12:13) <u>after</u> believing while depraved (John 3:16; Acts 16:31; Romans 10:9):

> *"For God so loved the world, that He gave His only begotten Son, that whoever believes in Him should not perish, but have eternal life.* (John 3:16)

> *And they said, "Believe in the Lord Jesus, and you shall be saved,...* (Acts 16:31)

> *that if you confess with your mouth Jesus as Lord, and believe in your heart that God raised Him from the dead, you shall be saved;* (Romans 10:9)

> *For the wages of sin is death, but the free gift of God is <u>eternal life in Christ Jesus</u> our Lord.* (Romans 6:23)

> *Therefore if any man is <u>in Christ</u>, he is a new creature; the old things passed away; behold, new things have come.* (2Corinthians 5:17)

> *For by one Spirit we were all baptized into one body, whether Jews or Greeks, whether slaves or free, and we were all made to drink of one Spirit.* (1Corinthians 12:13)

Thus, Piper and his fellow Reformed theologians' spiritual regeneration leaves the "elect" unjustified (unsaved), yet the Scriptures teach that spiritual regeneration and salvation are one and the same. Faith never follows spiritual regeneration/salvation. Faith always precedes justification/salvation/spiritual regeneration according to Romans 5:1:

> *Therefore having been justified by faith, we have peace with God through our Lord Jesus Christ,* (Romans 5:1)

We observe once again the dilemma facing Reformed Theology as it attempts to validate the "T" of the TULIP, Total Depravity.

Isn't it exciting to think through what we believe, allowing the whole body of truth contained in God's Word to eradicate all inconsistency? The absolutes we are ingesting will greatly enhance our study of Unconditional Election, the "U" of the TULIP—the subject to be addressed following Total Depravity, the "T".

Romans 10:17 and Depravity

So faith comes from hearing, and hearing by the word of Christ.
(Romans 10:17)

Reformed theologians have used this verse in an attempt to justify their definition of total depravity. They teach that, through the Scriptures, God gives the gift of faith to the depraved whom He spiritually regenerates (a spiritual regeneration that occurs prior to salvation). They incorrectly conclude, therefore, that the faith exercised prior to salvation is God's gift to those whom He has rescued from their depraved state through spiritual regeneration.

This argument is easily diffused by considering the following verses. We will begin by addressing Romans 10:8:

...the word of faith which we are preaching, that if you confess
with your mouth Jesus as Lord, and believe in your heart that God
raised Him from the dead, you shall be saved; (Romans 10:8-9)

By using the phrase, *"the word of faith,"* Paul is not saying that God's Word produces *"faith,"* but rather that *"the word of faith"* is preached—which if obeyed through confession and belief in Jesus while depraved, results in salvation.

In addition, Hebrews 4:2 bears out that all who hear God's Word are not profited by it:

...the word preached did not profit them, not being mixed with
faith in them that heard it. (Hebrews 4:2 KJV)

Rather than the word producing faith, *"faith"* must be *"mixed"* with *"the word"* for the word to be profitable when *"heard."* Don't misunderstand. The Spirit's conviction (John 16:8), the Father's drawing (John 8:44), along with the Son's drawing (John 12:32), combine with the word to prompt faith. A great disparity exists, however, between "prompting" faith and "producing" faith. Should God's Word be required to produce faith in the spiritually regenerated (due to an inability within the depraved to exercise "saving faith"—the Reformed view), all who hear the Scriptures would believe—that is, if the decision as to who will believe is left to God alone (the Reformed view). He desires that all be saved (1Timothy 2:4; 2Peter 3:9). However, all who hear His Word do not believe, as is again verified by Jesus' statements to the Jewish leaders in John 5:39-40:

You search the Scriptures, because you think that in them you have
eternal life; and it is these that bear witness of Me; (John 5:39)

These leaders had saturated themselves in Old Testament Scripture. Yet, they did not believe, as evidenced by Jesus' words in John 5:40, the very next passage:

> *and you are unwilling to come to Me, that you may have life.* (John 5:40)

These men refused God's offer of salvation due to their unwillingness to believe, not due to the depths of their depravity (and God's rejection of them from eternity past), as Reformed Theology advocates. Jesus places the blame squarely on the Jewish leaders—meaning that if extreme and hyper Calvinists are correct, Jesus, Who is God (Hebrews 1:8), was rebuking men who were incapable of believing, for failing to believe (only the elect can believe, in Reformed Theology's view). If this scenario were true, what would it make God out to be? For sure, not the loving, stable, just, and wise God the Scriptures portray! God doesn't play games with my life, your life, or anyone's life—which would be the case should the Reformed view be correct.

Considering our findings, let's examine what Reformed Theology's view of salvation does to God's sovereignty. First, God (according to their ideology) must spiritually regenerate the depraved and grant them repentance and faith <u>before</u> they can repent and believe. Their view also includes the idea that the spiritually regenerated receive God's gift of faith through hearing God's Word. Thus, they perceive God as using His Word to produce the faith He gives those whom He has prepared (through spiritual regeneration) to hear the message. If this case were true, and since God is not willing for any to perish, but that all come to repentance (1Timothy 2:4; 2Peter 3:9), all should be saved—that is, if God is to remain sovereign. How could a sovereign God, should He be the cause of all things (the Reformed view), not bring to fruition what He desires? If He is truly sovereign, and desires all to be saved, why would He not save all—that is, if His decision determines where man will spend eternity? Therefore, instead of Reformed Theology establishing God's sovereignty, it destroys it by portraying Him as being forced to tolerate what He does not desire. Could He not spiritually regenerate all, and spread the hearing of His Word to everyone, should man's destiny be based on His sovereign decision alone? (Can you see how the Reformed view of the Scriptures could easily lead a person into Universalism—the idea that all mankind will be saved?)

The Scriptures do, in some way, <u>prompt</u> faith in the depraved. For example, the Law, which is part of God's Word, is used to convict the depraved of their sin and so they might repent, believe, and be saved (Galatians 3:24). However, <u>prompting</u> faith and <u>producing</u> faith are two completely different, unequal actions. The Scriptures also <u>strengthen</u> the faith that exists within the <u>redeemed</u>.

God's Word not only teaches that the depraved are to exercise repentance and faith, but that the choice to repent and believe is theirs alone. However, God doesn't leave them totally to themselves. As was confirmed earlier, the Holy Spirit convicts the depraved of their need for a Savior (John 16:8), as does God's Law (Galatians 3:24; 1Timothy 1:9-10).

> *And He* [the Holy Spirit], *when He comes, will convict the world concerning sin, and righteousness, and judgment;* (John 16:8)

> *Therefore the Law has become our tutor to lead us to Christ, that we may be justified by faith.* (Galatians 3:24)

> *realizing the fact that law is not made for a righteous man, but for those who are lawless and rebellious, for the ungodly and sinners, for the unholy and profane, for those who kill their fathers or mothers, for murderers and immoral men and homosexuals and kidnappers and liars and perjurers, and whatever else is contrary to sound teaching.* (1Timothy 1:9-10)

God's Word also reproves the believer:

> *All Scripture is inspired by God and profitable for teaching, for reproof, for correction, for training in righteousness; that the man of God may be adequate, equipped for every good work.*
> (2Timothy 3:16-17)

The Scriptures are a sharp "*sword,*" used by God to reveal truth as well as error:
> *For the word of God is living and active and sharper than any two-edged sword, and piercing as far as the division of soul and spirit, of both joints and marrow, and able to judge the thoughts and intentions of the heart.* (Hebrews 4:12)

However, one must be attentive to God's Word if it is to be beneficial; Hebrews 4:2 (as noted previously) confirms that not all who are exposed to the truth are profited by it at the time they hear it:

> *"...the word preached did not profit them, not being mixed with faith in them that heard it."* (Hebrews 4:2 KJV)

Thus, faith is not God's gift to the spiritually regenerated through their exposure to the Scriptures (as Reformed Theology supposes), but rather faith is generated by the depraved prior to God making them new—prior to God giving them the gift of salvation/spiritual regeneration.

that if you confess with your mouth Jesus as Lord, and believe in
your heart that God raised Him from the dead, you shall be saved;
(Romans 10:9)

The faith exercised prior to salvation is generated within the *"heart"* (Romans 10:9) of the depraved. John 5:40 also applies:

and you are unwilling to come to Me, that you may have life. (John 5:40)

One must choose to *"come to"* Christ before he can possess *"life"*/salvation—the exact opposite of the Reformed view, which depicts the depraved as being spiritually regenerated and receiving "life" prior to coming to Christ for salvation/justification.

Conclusion

God's Word prompts faith within those who choose to believe, God using the Law (Galatians 3:24; 1Timothy 1:9-10) to convict the depraved of sin. However, no matter what part God's Word plays in prompting this faith, the depraved produce it—a requirement of the Scriptures. Therefore, Romans 10:17 does not teach that God produces faith (through the Scriptures) in those He has already rescued from depravity through spiritual regeneration (as Reformed Theology advocates).

God's Word not only prompts faith in the depraved, but also strengthens the faith of those already saved/justified. A consistent dose of truth does wonders for the souls of the saints. In fact, with the assistance of the Holy Spirit, it grants one the view from above—wisdom indeed.

Philippians 1:6 and Depravity

For I am confident of this very thing, that He who began a good
work in you will perfect it until the day of Christ Jesus.
(Philippians 1:6)

This passage is used by Reformed theologians in an attempt to substantiate their view of total depravity, unconditional election, and in turn, the "P" of the TULIP, Perseverance of the Saints. John MacArthur, in *"The Love of God,"* page 156 states:

‖ ...The sinner is...trapped in his own insuperable lostness, unless

213

> God intervenes to save him...
>
> ...that is precisely what happens. God Himself orchestrates salvation from eternity past to eternity future...
>
> Every stage of the process is God's work. There's a tremendous amount of security in that. If our salvation is God's work, not our own, we can be sure that He will see it to full fruition. "He who began a good work in you will perfect it until the day of Christ Jesus" (Phil. 1:6)[103]

"Salvation" is clearly God's work, but we must be aware of what MacArthur does <u>not</u> include in these statements. He fails to mention that he views the depraved as incapable of exercising repentance and faith—needing to be spiritually regenerated and given repentance and faith before they can repent, believe, and be saved. He also views the New Testament believer as having been elected to salvation by God, by means of an eternal decree. This background allows us to understand why he would write, "God Himself orchestrates salvation from eternity past to eternity future," and "Every stage of the process is God's work." Hence, MacArthur perceives Philippians 1:6 as not only addressing his view of total depravity, which prohibits the depraved from repenting and believing, but his view of election and perseverance as well. We will point out the contradictions in his conclusions shortly.

It naturally follows that R.C. Sproul (also a Reformed theologian) would record in *Grace Unknown,* page 210:

> Were the Bible to say nothing about perseverance, what it says about God's electing grace would be sufficient to convince us of the doctrine of perseverance. But the Bible is not silent on these matters, declaring clearly and often that God will finish what he has begun for us and in us....[Sproul then references Philippians 1:6 in an attempt to make his point].
>
>   God's preservation of the saints is not based on a mere, abstract deduction from his decree of election. It rests also on his immutable and free love, a love that is abiding, a love of complacency that nothing can sever....[104]

These statements demonstrate that Sproul, like MacArthur, believes that God's "electing grace," or "decree of election" (election by means of an eternal decree) is necessary due to a depravity which (in their minds) prevents the depraved from exercising repentance and faith. This improper view of depravity and election causes them to yield to the "P" of the TULIP, Perseverance of the Saints, a false idea that portrays God as completing the salvation of the elect that began from eternity past through the "U" of the TULIP, Unconditional Election.

Reformed theologians, if they are candid, have a difficult time determining if they are part of the elect. This detail is true of all forms of Calvinism. If one's perseverance is the proof of one's election, to what degree must one persevere to confirm his election? The answer is found nowhere in the Scriptures. Unconditional Election, the "U" of the TULIP, is contradictory to the full counsel of God's Word and, thus, erroneous, which causes the Calvinists to struggle so intensely with this issue—that is, if they are straightforward about the matter.

One of the major problems with perceiving Philippians 1:6 as confirming Reformed Theology's total depravity and unconditional election has to do with the word *"began"*:

> *For I am confident of this very thing, that He who <u>began</u> a good*
> *work in you will perfect it until the day of Christ Jesus.*
> (Philippians 1:6)

As we addressed in our study of *God's Heart as it Relates to Foreknowledge-Predestination,* Reformed Theology (all forms of Calvinism in fact) believe that God predestined all of the elect to salvation from eternity past by means of an eternal decree. Therefore, John MacArthur, regarding God's love for the elect, in *The Love of God*, page 17, states:

> God's love for the elect is an <u>infinite, eternal</u>, saving love.[105]

MacArthur believes that God loves "the elect" with an "infinite, eternal, saving love." In other words, he views God as loving the elect from eternity past—before they were born. How can this situation be true when a person doesn't become a person until he is conceived in the womb? Does MacArthur believe that God fell in love with an idea? Yet, MacArthur and John Calvin are in agreement, for Calvin also believed that God predestined the elect to salvation by means of an eternal decree:

> By predestination we mean the <u>eternal decree of God</u>, by which he determined with himself whatever he wished to happen with regard to every man. All are not created on equal terms, but some [the elect] are preordained to eternal life... (*Institutes*: Book 3; Chapter 21; Section 5—emphasis added)[106]

> We say, then, that Scripture clearly proves this much, that God by <u>his eternal and immutable counsel</u> determined once for all those whom it was his pleasure one day to admit to salvation...

> We maintain that this counsel, as regards <u>the elect</u>, is founded on his free mercy, without any respect to human worth.... In regard to <u>the elect</u>, we regard calling as the evidence of <u>election</u>, and justification as another symbol of its manifestation, until it is fully accomplished by the attainment of glory...the Lord seals his <u>elect</u> by calling and justification... (*Institutes*: Book 3; Chapter 21; Section 7—emphasis added)[107]

> ...that <u>God, by an eternal decree</u>, fixed the number of those whom he is pleased to embrace in love...Moreover, he enlightens those whom he has predestinated to salvation. Thus the truth of the promises remains firm and unshaken, so that it cannot be said there is any disagreement between the <u>eternal election of God</u> and the testimony of his grace which he offers to believers. (*Institutes*: Book 3; Chapter 24; Section 17—emphasis added)[108]

We discovered earlier, in *God's Heart as it Relates to Foreknowledge-Predestination*, the impossibility of God electing the elect to salvation by means of an eternal decree. Peter writes in 1Peter 1:2:

Elect according to the foreknowledge of God the Father, through sanctification of the Spirit, unto obedience and sprinkling of the blood of Jesus Christ: Grace unto you, and peace, be multiplied. (1Peter 1:2 KJV)

The phrase, *"Elect according to the foreknowledge of God,"* proves that God's *"foreknowledge"* must <u>precede</u> one's election. If so, the election of the New Testament believer cannot be by means of an eternal decree (as supposed by the Calvinists), for God's eternal decrees have always existed within His heart (Jeremiah 5:22)—leaving no room for His foreknowledge to precede them (note Diagram 2 in the Reference Section).

When, then, does election take place? Election must occur in <u>time</u>, <u>after</u> the depraved exercise repentance and faith—that is, if the Scriptures are to remain non-contradictory. In fact, election occurs during the church age in conjunction with becoming a new creation—through being placed in Christ by the Holy Spirit (1Corinthians 12:13) subsequent to exercising personal repentance and faith while depraved. Election can occur in this manner due to Jesus being the Father's *"elect"* KJV or *"chosen one"* NASB (Isaiah 42:1). Therefore, the New Testament believer becomes part of the elect as a result of being placed in the Father's Son, who was elected (chosen) to the office of Messiah (observe Diagram 8 in the Reference Section). And to what are New Testament believers elected (chosen) once they are placed in Christ—after repenting and believing while depraved? They are elected (chosen) to a special position (office) within the body of Christ. This arrangement leaves ample room for God's foreknowledge to precede the New Testament believer's election, fulfilling the requirements of 1Peter 1:1-2 flawlessly. (Note: Our earlier study, titled *God's Heart as it Relates to Foreknowledge-Predestination,* has more to say regarding this subject; so we will yield to that resource for the sake of time and space.) Keep all of this input fresh in your mind, for it will serve us well when we address election as an independent topic later in this series.

Let's take this wonderful truth and apply it to Philippians 1:6:

> *For I am confident of this very thing, that He who <u>began</u> a good*
> *work in you will perfect it until the day of Christ Jesus.*
> (Philippians 1:6)

This passage <u>can't</u> validate Calvinism's "T," Total Depravity, and in turn its "U," Unconditional Election, as they suppose. The word *"began"* in the phrase, *"<u>began</u> a good work in you,"* is profoundly problematic for the Calvinists. If the Calvinists are going to frame any argument based on the context of Scripture, they must properly, as well as consistently, define the terms used in the presentation of their argument—that is, if their theology is to be found valid. Let's consider for a moment why their reasoning lacks credibility.

John MacArthur defines salvation (in his previous quotes) as a "process" from "eternity past." Consequently, Calvinism cannot allow the "process" (MacArthur's word) of salvation to have a beginning without adding inconsistency ("mystery") to their argument. Calvinism's election (an election to salvation) occurs by means of God's eternal decree. Should this idea be true, the elect have always been the elect since God's decrees have no beginning! In other words, the elect cannot "become" the elect should they have been elected to salvation by means of an eternal decree. Thus, their definition of election contradicts Paul's words in Philippians 1:6— *"...He who <u>began</u> a good work in you."* How could God begin a work that has no beginning? Nonetheless, MacArthur, failing to pick up on his inconsistent reasoning, views Philippians 1:6 as validating Reformed Theology's definition of election. What causes him to overlook this error? Reformed Theology (extreme and hyper-Calvinism), moderate Calvinism, and Arminianism teach that the elect were elected to salvation by means of an eternal decree (note Diagram 11 in the Reference Section). Yet, at the same time, they advocate that God's decrees are sequential—a contradiction in itself (observe Diagram 12 in the Reference Section).

A vast difference exists between individuals being elected to salvation by means of an eternal decree, meaning that they have always been elected, versus being elected to salvation at a point in eternity past. Therefore, Calvinism's view of election is self-defeating. Let's work through these inconsistencies one more time by stating the same thing in a different way.

Calvinism teaches that God elects the elect to salvation by means of an eternal decree. We have verified, however, that God's eternal decrees have no beginning. Consequently, if the Calvinists are held accountable to what they presume, the elect have always been the elect. Nevertheless, they teach that the elect become the elect at a point in eternity past (review our study of Supralapsarianism, Infralapsarianism, and Sublapsarianism—Diagram 12 in the Reference Section). How can a work which has no beginning have a starting point? Hence, they teach a contradiction.

I view Philippians 1:6 as teaching something totally different. The repentance and faith exercised by the depraved do not save them. Man does the repenting and believing; God does the saving. Therefore Paul, in Philippians 1:6, is advocating that once the depraved exercise personal repentance and faith, God saves them subsequent to their repenting and believing. This salvation is God's work entirely, for the faith exercised by the depraved is not a work (Romans 4:5). Neither is faith something that the church saint can boast about (Romans 3:27). Thus, the fact that God *"began"* the *"work"* of the believer's salvation does not mean, as Reformed Theology incorrectly supposes, that the depraved are incapable of repenting and believing.

God will also complete the *"work"* of salvation that He *"began"* in all who repent and believe (Philippians 1:6). Therefore, church saints are not required to "persevere" under some unworkable system of rules in an attempt to prove that they are part of the elect (as advocated by Reformed Theology). Their High Priest, Jesus Christ, promises to *"save"* them *"forever"*:

> *Hence, also, He is able to save forever those who draw near to*
> *God through Him, since He always lives to make intercession for*
> *them.* (Hebrews 7:25)

Yet, Calvinism's "P" of the TULIP, the letter of the acrostic defined as "Perseverance of the Saints," advocates something else when taken through the full counsel of God's Word. We will address this issue in greater depth when we examine the "P" of the TULIP as an independent subject.

Isn't it encouraging to use what we have learned in past lessons to expand our understanding of God's Word? Truth is our most precious possession, but for truth to be classified as truth, it must be void of contradiction. An abundance of input will be introduced in the remainder of this series. However, with the assistance of our expanded understanding, the journey should be the adventure of a lifetime.

2Timothy 3:15 and Depravity

*and that from childhood you have known the sacred writings which
are able to give you the wisdom that leads to salvation through
faith which is in Christ Jesus.* (2Timothy 3:15)

The word *"salvation"* (or *"saved"*) is used in a variety of ways in the Scriptures. It can point to being saved from the <u>penalty</u> of sin (Romans 1:16) as well as being saved on a daily basis from the <u>power</u> of sin—by the living Word of God, Jesus Himself (Romans 5:10). "Salvation" can also point to being saved from the <u>presence</u> of sin, something that occurs when the believer leaves his earthly body and enters heaven (1Peter 1:5). Therefore, for proper interpretation, we must always determine the type of salvation and its context.

Some people view 2Timothy 3:15 as teaching that the depraved <u>can</u> exercise faith prior to *"salvation."* They advocate that man is convicted by God's Word while depraved, and must choose to repent and believe (while depraved), <u>before</u> salvation is bestowed. They cite the phrase, *"to salvation through faith,"* as proof that one is saved (from the penalty of sin) <u>after</u> one believes while depraved. According to the full counsel of the Scriptures, the depraved are capable of exercising personal repentance and faith. Hence, I agree with their theology regarding that particular issue: the depraved can either reject the conviction brought about by God's Word and remain lost, or accept it and experience God's gift of life. I do differ, however, with their view of Paul's use of the term, *"salvation,"* in 2Timothy 3:15. The context of this passage seems to be pointing to Timothy's daily salvation from the <u>power</u> of sin rather than his salvation from the <u>penalty</u> of sin at justification—since Timothy was already a believer by the time Second Timothy was written (note Paul's use of the pronoun *"you,"* pointing to Timothy specifically).

This verse <u>cannot</u> be used in an attempt to prove that God must spiritually regenerate the depraved, and give them repentance and faith, <u>before</u> they can repent and believe—the repentance and faith coming as gifts from God through the Scriptures rather than from the heart of the depraved.

John 12:46 and Depravity

*"I have come as light into the world, that everyone who believes in
Me may not remain in darkness.* (John 12:46)

This passage affirms that the repentance and faith exercised by the depraved allow them to exit spiritual *"darkness"* through God's salvation. In other words, the depraved can exercise repentance and faith <u>prior</u> to spiritual regeneration/salvation/justification.

Ephesians 5:8 and Depravity

> *for you were formerly darkness, but now you are light in the Lord;*
> (Ephesians 5:8)

Paul confirms that the lost are in *"darkness"* in their depraved state, but does not say that their depravity prevents them from repenting and believing. He also teaches that the depraved (during the church age) exit *"darkness"* and become *"light"* (Ephesians 5:8), become *"new"* creations (2Corinthians 5:17), through being placed *"in the Lord"* (Ephesians 5:8)—the phrase, *"in the Lord,"* pointing to <u>where</u> the Holy Spirit places the New Testament believer once repentance and faith are exercised (1Corinthians 12:13). In other words, believers during the church age are *"light"* due to having been placed *"in the Lord"* after submitting to Christ in the midst of their depravity *("darkness").* This order lines up perfectly with Jesus' words in John 8:12:

> ... *"I am the light of the world; he who follows Me shall not walk in the darkness, but shall have the light of life."* (John 8:12)

The church saint is *"light in the Lord"* (Ephesians 5:8) due to having been placed into the very source of *"light"* (John 8:12), Jesus Himself.

In the passages which follow, Paul uses the words *"in Christ,"* which carry the same meaning as *"in the Lord"* (Ephesians 5:8), to emphasize <u>where</u> New Testament believers are saved and blessed:

> *being justified as a gift by His grace through the redemption which is <u>in Christ</u> Jesus;* (Romans 3:24)

> *...the free gift of God is eternal life <u>in Christ</u> Jesus our Lord.* (Romans 6:23)

> *...to those who have been sanctified <u>in Christ</u> Jesus,...* (1Corinthians 1:2)

> *Therefore if any man is <u>in Christ</u>, he is a new creature; the old things passed away; behold, new things have come.* (2Corinthians 5:17)

Blessed be the God and Father of our Lord Jesus Christ, who has blessed us with every spiritual blessing in the heavenly places <u>in Christ</u>, (Ephesians 1:3)

and raised us up with Him, and seated us with Him in the heavenly places, <u>in Christ</u> Jesus, (Ephesians 2:6)

For we are His workmanship, created <u>in Christ</u> Jesus for good works,... (Ephesians 2:10)

Romans 6:6 applies as well:

knowing this, that our old self was crucified <u>with Him</u>, that our body of sin might be done away with, that we should no longer be slaves to sin; (Romans 6:6)

Paul, in Romans 6:6, teaches that once the depraved (who live during the church age) repent and believe, they are *"crucified with Him"* (with Christ). How can this be? We confirmed earlier that the Holy Spirit places the depraved into the eternal Son once they exercise personal repentance and faith. Once there, they are *"crucified"* and made *"new"* (2Corinthians 5:17; Galatians 2:20). This new creation possesses eternal life, life with no beginning or end. Therefore, New Testament believers are viewed by the Father as having always been in Christ—when Christ was *"crucified"* (Galatians 2:20), when He was *"buried"* (Romans 6:4; Colossians 2:12), and when He was *"raised"* (Ephesians 2:6)—but their point of entry into Christ occurred when they chose (in their depravity) to repent and believe. Let's take this thought and draw some very important conclusions.

No intermediate stage between depravity and salvation exists—yet Reformed Theology requires a gap. In other words, Scripture leaves no room for God to spiritually regenerate the depraved, and follow by granting them repentance and faith, <u>before</u> they can repent, believe, and be saved (the Reformed view). Nevertheless, Wayne Grudem, a Reformed theologian, writes, in *Bible Doctrine, Essential Teachings of the Christian Faith,* pages 301-302:

> And it is incorrect to say that all that happens in regeneration is that our spirits are made alive (as some would teach), for *every part of us* is affected by regeneration: "If any one is in Christ, he is a new creation; the old has passed away, behold, the new has come" (2Corinthians 5:17).[109]

Grudem views Reformed Theology's spiritual "regeneration" as equivalent to becoming a "new creation" "in Christ." If true, New Testament believers would be saved when they are spiritually regenerated prior to repenting and believing, and saved a second time after believing—that is, if the Reformed view is held accountable to the scriptural definition of spiritual regeneration. Again, we see that extreme and hyper-Calvinism's view of total depravity is unacceptable.

Acts 26:18 and Depravity

> *to open their eyes so that they may turn from darkness to light and from the dominion of Satan to God, in order that they may receive forgiveness of sins and an inheritance among those who have been sanctified by faith in Me.' (Acts 26:18)*

The context of Paul's words is extremely intriguing, for he was addressing King Agrippa prior to his voyage to Rome. In fact, Paul was describing God's calling on his life—that of preaching the gospel. Dave Hunt's words from *What Love Is This?*, page 476, confirm that Acts 26:18 refutes Reformed Theology's view of total depravity:

> What would be the need of Paul opening men's eyes and turning them from darkness to light through the Spirit-empowered preaching of the gospel if it all happens through sovereign regeneration, with Irresistible Grace and faith imposed as a result? Calvinism is refuted by the very commission Christ conferred upon Paul and the other Apostles.[110]

The redeemed turn from *"darkness to light,"* from depravity to salvation—not from spiritual regeneration to salvation.

Genesis 3:8-10 and Depravity

> *And they heard the sound of the LORD God walking in the garden in the cool of the day, and the man and his wife hid themselves from the presence of the LORD God among the trees of the garden. Then the LORD God called to the man, and said to him, "Where are you?" And he said, "I heard the sound of Thee in the garden, and I was afraid because I was naked; so I hid myself." (Genesis 3:8-10)*

The fact that the depraved <u>can</u> hear God's voice is confirmed in Genesis 2:17—
3:10. After sinning in Genesis 3:1-7, which resulted in spiritual death (Genesis
2:17), Adam and Eve <u>could hear God's voice in the midst of their depravity</u>.

James 1:18 and Depravity

In the exercise of His will He brought us forth by the word of truth,
so that we might be, as it were, the first fruits among His creatures.
(James 1:18)

Wayne Grudem (a Reformed theologian), in *Bible Doctrine, Essential Teachings
of the Christian Faith,* page 300, records:

> The fact that we are passive in regeneration is also evident
> when Scripture refers to it as being "born" or being "born again"
> (cf. James 1:18...). We did not choose to be made physically
> alive and we did not choose to be born—it is something that
> happened to us; similarly, these analogies in Scripture suggest
> that we are entirely passive in regeneration.[111]

In attempting to protect his view of total depravity, Grudem makes the mistake
of viewing physical birth as similar to spiritual birth. We confirmed why this view
is improper in our study of John 1:11-13, so a review of those notes might be
profitable at this time. Grudem (based on his previous quote) views the depraved
as "entirely passive in regeneration," holding true to the Reformed view of total
depravity, unconditional election, and irresistible grace.

James White (a follower of Reformed Theology), in *The Potter's Freedom,*
records John Calvin's view of James 1:18 and how it relates to faith, spiritual
regeneration, and in turn, total depravity:

> ...God begat us WILLINGLY (James 1:18), that is, from
> undeserved love. Hence it follows, first, that faith does not
> proceed from ourselves, but is the fruit of spiritual
> regeneration....[112]

Reformed theologians perceive James 1:18 as endorsing their view of total
depravity. Is this proper, or is James communicating something else? What
follows presents the contextual view of this passage.

James 1:18 confirms, beyond doubt, that God does the saving—that He has
always been, and will always be, the Source of the believer's salvation. Dave Hunt,
in *What Love Is This?,* pages 446, writes:

> ...Clearly James...is saying that regeneration was God's idea, "of his own will," and that He effects it ("begat he us"). James likewise confirms... that we are born again by "the word of truth," i.e., through believing the gospel of Jesus Christ...[113]

Hunt continues (on page 448) by addressing the contradictory nature of Reformed Theology's total depravity:

> ...what need is there to preach the gospel to *anyone,* since the elect are regenerated without it and the non-elect cannot believe it?[114]

Hunt also writes on page 451:

> Unquestionably, not only James 1:18 ("begat he us with the word of truth") but numerous other passages teach that believing "the word of truth" is essential for and must precede the new birth. The gospel is the specific "word of truth" that must be believed for the new birth to occur: "Believe on the Lord Jesus Christ, and thou shalt be saved" (Acts 16:31).[115]

The lost (depraved) first hear the *"word of truth,"* and those who receive it follow by exercising repentance and faith while depraved. At this time God, by *"the exercise of His will,"* saves them—which is the meaning of, *"In the exercise of His will He brought us forth by the word of truth"* (James 1:18).

Norm Geisler, in *Chosen But Free,* page 96, is in agreement with this view of James 1:18—even though he is a moderate Calvinist. Remember, moderate Calvinists view the depraved as capable of exercising repentance and faith:

> Here again, there is no question that God is the *source* of salvation. Had He not chosen to save, then no one would be saved. But the question remains as to the *means* by which we *receive* that salvation. That is, does God save us *apart* from our free choice or *through* it? Nothing in this text [James 1:18], or any other for that matter, declares that God chooses to save us against our will. Just the contrary is true...[116]

The depraved <u>can</u> most definitely exercise repentance and faith, as is confirmed many times over by God's infallible Word.

CHAPTER TWENTY ONE

CLOSING REMARKS

I WOULD LIKE TO TAKE A MOMENT TO REVIEW a quote from Charles Spurgeon, a Reformed theologian who struggled with the extremes of Calvinism. This quote was introduced earlier in *God's Heart as it Relates to Foreknowledge-Predestination.*

> If I am to preach faith in Christ to a man who is regenerated, then the man, being regenerated, is saved already, and it is an unnecessary and ridiculous thing for me to preach Christ to him, and bid him to believe in order to be saved when he is saved already, being regenerate. Am I only to preach faith to those who have it? Absurd, indeed! Is not this waiting till the man is cured and then bringing him the medicine? This is preaching Christ to the righteous and not to sinners.[117]

Can you better understand Spurgeon's concerns as an evangelist? How can the Scriptures teach that the depraved must be spiritually regenerated "before" they can repent, believe, and be saved, when such an arrangement would have man saved, not once, but at least twice? This bottom button (bottom line) logic inundates Reformed Theology. Yes, portray man as incapable of believing while depraved and you portray God as not only a contradiction, but totally undeserving of our believing.

In transitioning out of the "T" (Total Depravity) to the "U" (Unconditional Election) of the TULIP, R.C. Sproul's quote from *"Grace Unknown,"* page 152, is increasingly appropriate. In fact, let's take what we have learned in this series, plug it into Sproul's statements, and determine if we are equipped to detect the flaws in his reasoning:

> Those who favor a conditional view of election or some sort of prescience [foreknowledge] as the basis of election face a serious difficulty. They must assume that fallen persons are morally capable of responding positively to the gospel. This assumption is semi-Pelagian because it presupposes that original sin weakens the will but does not render it morally unable to incline itself to the things of God. Original sin notwithstanding, there remains some spontaneous power in the flesh that can incline itself to spiritual things. We said earlier that if one agrees with the doctrine of total depravity, the T of the TULIP, then the U of unconditional election follows necessarily. If one is incapable of meeting the conditions, then election must be unconditional. If the Reformation view of original sin is correct, then God would see no fallen creature choose Christ in the future. God would know from all eternity that, left to themselves, fallen creatures will not choose Christ.[118]

Can you detect the error in Sproul's argument? He must eliminate "prescience" (foreknowledge), for according to Reformed theologians, God is not required to foreknow any choice that the depraved might exercise in repenting and believing. From their vantage point, the depraved can't repent and believe—so no such choice could be made. Sproul also views the depraved (who remained lost) as being "left to themselves" with no hope of conviction of sin—a mindset that grossly violates John 16:8, Galatians 3:24, and Romans 1:20. He, therefore, perceives "freewillers" (the label Reformed theologians frequently attach to those in disagreement with their ideology) as advocating that the depraved can choose Christ while being "left" totally "to themselves." Sproul's previous statement:

> God would know from all eternity that, <u>left to themselves</u>, fallen creatures will not choose Christ.[119]

Have I advocated that the depraved are "left to themselves" in their pursuit of God? Of course not! In fact, I have stated on numerous occasions that the depraved are incapable of coming to Christ without the conviction of the Holy Spirit and the drawing of the Father—a truth that is readily accepted by many within Christ's body. This assistance does not mean, however, that the depraved are incapable of choosing to repent and believe.

Additional inconsistencies inundate Sproul's statements, but we must move on for the sake of time. Sproul's need is a deeper understanding of what "freewillers" advocate. Once this understanding occurs, I trust that he will be equipped to properly portray our views, and even better, trade Reformed Theology for a theology void of gross inconsistencies.   Should his theology change, he will reclassify "freewillers" as those who hold to the contextual view of the Scriptures. He will also reject the presupposition that unconditional election naturally follows total depravity.

Our examination of "Total Depravity" (as a separate subject) will cease for now. However, in covering "Unconditional Election," "Limited Atonement," "Irresistible Grace," and "Perseverance of the Saints" in subsequent lessons, we will address additional verses that reinforce what has already been established—that the depraved <u>can</u> exercise personal repentance and faith, refuting Reformed Theology's "Total Depravity" altogether.   The remaining letters of the TULIP (ULIP) are totally dependent on the soundness of the "T."   Having observed how thoroughly the Scriptures refute the "T," we should expect the Scriptures to easily refute the U-L-I-P as well. Thus, what lies ahead should be exceptionally stimulating.

Thanks for your time!   I trust that you have been encouraged, and most importantly, will walk away with a deeper understanding of the heart of the Creator—Who loves us more than can be imagined!

Diagram 1

Eternity
No Beginning And No End

∞   ∞

Diagram 2

Why God's Foreknowledge Cannot
Precede His Eternal Decrees

Calvinism and Arminianism adhere to the idea that the elect are elected (chosen) and predestined to salvation from eternity past by means of an eternal decree. This arrangement is impossible, and the following explains why.

Scripture teaches that God's decrees are eternal (Jeremiah 5:22), having always existed in His heart.

> *'Do you not fear Me?' declares the LORD. 'Do you not tremble in My presence? For I have placed the sand as a boundary for the sea, An eternal decree, so it cannot cross over it. Though the waves toss, yet they cannot prevail; Though they roar, yet they cannot cross over it.* (Jeremiah 5:22)

Scripture also requires God's foreknowledge (which means to know beforehand) to precede the predestination and election (choosing) of a New Testament believer.

> *For those whom He foreknew, He also predestined to become conformed to the image of His Son, so that He would be the firstborn among many brethren;* (Romans 8:29)

> *Peter, an apostle of Jesus Christ, To those who reside as aliens, scattered throughout Pontus, Galatia, Cappadocia, Asia, and Bithynia, who are chosen according to the foreknowledge of God the Father, by the sanctifying work of the Spirit, to obey Jesus Christ and be sprinkled with His blood : May grace and peace be yours in the fullest measure.* (1Peter 1:1-2)

Should God's foreknowledge, meaning "to know beforehand," precede His eternal decrees, eternity would have a beginning (a starting point)—a total impossibility.

Because God's decrees are eternal (Jeremiah 5:22), and foreknowledge is required to precede the predestination and election (choosing) of the New Testament believer (Romans 8:29; 1Peter 1:1-2), it is impossible for Him to have predestined or elected (chosen) New Testament believers to salvation from eternity past by means of an eternal decree.

Thus, the Scriptures teach that New Testament believers are elected and predestined to blessings (rather than to salvation) subsequent to exercising personal repentance and faith while depraved, which allows God's foreknowledge to precede such an arrangement. This is displayed graphically below.

FOREKNOWLEDGE	Predestination of New Testament Believers Election/Chosenness of New Testament Believers

∞

Diagram 3

God, The Eternal I AM

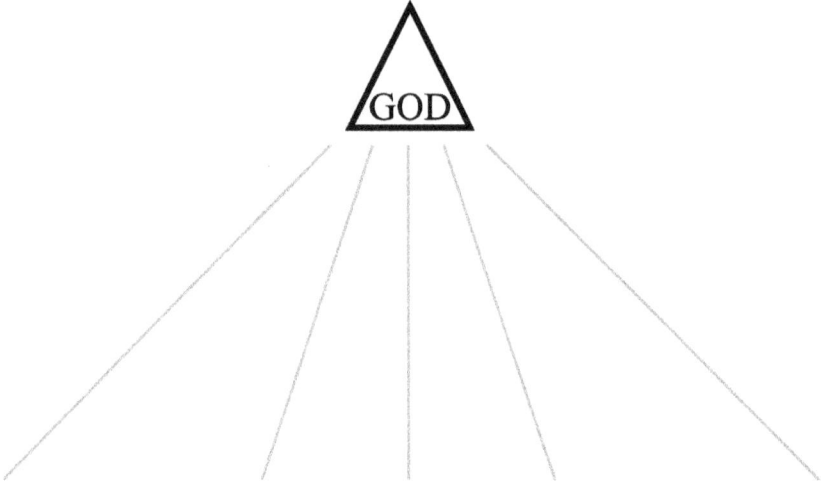

∞   ETERNITY   ∞
(without beginning or end)

God sees all events, from eternity past through eternity future throughout His eternal existence. In other words, He possesses the ability to see all things at once. He therefore, is never caught off guard since He possesses foreknowledge of all past, present, and future events. God is not required to cause these events to foreknow them.

Diagram 4

Arminius' Beliefs

Election
Predestination

| FOREKNOWLEDGE |

∞

Arminius' belief regarding foreknowledge affected his view of salvation. He believed that God looked into the future and, by means of His eternal foreknowledge, saw who would choose to repent and believe while depraved. God then, based on Arminius' theology, elected (chose) and predestined them to salvation from eternity past by means of an eternal decree.

Diagram 5

What Arminius' Belief System Actually Communicated

Election
Predestination
God's Foreknowledge

∞   ∞

Arminius believed that God's decrees, as well as His foreknowledge, are eternal. He also believed that individuals are elected (chosen) and predestined to salvation by means of an eternal decree. This order, however, leaves no room for God's foreknowledge to precede the New Testament believer's election and predestination. Arminius' theological chronology actually stacked election, predestination, and God's foreknowledge on top of each other, when Romans 8:29 and 1Peter 1:1-2 require God's foreknowledge to precede the election and predestination of a New Testament believer. Arminius arrived at this contradiction due to equating the blessings associated with salvation with salvation itself.

Diagram 6

Calvin's Beliefs

Election
Predestination
(God's Foreknowledge = Foreordination or Predestination)

∞   ∞

Calvin believed that God, from eternity past and by means of an eternal decree, elected (chose) and predestined the elect to salvation. This view contradicts Romans 8:29 and 1Peter 1:1-2, both of which require God's foreknowledge to precede the election (chosenness) and predestination of a New Testament believer. Thus, according to Calvin's theology, room does not exist for foreknowledge to precede the election (chosenness) and predestination of a New Testament believer. Therefore, Calvin deemed foreknowledge as synonymous with foreordination or predestination. In other words Calvin redefined foreknowledge as foreordination or predestination, which required the writing of volumes of materials in an effort to remedy such contradiction. Calvin arrived at the contradiction due to equating the blessings associated with salvation with salvation itself.

Diagram 7

The Remedy to Calvin's and Arminius' Error

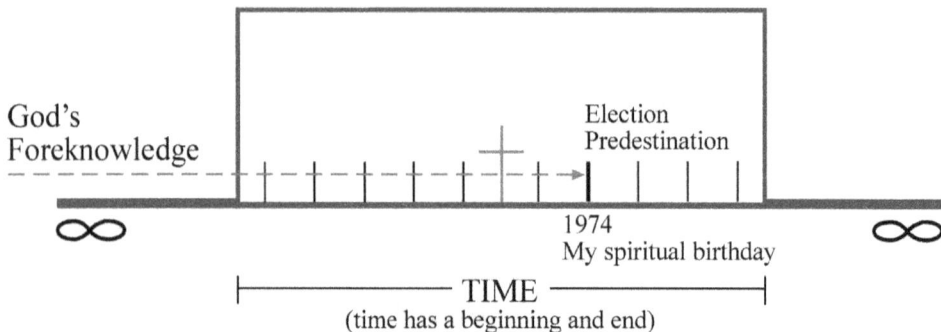

God's
Foreknowledge

Election
Predestination

∞

1974
My spiritual birthday

∞

├──────────────── TIME ────────────────┤
(time has a beginning and end)

The remedy to Calvin's and Arminius' error is found in allowing God's foreknowledge in this case to point to His foreknowledge of the thoughts, actions, and decisions of those who choose to repent and believe during the church age. Once they exercise repentance and faith while depraved, they are placed in Christ. God then predestines them to one day receive a glorified body (Romans 8:23; Ephesians 1:5). He also elects (chooses) them in Christ (Ephesians 1:4), after they repent and believe while depraved, bestowing upon them the office (gifting--1Peter 4:10) to which he elects them.

New Testament believers are placed in Christ, subsequent to repenting and believing while depraved, and only then are elected (chosen) and predestined. At that point they receive eternal life, life with no beginning and no end, and are viewed by the Father as having always been in Christ (Ephesians 1:4).

238

Scriptural Election/Chosenness and Predestination

The Father sees all New Testament believers, subsequent to their exercising personal repentance and faith while depraved and being made new, as having always been in Christ. This is due to the type of life they receive at the point of salvation - eternal life.

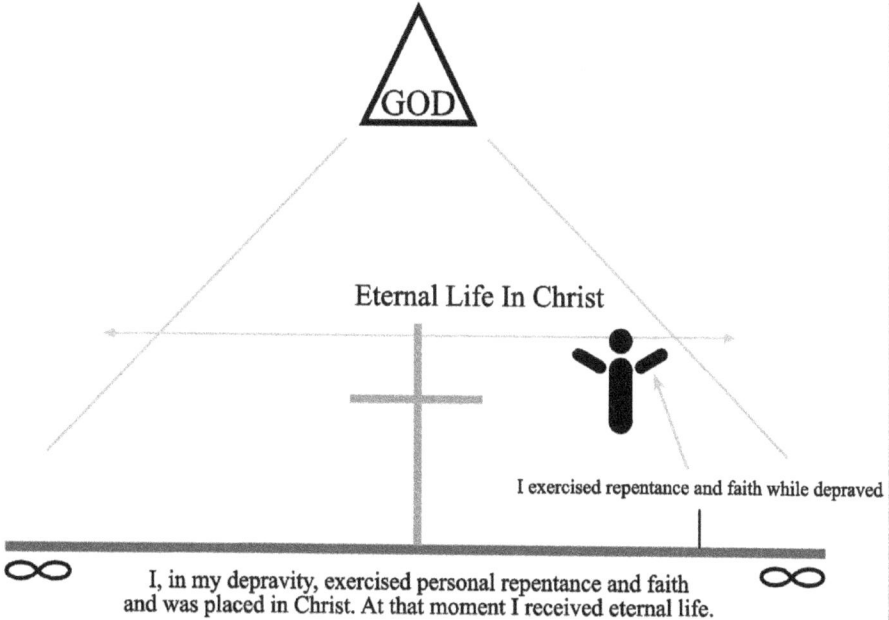

Eternal Life In Christ

I exercised repentance and faith while depraved

∞   I, in my depravity, exercised personal repentance and faith   ∞
             and was placed in Christ. At that moment I received eternal life.

The Holy Spirit places those seeking salvation into Christ when they repent and exercise faith while depraved (1Corinthians 12:13). Once this occurs, God makes them new (2Corinthians 5:17). He also predestines them (at that time) to receive a glorified body at the Rapture of the church (Ephesians 1:5; Romans 8:23; 1Corinthians 15:35-58; 1Thessalonians 4:13-18). They are also elected/chosen (at that time) to office due to having been placed into Christ, the Father's elect/chosen one (Luke 9:35; Isaiah 42:1), Who was elected/chosen to the office of Messiah. The office to which New Testament believers are elected/chosen is the special office or position (gift) they receive (1Peter 4:10) once they are placed in Christ and made new. Therefore, we were not predestined and elected/chosen to salvation from eternity past by means of an eternal decree. We were predestined the moment we were made new in Christ subsequent to repenting and believing while depraved; predestined to receive a new body (Ephesians 1:5; Romans 8:23) at the Rapture of the church. We were also elected/chosen to office when we were placed in Christ, subsequent to repenting and believing while depraved, Who was elected/chosen to office, the office of Messiah. Ephesians 1:4 states:

> *just as He chose us in Him before the foundation of the world, that we should be holy and blameless before Him. (Ephesians 1:4)*

Once we were placed in Christ, we received His kind of life, eternal life (Romans 6:23; Colossians 3:4), life with no beginning and no end. As a result, the Father sees us as having always been in Christ, even *"before the foundation of the world"* (Ephesians 1:4). Consequently, our point of entry into Christ was when we repented and believed while depraved, but once we were placed in Him through the power of the Holy Spirit, the Father saw us as having always been in His holy Son. He will continue to view us in this manner throughout eternity.

Diagram 9

The Predestination of Jesus' Death and the Hidden Wisdom
Acts 4:27-28; 1Corinthians 2:7

For trully in this city there were gathered together against Your holy servant Jesus, whom You annointed, both Herod and Pontius Pilate, along with the Gentiles and the peoples of Israel, to do whatever Your hand and Your purpose predestined to occur. (Acts 4:27-28)

but we speak God's wisdom in a mystery, the hidden wisdom which God predestined before the ages to our glory; (1Corinthians 2:7)

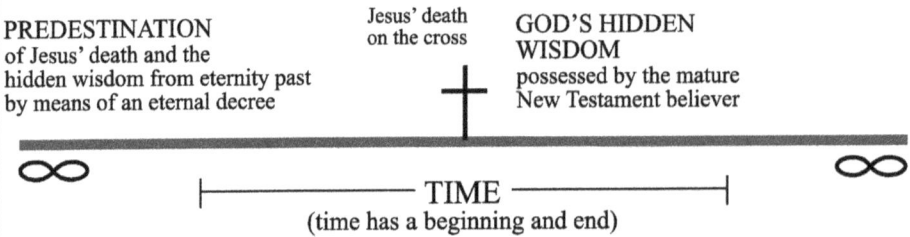

PREDESTINATION
of Jesus' death and the
hidden wisdom from eternity past
by means of an eternal decree

Jesus' death
on the cross

GOD'S HIDDEN
WISDOM
possessed by the mature
New Testament believer

∞   ⊢——— TIME ———⊣   ∞
(time has a beginning and end)

The Scriptures do not require that the predestination of the cross (Acts 4:27-28) and the hidden wisdom of God (1Corinthians 2:7) be preceded by God's foreknowledge. This difference leaves room for God to predestine the cross and the hidden wisdom of God from eternity past by means of an eternal decree. Such an arrangement is unlike the predestination of the New Testament believer, which occurs in time, and requires that God's foreknowledge precede it.

Diagram 10

Reformed Theology (Extreme and Hyper-Calvinism)

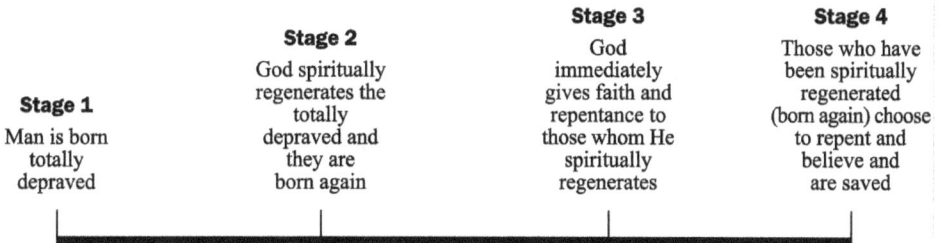

	Stage 2	**Stage 3**	**Stage 4**
Stage 1	God spiritually regenerates the totally	God immediately gives faith and repentance to	Those who have been spiritually regenerated (born again) choose
Man is born totally depraved	depraved and they are born again	those whom He spiritually regenerates	to repent and believe and are saved

This view is contradictory because Scripture equates spiritual regeneration and being born again with salvation. With Reformed theology's configuration, believers would be saved twice - a total impossibility.

The Scriptual View

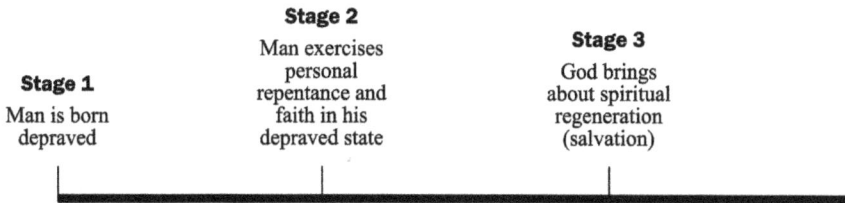

	Stage 2	**Stage 3**
Stage 1	Man exercises personal repentance and	God brings about spiritual regeneration
Man is born depraved	faith in his depraved state	(salvation)

Be aware that man is brought out of his state of depravity and into the kingdom in a flash, in fact, less than a flash. Therefore, the brevity of time between man's choice to repent and believe while depraved and God's act of spiritual regeneration (salvation) is impossible to imagine.

241

Diagram 11

Hyper-Calvinism (One Brand of Reformed Theology)

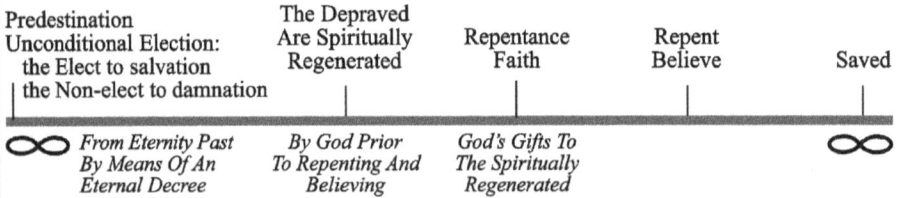

Predestination
Unconditional Election:
  the Elect to salvation
  the Non-elect to damnation

The Depraved Are Spiritually Regenerated   Repentance Faith   Repent Believe   Saved

From Eternity Past By Means Of An Eternal Decree   *By God Prior To Repenting And Believing*   *God's Gifts To The Spiritually Regenerated*

Strong (Extreme) Calvinism (A Second Brand of Reformed Theology)

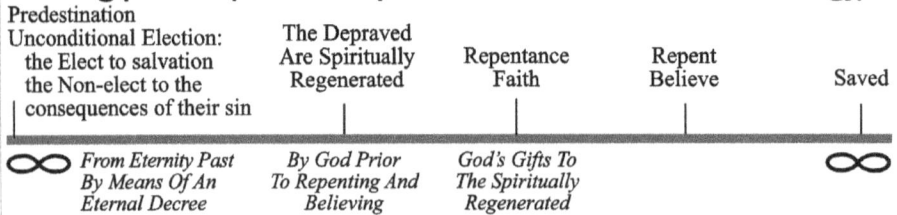

Predestination
Unconditional Election:
  the Elect to salvation
  the Non-elect to the
  consequences of their sin

The Depraved Are Spiritually Regenerated   Repentance Faith   Repent Believe   Saved

From Eternity Past By Means Of An Eternal Decree   *By God Prior To Repenting And Believing*   *God's Gifts To The Spiritually Regenerated*

Moderate Calvinism

Predestination
Unconditional Election:
  the Elect to salvation

Repent Believe   Saved

From Eternity Past By Means Of An Eternal Decree   *While Depraved*

Arminianism

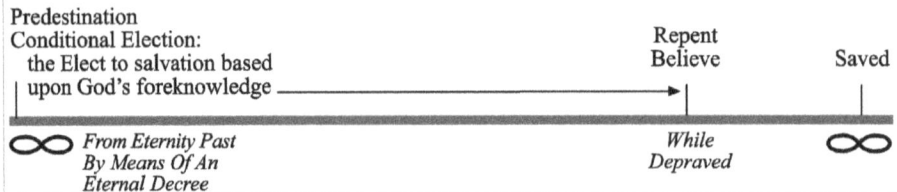

Predestination
Conditional Election:
  the Elect to salvation based
  upon God's foreknowledge

Repent Believe   Saved

From Eternity Past By Means Of An Eternal Decree   *While Depraved*

242

Diagram 12

Hyper Supralapsarianism	Strong (Extreme) Infralapsarianism	Moderate Sublapsarianism	Arminian Wesleyanism
(1) Decree to elect some and reprobate others	(1) Decree to create all	(1) Decree to create all	(1) Decree to create all
(2) Decree to create both the elect and the non-elect	(2) Decree to permit the Fall	(2) Decree to permit the Fall	(2) Decree to permit the Fall
(3) Decree to permit the Fall	(3) Decree to elect some and pass others by	(3) Decree to provide salvation for all	(3) Decree to provide salvation for all
(4) Decree to provide salvation only for the elect	(4) Decree to provide salvation only for the elect	(4) Decree to elect those who believe and pass by those who do not	(4) Decree to elect based on the foreseen faith of believers
(5) Decree to apply salvation only to the elect	(5) Decree to apply salvation only to the elect	(5) Decree to apply salvation only to believers (who cannot lose it)	(5) Decree to apply salvation only to believers (who can lose it)

243

Diagram 13

Sin in Control
Romans 6:12

Walking (or Living) According to the Flesh
Romans 8:4-5

Spirit

The Power of Sin will take advantage of any stimulus and attempt to deceive us: clouds, people, places, etc.

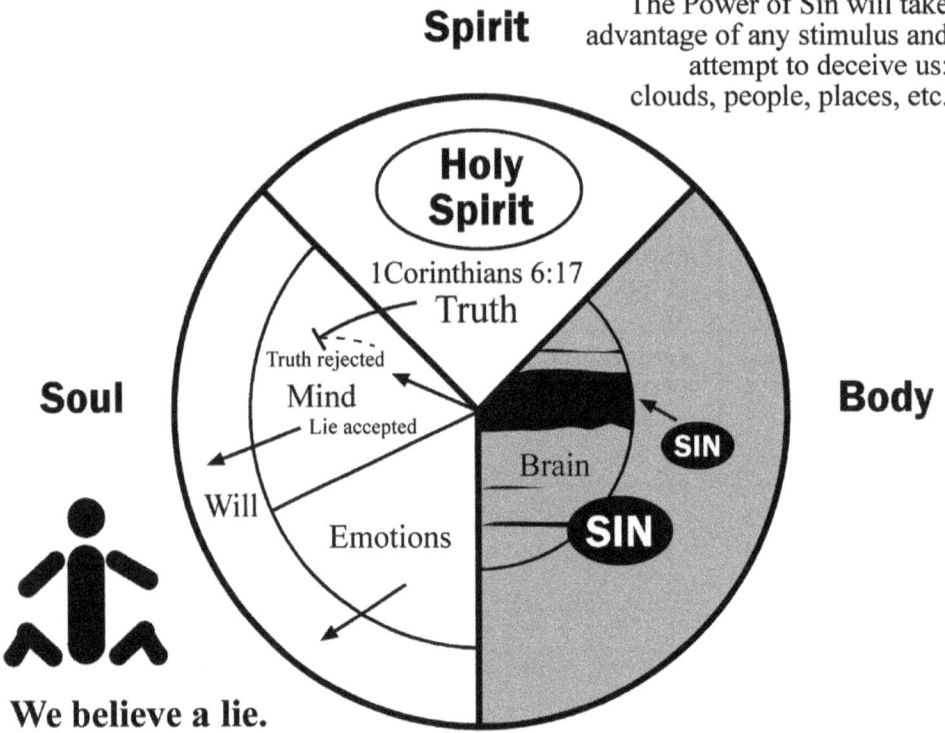

Holy Spirit

1Corinthians 6:17
Truth

Truth rejected
Mind
Lie accepted

Soul

Will

Brain

Emotions

SIN

SIN

Body

We believe a lie.

When we walk according to the flesh, we have failed to consider ourselves dead to the lie that the Power of Sin has sent into our minds (Romans 6:11). We have also failed to respond to the truth that the Spirit of God has sent in our minds. Thus, when this occurs, the new man sins.

> *Therefore do not let sin reign in your mortal body that you should obey its lusts,* (Romans 6:12)

> *in order that the requirement of the Law might be fulfilled in us, who do not walk according to the flesh, but according to the Spirit. For those who are according to the flesh set their minds on the things of the flesh, but those who are according to the Spirit, the things of the Spirit.* (Romans 8:4-5)

When we walk according to the flesh, we have believed the Power of Sin's lie and walked according to one of our ungodly habit patterns stored in our brain (the brain being a piece of flesh).

244

Diagram 14

Spirit in Control
Romans 6:13

Walking (or Living) According to the Spirit
Romans 8:4-5

Spirit

The Power of Sin will take advantage of any stimulus and attempt to deceive us: clouds, people, places, etc.

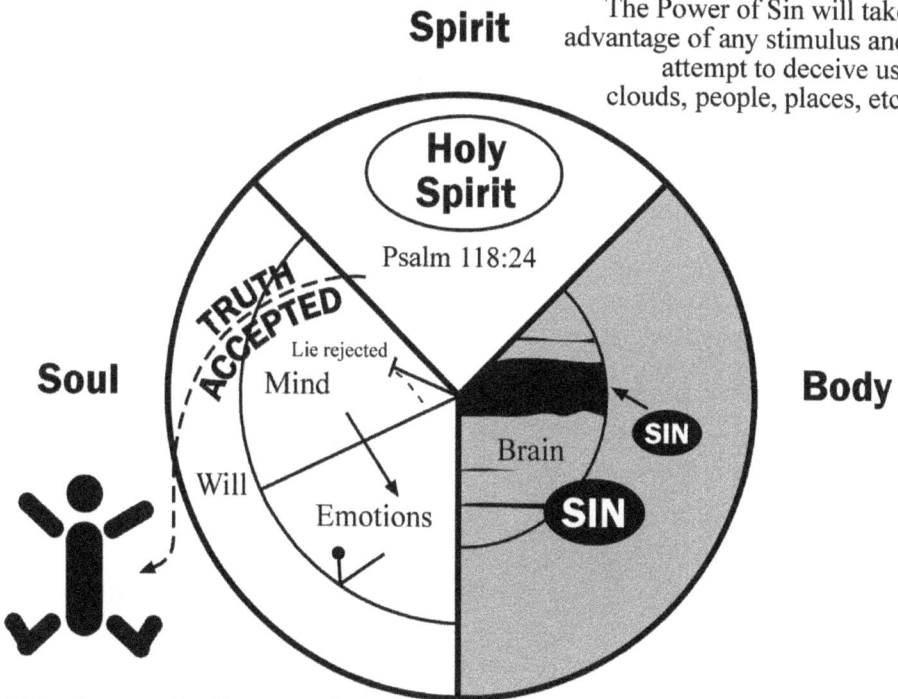

Soul

Body

Holy Spirit

Psalm 118:24

TRUTH ACCEPTED

Lie rejected

Mind

Will

Brain

Emotions

SIN

SIN

We <u>do not</u> believe a lie!

My mind is no longer enslaved to the evil thoughts generated by the Power of Sin. My new spirit and the Holy Spirit are one (1Corinthians 6:17).

When we walk according to the Spirit, we have considered ourselves dead to the lie that the Power of Sin has sent into our minds (Romans 6:11). We have also responded to the truth that the Spirit of God has sent into our minds and, thus, have not allowed the Power of Sin to reign (Romans 6:12).

> *And do not go on presenting the members of your body to sin as instruments of unrighteousness; but present yourselves to God as those alive from the dead, and your members as instruments of righteousness to God.* (Romans 6:13)

> *in order that the requirement of the Law might be fulfilled in us, who do not walk according the flesh, but according to the Spirit. For those who are according to the flesh set their minds on the things of the flesh, but those who are according to the Spirit, the things of the Spirit.* (Romans 8:4-5)

245

Bibliography

[1] Dave Hunt, *What Love Is This?*, Third Edition, Published by The Berean Call, 2006, pages 108-109, Used by permission.

[2] Ibid., 154-155.

[3] Charles Spurgeon sermon titled *The Holy Spirit in the Covenant*, delivered by C. H. Spurgeon, at New Park Street Chapel, Southwark, London, 1856.

[4] Dave Hunt, *What Love Is This?*, Third Edition, Published by The Berean Call, 2006, page 158, Used by permission.

[5] Ibid., page 36.

[6] Ibid.

[7] *Why I Am Not a Calvinist*, Jerry L. Walls, Joseph R. Dongell, InterVarsity Press, www.ivpress.com, © 2004, page 11, Used by permission.

[8] Norman L. Geisler, *Systematic Theology, Volume Three, Sin, Salvation*, pages 143- 144, Published by Bethany House, a division of Baker Publishing Group, Copyright 2004, Used by permission.

[9] Thehighway.com, A Brief Comparative Study of: Arminianism and Calvinism, Used by permission.

[10] Jacobus Arminius, *The Works of James Arminius;* Volume 1; Translated from the Latin by James Nichols; *A Declaration of the Sentiments of Arminius, 6. My own Sentiments on Predestination.*

[11] Norman L. Geisler, *Systematic Theology, Volume Three, Sin, Salvation*, page 144, Published by Bethany House, a division of Baker Publishing Group, Copyright 2004, Used by permission.

[12] John Piper, *TULIP: The Pursuit of God's Glory in Salvation*, DVD, Disk 2, Title 1, Chapters 1-3, Used by permission.

[13] Thehighway.com, A Brief Comparative Study of: Arminianism and Calvinism, Used by permission.

[14] Arnold Fruchtenbaum, God's Will – Man's Will audio series, © February 19, 2008, Used by permission.

[15] Edwin H. Palmer, *The Five Points of Calvinism*, Twentieth Printing, Forward, Published by Bethany House, a division of Baker Publishing Group, Copyright 1999, page 16, Used by permission.

[16] Norman L. Geisler, *Systematic Theology, Volume Three, Sin, Salvation*, page 147, Published by Bethany House, a division of Baker Publishing Group, Copyright 2004, Used by permission.

[17] *The MacArthur Study Bible*, John MacArthur, © 2006, Thomas Nelson Inc. Nashville, Tennessee. All rights reserved. Commentary on John 16:8, page 1617, NKJV. Reprinted by permission.

[18] R.C. Sproul Jr., *Almighty Over All: Understanding the Sovereignty of God*, pages 46-47, Published by Baker Books, a division of Baker Publishing Group, Copyright 1999, Used by permission.

[19] John Piper, *TULIP: The Pursuit of God's Glory in Salvation*, DVD, Disk 2, Title 6, Chapters 4-5, Used by permission.

[20] *The Love of God: He Will Do Whatever It Takes to Make Us Holy,* Appendix, John MacArthur Jr, © 1998, Thomas Nelson Inc. Nashville, Tennessee. All rights reserved. Reprinted by permission.

[21] John Piper, *TULIP: The Pursuit of God's Glory in Salvation*, DVD, Disk 1, Title 6, Chapter 1, Used by permission.

[22] Ibid., Disk 1, Title 6, Chapter 4.

[23] Norman L. Geisler, *Systematic Theology, Volume Three, Sin, Salvation*, pages 484-485, Published by Bethany House, a division of Baker Publishing Group, Copyright 2004, Used by permission.

[24] Taken from *Chosen by God,* by R.C. Sproul, page 72, © 1986 by Tyndale House Publishers, Used by permission of Tyndale House Publishers, Inc. All rights reserved.

[25] Ibid.

[26] Commentary on Titus 3:5. *Notes: Explanatory and Practical,* is the work of Albert Barnes (1798-1870), and published in 1872. The commentary is in the public domain and may be freely used and distributed.

[27] Charles Spurgeon sermon titled *The Warrant of Faith*, delivered on Sunday Morning, September 20th, 1863, by C. H. SPURGEON, at the Metropolitan Tabernacle, Newington Causeway, London, England.

[28] Taken from *Chosen by God,* by R.C. Sproul, page 72, © 1986 by Tyndale House Publishers, Used by permission of Tyndale House Publishers, Inc. All rights reserved.

[29] Edwin H. Palmer, *The Five Points of Calvinism,* Twentieth Printing, Forward, Published by Bethany House, a division of Baker Publishing Group, Copyright 1999, page 19, Used by permission.

[30] Dave Hunt, *What Love Is This?*, Third Edition, Published by The Berean Call, 2006, pages 445-446, Used by permission.

[31] Ibid., page 451.

[32] Ibid.

[33] Calvin on from his *Commentary on John – Volume 1*, John 1:13.

[34] Dave Hunt, *What Love Is This?*, Third Edition, Published by The Berean Call, 2006, page 450, Used by permission.

[35] Norman L. Geisler, *Systematic Theology, Volume Three, Sin, Salvation*, pages 133-134, Published by Bethany House, a division of Baker Publishing Group, Copyright 2004, Used by permission.

[36] Dave Hunt, *What Love Is This?*, Third Edition, Published by The Berean Call, 2006, page 338, Used by permission.

[37] Ibid., pages 451-452.

[38] John Piper, *TULIP: The Pursuit of God's Glory in Salvation*, DVD, Disk 1, Title 6, Chapter 4, Used by permission.

[39] Ibid., Disk 1, Title 6, Chapter 5.

[40] Charles Spurgeon sermon titled *Exposition of the Doctrines of Grace*, delivered on Thursday afternoon, April 11th, 1861, by C. H. SPURGEON, at the Metropolitan Tabernacle, Newington Causeway, London, England.

[41] John Piper, *TULIP: The Pursuit of God's Glory in Salvation*, DVD, Disk 1, Title 7, Chapters 2- 4, Used by permission.

[42] Ibid.

[43] Ibid.

[44] Ibid.

[45] Ibid.

[46] Ibid.

[47] Ibid.

[48] Johann Carl Friedrich Keil, Franz Delitzsch, *Keil & Delitzsch Commentary on the Old Testament*, page 2436, Used by permission.

[49] John Piper, *TULIP: The Pursuit of God's Glory in Salvation*, DVD, Disk 2, Title 6, Chapters 4- 5, Used by permission.

[50] Norman L. Geisler, *Chosen But Free*, Second Edition, page 208, Published by Bethany House, a division of Baker Publishing Group, Copyright 2001, Used by permission.

[51] John Gill, *The Cause of God and Truth,* 1736, commenting on Matthew 23:37, Section 15, No. 4.

[52] Norman L. Geisler, *Chosen But Free*, Second Edition, pages 208-209, Published by Bethany House, a division of Baker Publishing Group, Copyright 2001, Used by permission.

[53] Dave Hunt, *What Love Is This?*, Third Edition, Published by The Berean Call, 2006, pages 461-462, Used by permission.

[54] Ibid., page 462.

[55] Ibid., pages 462-464.

[56] John Piper, *TULIP: The Pursuit of God's Glory in Salvation*, DVD, Disk 2, Title 7, Chapter 2, Used by permission.

[57] Norman L. Geisler, *Chosen But Free*, Second Edition, page 67, Published by Bethany House, a division of Baker Publishing Group, Copyright 2001, Used by permission.

[58] Edwin H. Palmer, *The Five Points of Calvinism,* Twentieth Printing, Forward, Published by Bethany House, a division of Baker Publishing Group, Copyright 1999, pages 14-15, Used by permission.

[59] Ibid., pages 85-86.

[60] RC Sproul, *Grace Unknown: The Heart of Reformed Theology*, Baker Books, a division of Baker Publishing Group, Copyright 1997, pages 156-157, Used by permission.

[61] Dave Hunt, *What Love Is This?*, Third Edition, Published by The Berean Call, 2006, pages 452-453, Used by permission.

[62] Calvin's *Commentary on the Epistle to the Ephesians,* in *the Comprehensive John Calvin Collection* Ages Digital Library, 1998.

[63] Taken from *Chosen by God,* by R.C. Sproul, page 117, © 1986 by Tyndale House Publishers, Used by permission of Tyndale House Publishers, Inc. All rights reserved.

[64] John Piper, *TULIP: The Pursuit of God's Glory in Salvation*, DVD, Disk 1, Title 6, Chapter 2, Used by permission.

[65] Taken from *The Gospel and Its Ministry*, page 54, © Copyright 1978 by Sir Robert Anderson. Published by Kregel Publications, Grand Rapids, MI. Used by permission of the publisher. All rights reserved.

[66] RC Sproul, *Grace Unknown: The Heart of Reformed Theology*, Baker Books, a division of Baker Publishing Group, Copyright 1997, pages 155-156, Used by permission.

[67] Samuel Fisk, *Divine Sovereignty and Human Freedom*, Neptune NJ: published by Loizeaux Brothers, © 1973, pages 25-29.

[68] RC Sproul, *Grace Unknown: The Heart of Reformed Theology*, Baker Books, a division of Baker Publishing Group, Copyright 1997, pages 155-156, Used by permission.

[69] *The Wycliffe Bible Commentary* Electronic Database. Copyright © 1962 by Moody Press. All rights reserved, Used by permission.

[70] John Piper, *TULIP: The Pursuit of God's Glory in Salvation*, DVD, Disk 1, Title 6, Chapter 2, Used by permission.

[71] Ibid.

[72] Ibid., Disk 1, Title 7, Chapter 2.

[73] Ibid., Disk 1, Title 6, Chapter 2.

[74] *The MacArthur Study Bible*, John MacArthur, © 2006, Thomas Nelson Inc. Nashville, Tennessee. All rights reserved. Commentary on 2Peter 1:1, page 1952, NKJV. Reprinted by permission.

[75] Norman L. Geisler, *Systematic Theology, Volume Three, Sin, Salvation*, page 487, Published by Bethany House, a division of Baker Publishing Group, Copyright 2004, Used by permission.

[76] *Vine's Expository Dictionary of Biblical Words,* page 45, Copyright © 1985 by Thomas Nelson Publishers. All rights reserved.

[77] RC Sproul, *Faith Alone: The Evangelical Doctrine of Justification*, page 26, © 1999 Baker Publishing. Used by permission.

[78] Norman L. Geisler, *Systematic Theology, Volume Three, Sin, Salvation*, pages 488-489, Published by Bethany House, a division of Baker Publishing Group, Copyright 2004, Used by permission.

[79] Ibid.

[80] Ibid., pages 184-185.

[81] Ibid., pages 185-186.

[82] Edwin H. Palmer, *The Five Points of Calvinism,* Twentieth Printing, Forward, Published by Bethany House, a division of Baker Publishing Group, Copyright 1999, page 19, Used by permission.

[83] John Calvin, *Institutes of the Christian Religion,* Book 2; Chapter 2; Section 18.

[84] Ibid., Book 2; Chapter 2; Section 22.

[85] Edwin H. Palmer, *The Five Points of Calvinism,* Twentieth Printing, Forward, Published by Bethany House, a division of Baker Publishing Group, Copyright 1999, page 15, Used by permission

[86] Reprinted from *The Five Points of Calvinism: Defined, Defended, and Documented,* by David N. Steele, Curtis C. Thomas, S. Lance Quinn, © 2004, P & R Publishing, Phillipsburg, NJ, page 54-55

[87] Ibid., page 53.

[88] Dave Hunt, *What Love Is This?,* Third Edition, Published by The Berean Call, 2006, page 141, Used by permission.

[89] *The MacArthur Study Bible,* John MacArthur, © 2006, Thomas Nelson Inc. Nashville, Tennessee. All rights reserved. Commentary on Romans 10:9, page 1712, NKJV. Reprinted by permission.

[90] Ibid., page 1692.

[91] Ibid., page 1805.

[92] Wayne Grudem, *Bible Doctrine, Essential Teachings of the Christian Faith,* Published by Zondervan, 1999, page 301, Used by permission.

[93] Edwin H. Palmer, *The Five Points of Calvinism,* Twentieth Printing, Forward, Published by Bethany House, a division of Baker Publishing Group, Copyright 1999, page 15, Used by permission.

[94] Norman L. Geisler, *Systematic Theology, Volume Three, Sin, Salvation,* page 479, Published by Bethany House, a division of Baker Publishing Group, Copyright 2004, Used by permission.

[95] Wayne Grudem, *Bible Doctrine, Essential Teachings of the Christian Faith,* Published by Zondervan, 1999, page 303, Used by permission.

[96] Ibid., pages 301-302.

[97] Ibid.

[98] Ibid.

[99] Taken from *Chosen by God,* by R.C. Sproul, page 72, © 1986 by Tyndale House Publishers, Used by permission of Tyndale House Publishers, Inc. All rights reserved.

[100] Dave Hunt, *What Love Is This?,* Third Edition, Published by The Berean Call, 2006, pages 374, Used by permission.

[101] Dave Hunt, *What Love Is This?,* Third Edition, Published by The Berean Call, 2006, page 310, Used by permission.

[102] Ibid., page 362.

[103] *The Love of God: He Will Do Whatever It Takes to Make Us Holy,* page 156, John MacArthur Jr, © 1998, Thomas Nelson Inc. Nashville, Tennessee. All rights reserved. Reprinted by permission.

[104] RC Sproul, *Grace Unknown: The Heart of Reformed Theology,* Baker Books, a division of Baker Publishing Group, Copyright 1997, page 210, Used by permission.

[105] *The Love of God: He Will Do Whatever It Takes to Make Us Holy*, page 17, John MacArthur Jr, © 1998, Thomas Nelson Inc. Nashville, Tennessee. All rights reserved. Reprinted by permission.

[106] John Calvin, *Institutes of the Christian Religion,* Book 3; Chapter 21; Section 5.

[107] Ibid., Book 3; Chapter 21; Section 1.

[108] Ibid., Book 3; Chapter 24; Section 17.

[109] Wayne Grudem, *Bible Doctrine, Essential Teachings of the Christian Faith,* Published by Zondervan, 1999, pages 301-302, Used by permission.

[110] Dave Hunt, *What Love Is This?*, Third Edition, Published by The Berean Call, 2006, page 476, Used by permission.

[111] Wayne Grudem, *Bible Doctrine, Essential Teachings of the Christian Faith,* Published by Zondervan, 1999, page 300, Used by permission.

[112] Calvin from his *Commentary on John – Volume 1*, John 1:13.

[113] Dave Hunt, *What Love Is This?*, Third Edition, Published by The Berean Call, 2006, page 446, Used by permission.

[114] Ibid., page 448.

[115] Ibid., page 451.

[116] Norman L. Geisler, *Chosen But Free*, Second Edition, page 96, Published by Bethany House, a division of Baker Publishing Group, Copyright 2001, Used by permission.

[117] Charles Spurgeon sermon titled *The Warrant of Faith*, delivered on Sunday Morning, September 20th, 1863, by C. H. SPURGEON, at the Metropolitan Tabernacle, Newington Causeway, London, England.

[118] RC Sproul, *Grace Unknown: The Heart of Reformed Theology*, Baker Books, a division of Baker Publishing Group, Copyright 1997, page 152, Used by permission.

[119] Ibid.

www.ingramcontent.com/pod-product-compliance
Lightning Source LLC
Chambersburg PA
CBHW021356090426
42742CB00009B/885